D0978149

FROM THE "PREFACE":

When the untrained mind must grapple with the broader historical problems, it finds its explanations in certain rudimentary concepts and gross oversimplifications.... Among these are the Great Man theory...the single-cause explanation for a complex event, the naïve good-evil or black-white judgment of people and issues, the application of a single formula to all problems, the use of absolutes, and others. This book is intended to speed up the replacement of such rudimentary ideas with more advanced ones....

The fifteen chapters are planned to run parallel with successive periods studied in modern European history. Each chapter deals with one aspect of historical reasoning (or of historical phenomena) and most of its illustrations are drawn from one particular period. The first two chapters deal generally with the nature of history, the way to study it, and the relevancy of the past to the present. Then the nature of social forces is examined, the material being drawn mostly from the Age of the Renaissance and the Age of Explorations. From this, it is easy to go to the nature of causation, and the Reformation offers a perfect opportunity to illustrate it. The place of continuity and change in history is studied in connection with the English revolutions of the seventeenth century. The period of divine-right kings provides a suitable subject for describing the institutional factor in history, and the French Revolution for a closer look at revolutions....

CARL G. GUSTAVSON is Professor of History at Ohio University. He received his Ph.D. degree from Cornell, where he was a student of the late Carl Becker. In addition to A PREFACE TO HISTORY, he has written on German nationalism and the techniques of college teaching of history.

McGRAW-HILL PAPERBACKS
IN HISTORY

H. S. GLADWIN   *Men Out of Asia*
$2.50

H. HOOVER   *The Ordeal of Woodrow Wilson*
$2.25

G. MOSCA   *The Ruling Class*
               (Elementi di Scienza Politica)
               Edited and Revised by Arthur Livingston
               $3.45

L. A. WHITE   *The Evolution of Culture*
               The Development of Civilization to the Fall of Rome
               $2.25

A PREFACE TO HISTORY

CARL G. GUSTAVSON
Professor of History, Ohio University

McGRAW-HILL BOOK COMPANY, INC.
New York
Toronto
London

D
16.8
.G87

A PREFACE TO HISTORY

Copyright © 1955 by the McGraw-Hill Book Company, Inc. Printed in the United States of America. All rights reserved. This book, or parts thereof, may not be reproduced in any form without permission of the publishers.

Library of Congress Catalog Card Number 54-12251

    1920 MUMU 76

ISBN 07-025279-3

Preface

The principal purpose of this book is to present an outline of the nature of historical-mindedness on a level sufficiently elementary to be suitable for first-year college students. The intent is to provide a bridge for freshmen students of history whereby they may pass, by natural and gradual steps, from the preparatory-school level to the more advanced forms characteristic of college courses.

History, when treated purely as book learning, can be deceptive, for, unlike work in economics, mathematics, or the sciences, the existence of inherent patterns of reasoning may escape the uninitiated almost completely. Thus the mature student reads between the lines in the textbook and sees social forces in action, the complexity of causation in an episode, the strands of continuity, and the relevancy of the past to the present, while the beginner, on the contrary, merely sees facts on a printed page that must be learned. Confronted with phenomena beyond his ability to analyze because he lacks a knowledge of the historical approach, the beginner will necessarily memorize capsule versions of generalizations without acquiring the mental capacities which should be a by-product of the course. He may seek the assistance of outline series, where others have digested the materials for him, and his rote learning gives the illusion of a valid achievement.

When the untrained mind must grapple with the broader historical problems, it finds its explanations in certain rudimentary concepts and gross oversimplifications based upon inadequate observation and strong subjective preferences. Among these are the Great Man theory (or at least the visualization of politics almost exclusively in terms of personali-

CONCORDIA COLLEGE LIBRARY
2811 N. E. HOLMAN ST.
PORTLAND, OREGON 97211

ties), the single-cause explanation for a complex event, the naïve good-evil or black-white judgment of people and issues, the application of a single formula to all problems, the use of absolutes, and others. This book is intended to speed up the replacement of such rudimentary ideas with more advanced ones by disentangling some of the major concepts from the general narrative and illustrating each in suitable instances. The exposition, couched in simple language, was based in the planning stage upon an analysis of essay answers culled from a sequence of classes and starts at the level of interest and approximate psychology revealed in freshman themes. That which is to be learned in any one chapter could be put into one small paragraph—and the professor would know exactly what was meant. By the use of simple analogies, by references to their environment, and by illustrations primarily from modern history, an attempt is made to familiarize students with the various elements of the historical approach.

The fifteen chapters are planned to run parallel with successive periods studied in modern European history. Each chapter deals with one aspect of historical reasoning (or of historical phenomena) and most of its illustrations are drawn from one particular period. The first two chapters deal generally with the nature of history, the way to study it, and the relevancy of the past to the present. Then the nature of social forces is examined, the material being drawn mostly from the Age of the Renaissance and the Age of Explorations. From this, it is easy to go to the nature of causation, and the Reformation offers a perfect opportunity to illustrate it. The place of continuity and change in history is studied in connection with the English revolutions of the seventeenth century. The period of divine-right kings provides a suitable subject for describing the institutional factor in history, and the French Revolution for a closer look at revolutions. The later chapters follow a similar pattern.

While each chapter is pointed directly at the period being studied, some illustrations are borrowed from earlier periods. Although the historian must necessarily teach in a general chronological sequence, this does have a pedagogical drawback: the student is usually permitted to learn history in compartmentalized sections, in contrast to those subjects where he must use earlier material in order to solve or master the later. In these chapters some review is constantly under way, allusions to and amplifications of the key ideas used in earlier chapters, for a student needs to see them mentioned in various contexts and to build up numerous associations before he has actually learned them.

The presentation of factual information in these chapters is incidental to its use in illustrating a historical concept. While any particular illustration may provide an introduction to a topic or serve as review, the account is usually too elementary to be an adequate informational unit in its own right. Concepts related to such phenomena as causation or revolution are not dealt with exhaustively enough to satisfy the expert; these are introductory sketches containing about all a student can reasonably assimilate at his stage of development. The edges of the topics are etched in rather deeply and they may be somewhat schematized in order to facilitate clearer perception of the salient ideas under discussion. The exposition is aimed at bringing the student to the point, and only to the point, where professor and student can function at maximum efficiency on the college level.

Essentially, the attempt made here to strengthen historical-mindedness, far from being revolutionary, is merely a logical extension, in a systematized form, of common practice. It would seem to be in the interests of the profession to stress the elements of the historical approach itself, which is basic in many courses besides history proper and which is an ingredient of the liberal arts mind. The greater the contribution to preparation for work in other fields besides history, the greater are the chances of survival of authentic history, with its chronological sequence and its frame of reference intact, in the lower college. At the same time, the mastery of historical concepts and generalizations, through a study of how society has functioned in the past, should provide a more effective understanding of contemporary politics also. Historians as a group assuredly possess a common fund of wisdom, born out of the nature of the subject and its materials, which is valuable to that great majority of students who will never use history professionally (and hence benefit little from the methodology of historical research) but who will find that a knowledge of the historian's reasoning will contribute to better citizenship.

For the counsel and assistance of various kinds given during the preparation of the manuscript, I wish to express my thanks to Professors A. T. Volwiler and John F. Cady of the Ohio University history department; the interest and help of Dean George W. Starcher and President John C. Baker are also deeply appreciated. I am particularly indebted to Professor Edward Hodnett, chairman of the English department, for his reading of the manuscript and his valuable suggestions. A few passages in the final chapter parallel closely a section in my article "Tojo Says History Will Judge," *The South Atlantic Quarterly*, April, 1947; permission is gratefully acknowledged. The grant of a Ford Foundation Fellowship for the Advancement of Education was of great assistance in the final phases of this project. The Foundation, naturally, is not to be construed as indicating, by virtue of the grant, approval of any of the statements made or the views expressed in this book.

CARL G. GUSTAVSON

Contents

1

The Novice Historian

We Americans are inveterate travelers. During the summer months we take to the road in vast numbers. Many students, returning to their classes in the autumn, carry with them memories of exciting days profitably spent in visiting different parts of the country.

The more observant individuals, in passing through various localities, must have sensed the presence of history; perhaps they have discovered that history, frequently regarded by students as book learning, is a living reality in the American community. Every city or area cherishes those events of its own past which render it distinctive, and the tourist is made aware of them through place names, highway markers, signboards, and even the names of restaurants and motels. Despite the similarity of all Main Streets and the universal prevalence of neon signs and air conditioning, each town derives a certain definite character from its past which marks it off from any other place. In retrospect, the often-flaunted historical survivals seem to blend into the modern scene and become as real and living as the most modern building or automobile.

Although the Eastern sections of our country have provided the background for most of the episodes of national importance, the traveler in the West will also be impressed by the ubiquity of history. A tourist who, heading along highway 50, finds himself in the region of Dodge City and Cimarron, will recognize the countryside, even though he may never have been there before. Memories of western movies come so forcefully to mind that Indians and covered wagons would seem natural among these hills. To the casual visitor, the past, in this instance, may have greater immediacy to himself than the visible present.

Certain spots evoke a particularly vivid picture of life as it was lived in the remote past. Mesa Verde, in southwestern Colorado, is one of these. The highway itself augurs the unusual as it winds up the side of the mesa, each turn revealing a panoramic view of the surrounding wilderness and distant mountains. The drive is a fitting prelude to entrance upon the plateau, which gives the illusion of a gigantic stage in the sky where many a forgotten Stone Age adventure must have occurred. Rangers conduct visitors into the cliff dwellings for which the mesa is famous. Standing in one of these, a person can readily conjure up in his imagination the scene as it was in A.D. 1200, when the Indians still lived there. If he first accompanies a ranger on a tour of the earlier sites, which begins with the most primitive and progresses in chronological order, he will more easily be able to visualize the daily life of the Indians. Should he later chance to visit the Hopi Reservation, he might stare in amazement as he recognizes parts of the ancient scene being reenacted among the present-day descendants of the cliff dwellers.

When the traveler drives out of the Wasatch Range of Utah and sees the green valley about Salt Lake City, he must inevitably wonder how this oasis was created in the midst of an inhospitable wasteland. In order to understand the presence of this city in the desert, the visitor would have to learn something about the origins and subsequent struggles of the Mormons. He would then have explanations for those dominant features, the Temple and the Tabernacle, would know the reason for the sea-gull monument, and understand the use of such names as Apostles, Stakes, and Deseret. He could also visualize, in a sweeping fashion at least, the sprouting of this sturdy plant, the Mormon commonwealth, in newly irrigated lands and the subsequent spread of runners in all directions, from whence new Mormon communities grew. Should he happen to arrive on Pioneer Day, July 24, and find stores and gasoline stations closed, he will be sharply reminded that these people continue to treat the history of their forefathers with the utmost reverence.

History gives perspective. After the tourist has seen the different points of interest in San Francisco, he will wish to visit Telegraph Hill, with its magnificent view of the bay area. At this elevation, the hitherto bewildering topography of the region falls into place, and the relation of each detail to the whole may be discerned. History, similarly, is a mountaintop of human knowledge from whence the doings of our own generation may be scanned and fitted into proper dimensions. History enables a person to see himself as part of that living process of human growth which has emerged out of the past and will inexorably project itself out beyond our own lifetime. We are the product of the past—but not the *completed* product.

Some time ago there appeared, in a letter from a high-school student to the editor of a leading national magazine, the following statement: "Today's youth is interested in the living present, not in the dead past!" There can be no quarrel with the first half of this declaration. Anyone who has an active, intelligent interest in our own times, however, will find many problems confronting him, and the search for the answers will inevitably draw him into the past. The living present is the extension of a past which in innumerable ways is still with us. Most of our problems, after all, originated in former decades or centuries. A person who has obtained a deeper insight into history will regard the phrase "the dead past" as indirect proof that the one using it actually has no vital interest in the present either.

We have inherited wisdom, as well as problems, from earlier ages, and we might respond to the above quotation with words uttered by Cicero two thousand years ago: "To be ignorant of what happened before you were born is to be ever a child." Unless we understand how present-day problems had their origins, our suggested remedies are apt to prove rather naïve. Most of the more flashy panaceas that are offered are usually put forth with little idea of origins, hence the real difficulty of the problem. He who heedlessly escapes into the present will always carry with him a flat, unbalanced picture of our day and an entirely inadequate impression of the nature of the social forces which ceaselessly impinge upon us. There may be considerable truth in the famous maxim of Santayana, the philosopher: "He who does not know history is fated to repeat it."

Even the psychiatrist goes into the past before he dares to prescribe a remedy. When he is asked to solve a personal problem, he invariably wants a case history. Just as an individual's personality represents the sum total of his experiences, so the present appearance and conduct of nations and institutions reflect the formative circumstances of their background.

In a sense, a history student is assembling a gigantic jigsaw puzzle. He is learning how the world he lives in was put together. Thus, we study the Reformation and learn how various religious denominations came into being. In the Enlightenment we see popularized some of the ideals in which we still believe. A survey of the Industrial Revolution and its aftermath reveals the evolution of the modern urban society of which we are a part. The materials of a history course, far from being a miscellany of antiquarian information, are selected for the specific purpose of showing the origins of our society and culture.

A novice in history must accustom himself to the thought that many things can be contemporary even though he is reading about the year 1850 or 1750. In such a case as the Roman Catholic Church, the year might be A.D. 750, for events occurring then may have helped to shape that Church as we know it today. Social and political institutions and human practices often have a far longer longevity than does a human life. Because they have a longer duration than a single lifetime, a study of their shapes and functions must embrace a greater time scope than our own lifetime. The human being, with his puny life span, is but a pygmy walking among giants whose growth and decline must be measured in terms of centuries.

A person who thinks of history as dead very probably does not concern himself with much of anything beyond his own immediate environment. Although he arrogates for himself citizenship in the busy, progressing world of the twentieth century, he lives in the present *moment,* not in the present age. It is not mere coincidence that the student who reads the front pages of the newspaper fairly regularly is usually the one who secures the best marks in history. Such an individual has a much better comprehension of the world in which he lives. Because he has accustomed himself to dealing with its social forms and forces, the subject materials and ways of thinking of a history course are not completely foreign to him.

The Historian's Road Map

We mentioned, a little earlier, the view from Telegraph Hill. Another analogy is suggested by the view of the ships in San Francisco harbor. In the days of the sailing vessel, the mariner who would bring his ship to port without disaster had to know the prevailing winds, the direction of the currents, the location of reefs and sand bars, and the nature of the prevalent storms in the region. Historical forces are to the ship of state, to organized society, what the natural forces of the ocean were to the old-time clipper. As the captains and navigators had to know the ways of the sea, so citizens of a republic need to know the social forces whose operations make up history. A ship such as the "Titanic" may blunder into catastrophe even in the twentieth century, and a nation may suffer a Pearl Harbor.

Not that history guides us with the clarity of a tourist's road map or a mariner's chart. The lessons of history are not as easy to discern as some people would have us believe. Any statement in which the prefatory "History teaches us that . . ." is used as a springboard should be very carefully scrutinized; the accompanying assertion may be quite valid and acceptable, but the odds are against it.

History looks deceptively easy—so much so that there is a widespread idea that anyone who can read a history textbook can also teach history. Such an assertion obviously would be ridiculous for the languages, natural sciences, or mathematics. In the social studies, however, mere memorization of the book too often passes for mastery of the subject.

Before a person can use historical information as a key to the understanding of present problems in a reasonably effective manner, he must understand certain fundamental processes and concepts—he must become historically-minded. Complete competency in it requires as arduous and exacting a training as that of a physician, engineer, or lawyer. A certain familiarity with the basic processes and concepts, however, should provide the student with an ability to differentiate between authentic leader and demagogue, and it should bring him a far clearer perception in judging public issues. In short, it should make him a more enlightened citizen.

Historical-mindedness is "a way of thinking," a form of reasoning when dealing with historical materials and present-day problems. Use of it occurs to a greater or lesser extent in other fields besides history proper; economics, political science, philosophy, literature, and geology are among these. In mastering this way of thinking, a student is also enhancing his capacities in these other fields.

We may, for present purposes, list the characteristics of historical-mindedness in seven categories. In the following chapters we shall try to explain and illustrate their meaning more fully.

1. It is possible to see history on two separate planes. One is a superficial observation of the actors and events, wherein the focus of attention is upon the story or narrative in itself, the colorful and dramatic episode and the excitement of the human struggle. Historical figures seem to be making their own decisions in reasonably free will out of the resources of their own personalities. Their actions are judged according to a moral code, perhaps, or according to their successes and failures. Even as the

reader enjoys the story, however, he may become uneasily aware that his judgments are too hastily concocted because he has based them only upon the immediate circumstances of the episode. He has caught a glimpse of other factors, perhaps unrealized by the historical figures themselves, which helped to determine the course of their careers.

The historian, while relishing the excitement of the adventure, remains unsatisfied until he penetrates into this second plane of broad causation. Here the figures on the historical stage are often to be seen as personal embodiments of powerful and terrible tensions and pressures within society. While the actor undoubtedly had alternatives to face in making his decisions, they were greatly limited by the set of circumstances in which he moved and by the resources at his disposal. Every historical figure has been forced to act within the limits of what was possible, and many a famous disaster was caused by failure to take this into account.

The first characteristic: *A natural curiosity as to what underlies the surface appearances of any historical event.*

2. The historically-minded person knows that events do not occur in isolation; every happening is brought about and conditioned by a series of events. He will, consequently, be impelled to seek for associations between the particular episode and others which may be connected with it. *In studying any present problem, idea, event, or institution, the mind of the historian inevitably gravitates in the direction of the past, seeking origins, relationships, and comparisons.*

3. The natural scientist studies the forces in the physical world. He learns what they are and has developed techniques for measuring them. *The student of society must try to discern the shapes and contours of the forces which are dynamic in society.* They are of various kinds. The needs of different economic classes are one of the foremost, and hence an understanding must be acquired of the outlook of the so-called middle classes, of the laboring groups, and of the old-time feudal aristocracy. Within each of these there are further differentiations, each with a varying outlook. Another type of social pressure derives from the various forms of loyalty, whether to a nation, region, dynasty, caste, or religion. The power and needs of government itself invariably exercise a major influence upon its community. The exigencies of military defense have, through all ages, played a tremendous role in determining social action.

4. Because the historian is profoundly aware that the past is still at work in the present, *he stresses the continuity of society in all its forms.* The present situation is simply a cross section of the whole story which

dates back to the remote beginnings of humanity and which will be projected into the future. The historian appreciates the conservative attitude that changes, too abruptly undertaken, create more inequities than they alleviate.

5. He is also convinced that in innumerable ways *society is perpetually undergoing a process of change*. No government, no social group, can permanently prevent this gradual transformation. The biologist teaches evolution, and Darwin is customarily regarded as the discoverer of this theory, yet the concept of evolution was being employed by historians before it was applied to the physical sciences. Institutions, also, change their shapes and functions with the passage of time as they adjust to a changing environment. One of the most fascinating problems of historians and sociologists is the analysis of the processes whereby social changes do occur.

6. The student of society, although he may have very definite ideas of what ought to be done (he should), must rigidly, first of all, concern himself with what *is*. *He must approach his subject in a spirit of humility, prepared to recognize tenacious reality rather than what he wishes to find.* Until the student of the physical world learned to do this, the fruit of his labors was astrology and alchemy. In the scientific method, the forces are carefully observed and measured, the results verified again and again. Only after this is done, can a real attempt be made to control and direct the forces of nature or society.

7. Finally, *the historian knows that each situation and event is unique*. He can scarcely hope to discover laws in history, because the elements and factors with which he deals are too variable. History is not a science, even though scientific methodology is used as much as possible. Although the historian will have good grounds for anticipating certain developments, he can make no positive predictions. He cannot phrase his conclusions beyond the probable.

The Novice Studies History

The above characteristics are, fundamentally, attainments of the practiced mind. Even as we learn muscular skills by practice, so we develop mental abilities by conscientious and repeated use of the reactions which we hope to make habitual. Like most learning activities, historical-mindedness develops gradually, almost imperceptibly, with many errors and hesitancies. The professor, reading quiz papers of an essay nature, can note the improvement, although the student may be unaware of it.

The mentor may teach by example, but the student must do his own thinking in order to achieve historical-mindedness.

Only knowledge that is actually used will become a part of oneself. This may explain why some students feel that history consists of innumerable facts to be memorized—the dead past. They feel this way because they let it become just that by not studying it properly. The caricature of history, still widely entertained, which depicts it as a study of names and dates and battles, of a dreary succession of events learned for a test and then forgotten, is due, above all, to the student's method of study. By memorizing only, he is trying to take a short cut to knowledge, and he himself reduces history to that level. He often stops studying at the precise point where he is finally ready to begin.

It is quite true that a history course contains a rather formidable array of facts which must be learned in one way or another. We call this orderly collection of knowledge about the past a *frame of reference*. This personal filing system of one's knowledge consists of fairly detailed information about the successive important events during the development of our society and culture. A great many of the facts have to be learned on faith, relying on the assurance that these have been screened, reduced to a workable minimum, while still presenting a useful frame of reference. As the student goes on in school, he will be surprised at how many of the facts will reappear in other courses, and the earlier knowledge will begin to pay immediate dividends. More important from a long-term point of view, an adequate frame of reference enables a person to derive full benefit from a book or newspaper or magazine, inasmuch as he is enabled to recognize allusions and can amplify, from his own memory, cursory references as he meets them.

One of the secrets of the education process is that the more one knows, the more one learns. The greater the amount of factual knowledge possessed, the easier it is to tie in new material, to associate the new with the old in such a way that it remains a permanent acquisition. Learning multiplies by a sort of mathematical progression as familiarity with the subject increases. An individual who is studying by means of associations is learning more pleasantly, more quickly, and more permanently than one who tries to take the deceptive short cut of rote memory of the printed page.

When a student memorizes names or an outline, he is preparing to study. He is like a student in a laboratory who is getting his materials ready for an experiment. When the latter has completed his preparations, he does not abruptly announce that the experiment is completed. The beginning history student, however, is prone to quit once he has the materials for thinking things out. He ought to force himself to sit quietly for a while longer, seeking associations which he can make, known knowledge which will help him remember the new material. If he cannot relate it to his historical frame of reference, let him apply information from other sources or from personal experiences. (Some examples of these will appear in later chapters.) The contemporary scene frequently lends itself to comparisons, and here is where a student who reads newspapers and magazines will have a decided advantage.

It may be objected that there is not time for such a procedure. The truth is that there is not time for any other method except this one; the student is actually learning, whereas otherwise he is only cramming for a quiz. The process will take a little longer at first. The beginner will very quickly, however, learn to combine the memorizing and thinking in such a way that both will require less time than a single one did formerly. This is what the top-grade student has learned to do. Much of the knack to studying history is to be found in knowing what *not* to learn. The beginner wastes time and energy because everything seems of equal importance. Only as greater perception develops will he be able to separate the more significant statements from material necessary to a balanced narrative but not vital in itself.

The real objection is often not with the time element but with a more intangible obstacle. Genuine thinking along intellectual lines may be rather painful to the novice. The situation can become intensely frustrating. A person may alert his nervous system and order his mind to think. Nothing happens. He fiddles with his pencils, combs his hair, cleans his fingernails, goes for a drink of water, comes back, fills his fountain pen, combs his hair again. Still no thinking. In these desperate circumstances, rote learning of the assignment offers an avenue of escape which also conveys the comforting illusion that the material is being mastered. (It is rumored that some students do not even bother to do this much work. Such academic hitchhikers ought to be abolished—and frequently are. These are the ones who permit the seeds of knowledge to fall on barren ground. Far from moistening the soil with the sweat of labor and thereby allowing the seeds an opportunity to germinate, they are apt to hold up the hard pellets and vigorously maintain that they are dead!)

The trick lies in knowing how to put the mind to work by providing something for it to think about. Asking oneself questions will accomplish this elementary and necessary purpose. This is the equivalent of cranking the old-fashioned motorcar, but it will start the wheels turning. A sporting element may be added to the project by attempting to guess what the questions of the instructor will be, then, with the book closed, attempting to answer them. While the initial queries in any session will undoubtedly be of the who-what-when variety, in order to check if the major points of the assignment have been absorbed, the questions ought eventually to broaden into such considerations as causation, motivation, and comparison. One might select one of the historical figures in the assignment and try, from memory, to visualize his career. Have any other men resembled him in ideas or deeds? What ideas or events spurred his actions in a certain direction? Was he a prime cause for a historical movement or just an accidental figurehead? And here we meet a certain idea of the age. Why was this idea so popular then? What are the reasons for the success of a certain movement? Which of these reasons was probably the most important? How did the various social groups in a country probably line up in a particular crisis?

As this procedure becomes habitual, the questions will increasingly and spontaneously suggest themselves during the initial reading of the text. The questions will emerge out of natural curiosity, rather than as the result of compulsive preparation for classroom discussion and tests. Comparisons and contrasts with his own environment will stimulate the student, and, while he is analyzing the problems of earlier generations and trying to understand their behavior, he will gain greater comprehension of his own society. Finally, he will discover that the nature of the subject is, broadly speaking, creating certain general patterns in his own thinking—those categories which were listed in the preceding section. The chapters of this book are intended to assist and hasten this process.

The development of historical-mindedness and the learning of a frame of reference go hand in hand; an adequate frame of reference is necessary for thinking along historical lines, while practice in reasoning through the various episodes will cause facts to be more surely remembered. Only knowledge that is actually used will become a part of oneself. As was stated earlier, historical-mindedness is created in very much the same fashion as other skills are developed, by practicing them until they become second nature. No formula has been developed, or ever will be, whereby proficiency is suddenly achieved. When one learns to play tennis, bowl, skate, or dance, the movements are awkward and embarrassing at first. There are many angular gestures and much waste motion. The piano teacher does not expect a finished performance by a new pupil. Nor does the history professor expect a student to develop his own thinking overnight. He does often wince at the childish, naïve explanations that the novice in a history course will perpetrate, but he rejoices, as the course continues, if the student begins to manifest a more mature understanding of historical events and movements.

2

The Past in the Present

"Do you happen to know if your grandmother was ever personally acquainted with Moses or Elijah?"

Silly question? Of course it is—for a college student. A child of eight, however, might take the question quite seriously in a Sunday-school class. In the intervening years the eighteen-year-old person has acquired a certain amount of historical perspective. This development is a matter of great importance for the study of the past, since history can have little reality for the individual until he has attained a relatively mature sense of time. Although an adult usually assumes that his conceptions of time, like his general powers of observation, have not changed greatly since early childhood, psychologists tell us that the average individual does not usually possess the *capacity* for complete understanding and measurement of time until he is about twelve years of age. The following years then see the application of this ability to the point where a genuine historical perspective may be achieved. The whole process is so gradual, however, that we remain virtually unaware of its development.

As the young child becomes conscious of the world, he organizes it about himself, his ego dominating his surroundings. His parents and playmates, his home and toys, all the observed environment are his personal property, existing only for his own sake. The thought that these surroundings existed before he did seems preposterous. The world *is;* there has been no past. Passage of time is first impressed upon him as a knowledge of when certain things happen in the daily routine of the household, and the small child reveals his awareness of this by an insistence that the correct order of events must be carefully preserved down to the smallest detail. Although a child of five realizes that there is a today, a yesterday, and a tomorrow, even the seven-year-old child seems incapable of absorbing such an abstract idea as the possibility of a past. Before he is seven, he has started to acquire an understanding of the true length of various time dimensions, beginning with the smallest, such as the hour, day, and week, and by the time he reaches his ninth birthday, he may possess enough experience to visualize the length of a year. He is now conscious of the past, although it remains an orderless jumble without any measurement of duration or any division into periods. Historical figures who lived hundreds of years apart may seem contemporary. Grandma may very well seem old enough to have known Julius Caesar personally. Stories about ancient heroes may be delightful tales, but they seem as much fiction as Aesop's *Fables*.

The cultural history of man's development runs parallel with this genetic growth. Ancient man, in his artistry, had reached the level of the nine-year-old boy. A rock carving of the deeds of an Assyrian monarch may depict him waging war; in the same picture he is seen fighting a battle, butchering his captives, and receiving tribute from the defeated king. At first glance, the picture seems to portray one scene only, but actually the artist is commemorating the past, the past viewed as a whole, rather than as a series of consecutive events. Even in medieval Europe, painters would show the same person engaged in several activities in the same scene. As late as the Renaissance, artists apparently saw nothing incongruous in portraying biblical scenes where the figures were dressed in the style of the Renaissance and the cities were obviously those of contemporary Italy.

A profound development of the sense of time occurs at about the age of ten or eleven. The child now has the advantage of more personal perspective. He still finds it difficult to visualize long duration in history, but he can see *points* of time, definite dates when things occurred, and he has become aware of events happening before and after a given point. By the age of eleven, most children can understand the subdivisions of history and the possibility of an extended series of successive ages. Apparently the most usual means whereby time is visualized is by the application of the knowledge of space. That is, the person has learned to measure nearness to himself of observed objects; he is now doing the same with time. Events of history are visualized in a linear manner, a straight line with events strung out upon it in chronological order.

Being able to recall a series of happenings in a chronological sequence is not enough for a proper study of history. In order to comprehend historical events, the time perception of the reader must be sharpened a bit more. He must be able to visualize *duration,* a passage of time, a stream of time flowing on and within it a series of connected episodes. A person should normally have attained the ability to apply duration to history by the time he reaches the twelfth or thirteenth year. Perhaps the best way to contrast the two viewpoints would be by comparing a travelogue as seen by a succession of slides and as seen in a motion picture. In the one case there are a series of still shots and episodes, rather disconnected and abrupt, while in the other the action flows smoothly, revealing all the scenes and events in sequence without breaking the action. The history student who merely masters a series of disconnected facts is learning by the use of slides and misses the continuity, the real flow and growth of the narrative in what he is observing.

Incidentally, considerable variation in the keenness of time perception exists among adults. Even among them a tendency persists to recall a personal experience as part of a blurred general past rather than as one in a definite series of happenings. The ability to judge duration varies greatly. Much may depend upon surroundings; a husband may have employment where he is constantly aware of the passage of the hours, while his wife, not under quite such compulsion of the clock, remains considerably less acute in her perception of the progression of time. In countries undergoing industrialization, factory managers invariably find it difficult to educate former peasants to the necessity of beginning promptly on the hour and to an understanding that time is valuable.

Only when the youth has arrived at a maturation of his sense of time is he ready to comprehend fully historical narration. The average college freshman has possessed this faculty for only five or six years. Even after high-school courses, even after learning the major milestones in human development, he may still, all unawares, be dominated by the child's conception of the past. The past may still be a jumble of chaotic facts, events may be only points of reference, no conscious effort having been made to apply a personal measuring stick of time comprehension to history. A sequence of related events remains an outline to be memorized. The much-hated dates, in themselves only the husks of learning, are all that is grasped out of the flow of time and temporal duration. This is likely to lead to a positive distaste for history in junior and senior high school. History, filtered through a child's time concepts, becomes only a caricature of its real, living nature.

Outcroppings of the Past

The student who has an acquaintance with geology is apt to have a decided advantage in developing his historical thinking. There may, at first glance, seem little relationship between the story of human society and the science of earth and rocks. Nor may it become readily apparent during the initial study of such phenomena of physical geology as erosion and weathering, of glaciation, and of the formation of various types of rocks. Then one day there may suddenly come—with the impact of a revelation—the overpowering comprehension that these same processes, seemingly so commonplace, so much a part of the everyday world, have been functioning uninterruptedly for a length of time stretching incredibly beyond human ken. Simultaneously, the idea is really grasped for the first time that the familiar hills and valleys, rivers and lakes, did not suddenly take form, but are the works of these same commonplace forces. The present forms take on new meaning, are endowed with a life of their own, cease to be a static and shadowy background for our own activities.

In an intellectual sense, of course, these things are already known. Yet, here too, it is hard to escape childhood conceptions. The small child's disposition to regard the inanimate as an appendage of himself is apt to be tenacious. Even as he grows older and learns otherwise, this is likely to remain surface knowledge only, his innermost being retaining his original feeling as a child. It has been proved that persons from age ten to fourteen tend to retain their naïve notions of the physical world even after they have learned the scientific explanations in school. As indicated earlier, the world of the child *is*; the biblical account of a sudden creation is natural to the childish and primitive mind. Our ideas seem to be drawn to the more primitive level by a mental force of gravity unless the person consciously assists the more complex and true explanations to gain the supremacy. Curiously enough, our minds appear to recapitulate the ancient and constant struggle between the primitive and the civilized. Hence, as narrated above, the sensation of revelation, of windows opening in the mind, when a new insight suddenly is absorbed and takes permanent possession of the thinking faculties.

A conscious effort is required in order to make ourselves at home, to orient ourselves, in a world of far greater dimensions than that to which we are accustomed. For this reason, geology can be good training for the study of history. Geology develops a sense of time and a "feel" for the pattern of history. It does this by relating the present to the past, showing them as part of the same, and, by showing how the familiar and ordinary extends into the past, opening a friendly gateway for the exploration of the past. The unknown, the miraculous, is minimized, and the haze of unreality that seems to cover the past evaporates. History ceases to be a part of fiction.

The analogy between the two can be made more precise. Over the hundreds of millions of years in which the work of erosion and sedimentation has been under way, successive layers or strata of sediments have been deposited. Soil so deposited, with time and pressure, becomes rock. The geologist is the historian of nature who can identify when and under what conditions the various features of the physical world came into existence. He knows the characteristic fossils in each layer of rocks, each the record of one age, and, recognizing these, can describe the conditions of the earth when these fossils were living creatures.

The geologist lives in a present world which is also the world of the past, for everywhere he goes, his trained eye reads in the present the presence of the past. Outcroppings of rocks in one hill may date from the age of the dinosaurs, while another outcropping nearby may go back to the first amphibians. Close at hand, layers of igneous rocks, which were laid down as lava, allow him to visualize the existence of volcanoes of which no other trace now remains. The geologist may look down into a valley and be able to declare that thirty thousand years ago a large river flowed there. He may discern evidences of catastrophes of nature, whose work still shows in the contours of our world. In such a case as the Grand Canyon, the rock chronicle of life from its earliest inception can be seen in one sweeping view.

Particularly in the analogy of successive layers and their outcroppings into our familiar surroundings are geology and history similar. The functioning of human societies is also producing "layers," which in turn are covered over by later societies, yet which in many instances leave "outcroppings" visible to the practiced eye. Various institutions, modified by later times, still remind of a past age. Ideas and social practices can be dated in origin. The disasters of bygone days have left their marks upon the actions and thoughts of our generation. He who knows history adds depth to his observation, knowing, as he does, the origins and life history of what he sees and thereby understanding a great deal about its purpose, how it functions, and why it operates in this particular way.

Place names of the United States furnish a good illustration of how historical layers can be detected. Someone who knew nothing about this country could reach certain conclusions about its history simply from looking at the names, on a map, of our cities, mountains, and rivers. He would find everywhere characteristic Indian names of natural features, such as Mississippi, Susquehanna, and Erie, and would immediately know by the uniform deposit of such names that Indians had at one time lived over the entire country. From the predominance of English names of our cities, he would be able to visualize an English people spreading over the country, conquering and settling it, a whole new deposit upon the map. He would notice with curiosity the sprinkling of names from the European continent and deduce, perhaps, that other nationalities had participated in a subordinate role. The density of Spanish names in the West would probably provoke special interest and lead to the conclusion that another deposit had been laid down there quite independently of the English. He might even compare the widespread usage of Spanish names for geographical features and the more restricted usage for cities and decide that the Spanish had explored large areas which they had not settled. Probably he would be interested also in the French names in Louisiana and Quebec and see still other independent deposits there.

It would be possible for the observer to do the same with the place names of Great Britain, thereby discerning the historical strata laid down, in turn, by the successive invaders of the island. Anthropologists, in fact, tell us that some of these layers are still visible in certain aspects of the physical make-up of the population. The Welsh, comparatively brunet and brown-eyed, are primarily the descendants of the pre-Celtic stock which had come from the Mediterranean. Moving eastward, the observer enters the belt of those who are predominantly of Anglo-Saxon descent and who show it by their lighter complexion. Then, along the northeast in old Northumberland, the still lighter coloring yields evidence of Danish invasion. Hence, in crude form, here are "outcroppings" of three different historical periods in the history of Britain which can still be discerned. What of the Roman conquest? If one wished to push the parallel still further, perhaps here is an example of erosion, for the Romans were partially expelled and partly absorbed to the extent that very little visible survived of their period beyond some place names. The pre-Roman Celts were also absorbed as a physical type, although their language remains as another form of outcropping. The Celtic or Gaelic language has never quite died out in Ireland, Wales, and Scotland. One might deduce that a great deposit of English-speaking people has occurred, from the Continent, covering over or "eroding" altogether the older Celtic; only out on the fringes of the west, the last place of refuge, does the older language still survive.

To the eye of the scholar, trained in the knowledge of past events, the map of Europe, political and ethnological, represents a living record of events that happened long ago. The ethnological map of European Russia contains numerous splotches of color indicating presence of Finnish-speaking folk. These patches are scattered, oftentimes surrounded by Russians, and spread from the Baltic to the Urals. At first glance the areas may simply seem scattered, but upon a closer examination, they look remarkably as though they were segments torn loose and dispersed by some gigantic explosion or by some propulsive force moving to the northeast in the central region of Russia. This is precisely what happened, although the actual explosion or impact was centuries in the making. Originally, the Finns inhabited central Russia. In the early centuries of the Christian Era, the Slavs began to move into the region, and as they did so, absorbed some of the Finns, while the others retreated to the northwest, north, and northeast. A few stood their ground and still live on their ancestral soil, islands in the Russian sea.

Anyone who studies both French and Spanish immediately discovers how similar their vocabularies are. He would find a like kinship in Italian and Portuguese. The student is here experiencing one of the consequences of the existence of an empire which perished fifteen hundred years ago. Though the Roman Empire passed, the Latin vulgar dialects continued to exist, gradually modified by local usage into the modern Romance languages. On the other hand, the failure of the Romans to conquer the Germans is still evident from the survival of the Germanic languages in Germany, Scandinavia, and Great Britain.

The map of the world is a jigsaw puzzle that took millenniums to put together. The Arabic world stretches from Morocco to the borders of Iran. This tremendous area, the entire southern shore of the Mediterranean and eastward, is testimony to one of the mightiest convulsions in human history, the great expansion of Islam after the time of Mohammed. Consequently, the deposits left by the Roman Empire and by the age of the conquering Caliphate still face each other across the great sea of the Old World. They are visible in language, in religion, in architecture, and in less obvious forms.

Sometimes the circumstances which helped to shape the jigsaw puzzle seem trivial, yet were lasting in effect. In the period of collapse of the Roman Empire, a huge forest, called the Silva Carbonari by the

Romans, covered the central portion of present-day Belgium as an extension of the heavily wooded Ardennes region. Through the whole region and stretching westward to the sea, the inhabitants spoke a provincial form of Latin. As the defenses of the empire weakened, Germanic invaders, the Franks, were allowed to settle on the Roman side of the Rhine in return for assistance against the depredations of their relatives. These newcomers were decidedly unpleasant neighbors for the more civilized, Latin-speaking natives, and many must have fled for refuge to the forest. Frankish warriors under Clovis later went on to conquer Gaul, future France, but were too weak numerically to give a Germanic language to that country. In western Belgium, however, Frankish dominion over several centuries led to the appropriation of the open farming country by German-speaking folk, the Franks themselves, and others, until the resultant Flemish tongue became the permanent language of the region. Meantime the Latin of the forest dwellers had been transformed into a dialect of the Latin-descended French. Consequently, the existence of a forest of fifteen hundred years ago determined that Belgium today has two languages. The strangest part of all is that they say the border between the two languages today is within a few miles of the outer limits of the ancient forest!

Are, perhaps, all of the great movements in the past? A second reflection, however, will suffice to recall that a great many Americans are only second- and third-generation, that our fathers and grandfathers participated in numerically the single greatest movement of peoples in all history, the making of North America into English-speaking terrain.

These illustrations of historical deposits are taken from linguistic or ethnological references. There are, of course, other forms also. As the British withdraw from certain of their possessions, one can see that they have left a political deposit in the political practices of Egypt, India, Pakistan, Ceylon, and Burma. The vast technological changes of the past century are building up, all over the world, a new form of society and are relentlessly eroding outcroppings of the past.

Some of the outcroppings can be dramatic contrasts to the age. The white man, coming into contact with the American Indian, was seeing how his own ancestors had lived a hundred generations before. There is a fascination to the work of the anthropologist, for he is dealing with the types of culture that more advanced peoples abandoned millenniums ago. He is, in a sense, visiting his remote ancestors, seeing how they lived and what they thought. The psychologist even reports that some of our ideas, in our twentieth-century minds, are actually reminiscent of those of our remote primitive ancestors.

Personal Contacts with the Past

All these illustrations may seem remote from our own lives, for we are dealing with wider perspectives and longer durations than we can readily grasp. Individually, we are a part of or affected by these greater movements and institutions, yet at times we find it difficult to comprehend them, and especially so in the fairly even tenor of existence in a stable society. Only at such a time as, say, when one is drafted into military service, do we feel acutely how closely we are a part of the larger historical movement.

Some of the outcroppings can be decidedly personal. The sight of the President of the United States, a governor, or a senator brings a momentary sense of contact with the larger dimensions of history. We may, as participants in a war, have been a part of the formal, traditional history. Beyond the realm of immediate personal recollections lie constant opportunities for extending our memory by means of accounts we hear from persons who have participated in historical events. The country is still so young that history by word of mouth from the pioneers remains common. Family histories constitute a type of personal acquaintance with history.

Museums offer an opportunity for the individual to dip into the past, seeing with his own eyes the costumes and tools of the forefathers and leisurely imagining a reconstruction of their lives. The author recalls vividly the sensation, when, after reading a history of ancient Egypt, he visited a museum in Chicago and came upon the mummy of one of the Pharaohs whose exploits had been narrated in the book. This was not merely a name in a book or a statue. This was *he* personally, the actual head and skin of one who had died more than three thousand years ago. (Paradoxically enough, the only king that the author has ever seen with his own eyes has been dead for more than three millenniums. Some people might say that this is rather appropriate for a historian!)

Another form of artificial retention of the past is the collection of antique furniture and the copying of styles of architecture. Even the changing fashions of dresses sometimes recall the past. It is a profound historical truth that a "new look," in whatever phase of life, usually represents a resurrection of the past.

Observances of holidays and anniversaries serve as frequent reminders of important historical events: in this country the Fourth of July, Armistice Day, Thanksgiving Day, Columbus Day, and birthdays of certain great men; in France, Bastille Day; Guy Fawkes Day and others in England. The hundredth anniversary of a state's admission to the Union calls for a special celebration. Religious anniversaries such as Christmas and Easter commemorate events of long ago. All these recall to our contemporaries the values and the struggles which helped to determine the contours of our society.

Physical survivals of the past which are still in use make up another category of historical outcroppings. Our foods have a story behind them as to their places of origin, how they were discovered by man, and how they were put to use. Prosaic as these may seem they deserve attention, for they are at the very basis of human life. For example, our various meats call up the memory of how early man became pastoral by learning to keep animals in captivity and so took a tremendous step in the direction of civilization. The cultivation of cereals was another great accomplishment. Common ordinary salt was the cause for many a tribal war. So ancient are these acquisitions that they are taken for granted; yet these are, in a sense, historical outcroppings.

In some instances, foods *have* played a part in our more recent history. Tobacco was a basic element in the story of the founding of the Virginia colony. Coffee, in Latin America, played a similar role. The potato and corn, of course, spread from the New World in relatively recent times. Spices, a word encountered in all histories of the Age of Discoveries and often read without meaning, are the pepper, cloves, and cinnamon found in every cupboard. Commonplace now, they were then so precious that they were largely responsible for the expansion of Europe into the Far East. It took the Second World War and the cutting of the route to the Far East to remind this generation that spices are still primarily a product of those fabulous Indies which Columbus, Vasco da Gama, and other men of their age dreamed about.

Clothing—again prosaic—yet other historical factors are existent in their background. We think about the Age of Discoveries in terms of great men and a map, though food and clothing were primary motives for the explorers. We learn about the Muscovy Company, the Hudson Bay Company, and the French penetration of America without always fully grasping that glamorous exploration and adventure were merely by-products of the search for such commodities as furs. Pictures of the Founding Fathers of the republic in knee breeches recall to us that the long trousers of our day are comparatively recent attire for polite society. Trousers were originally worn by the lower classes, while the short breeches were a symbol of superior rank for those who did not have to labor. The insipid reign of the drab male attire of our own day, reflective of the sober, industrious middle classes, was first ushered in by the overthrow of the aristocracy in the French Revolution. Communist leaders are oftentimes shown wearing caps; caps versus hats, another historic issue, for in Russia hats were associated with the upper classes, and the capitalist continues to be designated by a hat in Soviet cartoons. In the Spanish civil war of the 1930's, the wearing of a hat in Republican Spain was strongly inadvisable for the same reason.

Nearly all our familiar institutions are outcroppings of historical deposits. The days of the Old Testament are far past, yet orthodox Jewish religious practices are reminiscent of them. Although the Roman Empire has long since departed, the Roman Catholic Church stands like a mighty rock, formidable and enduring, in its language and officials recalling the days of that long-departed empire. The Reformation was well under way four hundred years ago; enter the Lutheran or Presbyterian churches and observe the forms of worship dating from that period. The Masonic temple stands as a monument to the form of religious and political philosophy born in the eighteenth century.

The world is a museum and mosaic of the past. The modern traveler has the privilege, virtually, of going in a time machine to regions where he finds himself in the ancient past. If he wishes to see agrarian methods as his ancestors practiced them in the medieval period, he can still find them in some areas of Europe. If he desires to go to the Old Testament times, he can find them in many parts of the Arabic world. If he would like to watch the Egyptian farm as he did in the days of the Pharaohs, let him go to Egypt today. The explorer, at least, has the privilege of seeing tribes where life remains fundamentally unchanged since the hunting and fishing period of humanity. Everywhere the traveler finds evidence of the modern age; everywhere he will find survivals of the past.

The first important idea to grasp in studying history is that in the world in which we live, the contours we accept as a part of our *modern* world are in reality the outcroppings of layers laid down in the past. As we read history, we are not merely scanning remote occurrences, but rather are studying the contours of our own environment as they were originally created. In our three-dimensional surroundings there is actually a fourth dimension, Time, whose evidences are not readily visible to the unpracticed eye, whose influences may be unconscious, yet which persistently permeate our lives.

3

The Nature of Social Forces

In the last chapter we used geology as an analogy to bring out certain aspects of history. Perhaps we can learn more of the relationships of ourselves to the historical processes by another analogy—the weather.

Although the weather is always with us and in one way or another influences our daily lives, most of us are not sufficiently mentally alert to know much about it. We think in simple terms of wind, rain, snow, and clouds, as men have always done. Wind is "wind" and that is self-explanatory, obvious and simple, a thing in itself as we learned it in childhood. We are not likely to recognize the wind as being the movement of air flowing from areas of greater air density to areas of lesser density. The high cumulus cloud of a summer day is seen purely as a cloud, rather than as visual evidence that where the cloud is located, the invisible upward draft of warm air is meeting colder air and is causing a condensation of water vapor. We perceive fog as a certain form of weather and it, too, is a distinct and separate sort of thing for us. Perhaps the first airplane ride through a cloud became an exciting experience when the clouds actually proved to be fog. A new experience brought together two hitherto separate objects of perception and proved them to be the same thing.

That is, we think in certain elemental terms and, unless spurred beyond them for some reason, are apt to continue using them. We take what the five senses give us out of immediate experience and do not bring into our mental pictures the less evident but more fundamental reality that lies beyond our customary perceptions. We do not make use of wind, clouds, and rain as manifestations that permit us to see, indirectly, such invisible phenomena as water vapor in the air and the high and low pressure areas. Yet we walk the earth surrounded by these comparatively intangible energies and are constantly affected by them.

In a very similar way, we think of the historical forces in the most simple terms of leading political figures, Congress, Republicans, Democrats, and so on. These also are the manifestations of a less obvious reality which, in fact, determines the events that pass before us. The energies and forces which play upon the established institutions assail our senses all the time, are ever-existent, yet form only a confused, meaningless, and scarcely observed series of impressions unless we have additional training. Their dimensions are too large for the untrained eye to grasp, and their nature is quite different from the physical phenomena about us, but they nevertheless exist and impinge upon us in thousands of ways, affecting our lives and perhaps determining our fate.

To some extent, of course, the shrewd observer can know a great deal about the weather without any training, and hence the "weather signs" and folklore about the weather. Some have been proved correct by science, while other ideas are sheer superstition. The same is true of the thoughts of men concerning society.

The meteorologist can essay a prediction about the coming weather. He cannot do so exactly, as everyone knows, yet he discerns what the possibilities are, what the component elements in a situation are, and what the odds are in favor of a certain development. He knows that there are large-scale climatic conditions covering the continent and beyond, pressure areas and "fronts," that will determine what the weather in his own locality will be like. By getting information of this sort from many areas, he secures the whole picture and is able to calculate the probabilities of the local weather.

The historian cannot predict, and he never will be able to do so. There are too many elements in the situation and too many variables. What he can do is to scan the whole picture, descry the trend of developments, and study the life history of institutions, classes, nations; he thereby becomes able to formulate a good estimate of what can be expected. Although history does not repeat itself, broad parallels can frequently be discerned. By carefully comparing these for similarities and differences, he may reach certain conclusions of a probable nature. When used cautiously, past development and experiences furnish a valuable guide to present-day conduct. Like the meteorologist, the historian gets information from far places, but they are in the time sense. His "weather map" covers years instead of square miles. He studies "pressure areas" and "storms" also as they are relayed to him by history.

Most people have accepted these social storms in the same spirit as storms of nature, feeling them to be inevitable and inescapable. Chroniclers and prophets through the ages ascribed them to the will of God: "God sent this scourge to punish us for our sins." Social calamities were deemed beyond human understanding or human control. The recurrent sentence in the old Russian tsarist anthem sums up the feeling: "Oh, Lord, give to us peace in our time!" At most, these storms are ascribed to the work of one man, and a Roosevelt or an Eisenhower, a Stalin or a Hitler is personally credited with being responsible for events. Up to a certain point this may be true, yet they would never be successful if powerful forces were not assisting them. The men who guide policies are not purely rational men meeting in solemn conclave with perfect freedom to decide what is just and proper; many forces play upon anyone in authority and determine his actions.

The contours and energies of our society are of the utmost importance to us. These are the surroundings college youth will later traverse and the influences they will feel throughout their lives, and in them are the social forces which may elevate or crush the individual. It is sensible for any person, as he prepares for the profession that he hopes will bring him success, to learn to scrutinize carefully the environment through which he must travel.

Society is dynamic. These contours change, however slowly. This may not be so clearly realized in America, where, in the midst of apparent stability, alterations are gradual and nonviolent. The few years in which a college freshman has been awake to events in his country scarcely provide sufficient perspective for an appreciation of how much even the American scene does change. Consider, however, the effect of social forces upon a German born, say, in 1900, when Germany was a well-ordered and prosperous empire. The First World War interrupted his normal pattern of life and probably brought death to one or more members of his family. He was very probably himself in the army before the end of the war. Its conclusion brought collapse of the seemingly firm foundations of his world. Germany abruptly became a republic, amidst considerable confusion, in which he had to adjust to very different political surroundings. Inflation, unemployment, and depression followed, all this in his twenties, when he was trying to secure a niche in society and begin a family. In his early thirties, the Nazis took over, bringing a new set of circumstances, including renewed prosperity, dictatorship, mass hysteria, and concentration camps. Then came another war, the destruction of his home city by air attack, and ultimate enemy occupation. If his home was in the eastern zone of Germany, a Communist regime was imposed upon him, and if he lived east of the Oder, he became a homeless refugee.

This is an extreme example of how the "storms" of human affairs interrupt and damage the career of the individual. The twentieth century, nevertheless, has a tempo as much more rapid than past centuries as our modern automobiles exceed the horse and buggy, and any person facing a lifetime in the second half of the century must expect to see continued stormy political weather. We live in that sort of age.

Social Forces Create Basic Historical Patterns

To the question of what makes history move, why events take the shape and direction that they do, no easy formula will ever provide an answer. Much is the result of accident, of coincidence, of the efforts of individual personalities; yet beyond these are the more constant social pressures and forces, which, playing upon individuals and institutions, oftentimes carry the human fate with them in a mighty stream regardless of individual will or program. History, seemingly chaotic when viewed through the single event, takes on a more understandable pattern when surveyed through these social forces.

For example, the city-states of ancient Greece, of Renaissance Italy, and of medieval Russia had certain things in common which were not caused by the copying of any original prototype but rather were due to the fact that they were all responding to a similar set of circumstances; the dominant groups in each had like motives, were animated by similar social forces, and responded in approximately parallel ways. The mercantile classes of Venice, of Lübeck, and of London were all driven by similar motives. The craft guilds of Milan and Florence as well as those of Bruges and Ghent had like problems and, often, corresponding responses to them. Although there were from fifty to a hundred Italian city-states, their individual patterns of evolution in the medieval and Renaissance periods often bear a remarkable resemblance to one another. The names of people and of parties vary, the individual crises and important episodes are all different, but in the sum total there is a basic pattern with which most of them roughly conform. Nomadic tribes, whether of Mongolia or Arabia, have tended to resemble one another in their mode of living and in their tribal histories. In all modern industrial nations like social forces emerge, and, in the long perspective, their histories show comparable patterns.

Social forces are human energies which, originating in individual motivations, coalesce into a collective manifestation of power. The initial personal motivation may be economic, religious, lust for power, intellectual curiosity, or any other impulses which drive men to action. Under certain circumstances, these energies will be combined in order to achieve purposes desired by a whole group of people. For present purposes, we may list six general types of social forces: *economic, religious, institutional* (mainly political), *technological, ideological,* and *military.* They are subject to considerable variation and are overlapping, as will be seen in later chapters.

Note that the presence of a social force of any importance nearly always involves the concomitant existence of a *social group.* In our constant references to such economic groups as the middle class, the workers, or the peasants, we are dealing with larger blocs of people than are likely to possess any single inclusive organization. Within such a group, however, one or more formally organized associations may appear which express the wishes of individuals motivated by this particular interest. The word *association* refers to *a social group whose members have certain interests in common and who organize for common purposes.* The churches obviously have been created by drives essentially of a religious nature; labor unions represent workers; Chambers of Commerce and kindred associations speak for businessmen; the list could be extended indefinitely to include such specific societies as the Farm Bureau, the American Legion, the American Medical Association, the Sons of the American Revolution, the American Association of University Professors, the Masonic lodges, and the Rotarians. Some of this latter group reflect economic purposes only partly or not at all, other social forces, perhaps not even among the above six, being responsible for their creation.

A college campus, incidentally, is a rather faithful copy of American society in this respect. Not only does a campus usually have its class and student-body government, analogous to state government, but it also includes fraternal groups, religious bodies, professional organizations, and honor societies which are parallel to the adult associations. Any undergraduate knows that there is competition among these groups for members, prestige, and important offices. A principal difference, however, is found in the less potent economic motives present in campus groups.

Our American associations are valuable in the proper functioning of the democratic system. They permit and usually stimulate the free expression of opinion, and they train democratic leadership. Whereas the lone individual may find difficulty in making his voice heard, as one of a number of similarly-minded persons his opinions will register at other times besides the official elections and in other matters than those purely political. The associations are the intermediate step of social organization between the individual and the state. They are the "grass roots" of democracy.

The different major groups of a country are in a constant state of competition with one another for economic advantages, for cultural influence, or for such privileges as political power can give. The growth and decline of these major groups is not normally sketched in sharp outlines in a history text, the gradual changes in strength of the competing groups becoming perceptible only at intervals. The conflicts are fought out primarily in the market place and in the various organs that influence public opinion. Such rivalry is usually an indication, in the modern society, of growth and vitality as well as of the emergence of new interests. An American would judge that the freedom of this rivalry has been a potent factor in the astounding progress of our country. Any rivalry becomes harmful, however, if it is permitted to turn into serious conflict; such a development may endanger the unity and stability of society and the well-being of its members. The Marxist doctrine of class struggle has been pushed to this extremity, the Marxists taking one single type of social conflict, oversimplifying it, minimizing other types of social rivalry, and emerging with a gross distortion of the true nature of society.

In popular parlance, we talk about Great Britain or France or Germany following a certain policy. In our history we tend to treat the role of a country in its international affairs as if it were a single entity. This is a conventional oversimplification. If we wished to speak precisely, we would have to specify which group or groups in the nation were so influential that they were able to move a country's affairs in a given direction. There can be no unanimity in a nation, and we are speaking only of the most forceful voices which for the moment become the voice of the country.

The remainder of this chapter and part of the following one will be devoted to illustrating the nature of the social forces of an economic nature. Religious and technological influences will be introduced in the next chapter also, while the others will be deferred for later analysis.

Economic forces will be illustrated first because they are probably the easiest to observe and because most present-day historians seem to feel that they form the strongest social forces in society as a whole. Economic groups tend to display a certain consistency in their behavior. By securing a generalized picture of their usual conduct, of the nature of their efforts, a student of society can at least have an idea of the direction of the social forces wherever his studies may be centered. The economic groups furnish us with certain rudiments, certain bases, from which we may probe more deeply into the structure of society and the causation in any given event.

Economic Groups in the Medieval City

The various polls of public opinion have become an established feature of American public life. Anyone who has studied them knows that the occupation and income of a person is apt to determine his political views. People tend to vote by their pocketbooks. There is, for example, a labor vote, a farm vote, and an upper-middle-class vote; the needs and outlook of persons in a common occupation are apt to be similar. In each of these there are some who do not share the group opinion, and this should serve as a warning that there are other factors besides the economic to be considered; yet in bulk they do tend to become a definite group and to serve as a factor in the life of the political community.

The tendency for individuals of a similar occupation to form a social group, which becomes assertive of its needs and claimed rights, is by no means limited to the American scene. The same tendency has been at work in every known society. Just as the geologic processes that we see today were operating in the distant past, so the social forces, varied by circumstances, have functioned throughout the length of recorded history. As mentioned earlier, urban life has repeatedly brought into existence certain economic groups whose direction of endeavor remains relatively constant. A brief survey of the typical successive developments in an average city of the later medieval period should provide some idea of these social forces.

The merchant, in the earlier feudal period, must at times have felt himself a stranger in a foreign world. The noble often looked with scorn upon the man who had no land, associated him with the lowly peddler and despised foreigner, and was apt to regard him as a runaway serf, meriting no consideration. His property, outside of the conventional limits of feudal usage, was likely to be pillaged.

A merchant needed personal liberty, the right to travel for the sake of business, and insurance against seizure by some greedy lord. The market place required protection. The richer people hoped for guarantees that they would not be subjected to forced loans. Failing to get these necessities from a lord, the merchants banded together into associations or guilds to provide proper safeguards for themselves, in what became the opening step in their fight for freedom. The guilds might offer their assistance or gold to one side in a war between nobles in return for a grant of privileges, they might help the king against his recalcitrant feudal vassals, or—frequently—they took advantage of the financial embarrassment of their superiors to purchase a charter. The list of demands that the traders wished granted is a catalogue of the differences between the feudal and mercantile worlds: the freedom to marry as they pleased, the freedom of movement, the right to purchase and sell and inherit property, the sanctity of contracts, exemption from monopolies, tolls, tonnage, right of hospitality, dues, and the *corvée*. These men needed a better law than the feudal, with its duels and ordeals; the practical merchant desired courts with judges who understood business practices and where proof was the compelling factor in decisions.

In countries with a strong king, the traders generally extracted town charters from the authorities, giving them these gains, while remaining subjects of the king. They could then elect their own officials. One of the worst hazards of the business, sudden demands for large financial contributions to the crown, was minimized when they procured the right to tax themselves, thereby assuring themselves of a set amount, rather than an arbitrary figure.

In areas of weak central government (or none), the merchants might seize complete control of a city and govern it as a virtually independent state. Frequently they ran afoul of the bishops. This prelate was often feudal lord of a town, the actual governor of it, and he would look with no mild eye on the rivalry of the merchants with interests so different from his own.

Once the merchants controlled a city, the town policy would reflect their needs. The merchants were no more likely to rule for the benefit of the lower classes than were the nobility. They were prone to resort to warfare in order to open up necessary lanes of traffic for their goods, regardless of the cost to the other inhabitants of the municipality. Rival cities struggled for possession of valuable markets and resources. Florence fought long wars with Pisa for the sake of an outlet to the sea, while

Venice and Genoa battled for control of the eastern Mediterranean waters, the winner taking over the greater part of the trade of the region. The merchants built roads, bridges, canals, and imposing civic edifices, these expensive public works being paid for by the lower classes as well as by themselves. Banks and stable currency were provided. The ruling group fixed prices, wages, and standards without much regard for the welfare of the workers. They carefully assured their own clique control of exports and imports and excluded merchants of other cities from their own markets. Trade secrets were guarded with great care. The surrounding countryside was subjected to the rule of the city, the nobles being defeated, in order to assure a steady supply of food.

The government was usually a republic. This was natural since only in this way could the large numbers of merchants all have their say. A town assembly, council, and a doge or burgomaster made up the government, although infinite variation in titles are found among the different cities. It follows that the merchants could be outvoted by the remainder of the citizens of the community, and therefore the trading princes took good care to weaken the assembly, to control the voters, or, at least, to keep the official posts within their own ranks. To prevent too many persons from entering their own merchant guilds, they limited admission to their own relatives, or to those with large fortunes.

While the commercial elements were rising to power, another economic group, the craftsmen, were also attaining importance. Although the traders and craftsmen usually worked together against their mutual oppressors and perhaps belonged to the same guild, the merchants eventually gained such predominance in affairs that the others found organizations of their own desirable. Attempts of the craftsmen to organize in their own self-interest were apt to be greeted by the merchants with as much indignation as the nobles had expressed toward the original guilds. The unrecognized groups of craftsmen also had needs—demands which often ran athwart the needs of the merchants: a guarantee of civil rights, an education in their own chosen craft, freedom to work where they wished, freedom to choose their own officers, recognition of their own property, and the autonomy of their own craft guilds. They also wanted a share in the government, since they paid a large proportion of the taxes and helped to man the armies and civil services.

As weapons, they could use the same tactics as the merchants had done. The craftsmen might ally with the king, rebel in conjunction with an enemy attack, or join one of the factions in an internecine struggle in return for concessions. They might simply rise in wild revolt, destroy-ing property and endangering the lives of the wealthy. Where they won, their demands were granted, and they were given representation in the government.

In the end, the process repeated itself. A new trend appeared in the craft guilds, once equality with the merchants was achieved. The masters of these groups made it increasingly difficult for apprentices and journeymen, the lesser ranks in the guilds, to rise to the rank of master. These latter became a part of the ruling oligarchy, while the lower classes remained disenfranchised.

The struggle for emancipation was resumed by the lower classes. New organizations were created, often camouflaged as religious orders. New revolts flared. The upshot was that the upper classes frequently abandoned democratic government in favor of a dictator or hereditary prince who would "keep order," that is, suppress the menace to upper-class domination. Sometimes the king took advantage of the disturbances to step in and restore his authority. Occasionally a captain of mercenaries joined the cause of the lower classes for his own purposes and ruled the town in the ostensible interests of the plebeians.

The above survey is drawn with too broad strokes to satisfy an exacting medievalist. It does, however, give an indication of the social forces at work, regardless of which Italian city is under consideration, and it does provide a basic frame of reference, useful for further learning. As more specific details are added, the pattern will be found to vary from city to city, sometimes drastically, but the foregoing does provide a general picture.

Social Forces in Florence

Now let us examine in more detail the social forces in one specific city, Florence, as they existed in the fourteenth century. Florence was at this time one of the great cities of Europe, numbering perhaps 130,000 souls, its banking interests and its textile industry being particularly important.

In effective control of the state were the seven more powerful guilds or associations of the city These *arti maggiore*, as they were called, were the judges and notaries, the importers of foreign cloth, the money-changers or bankers, the local cloth manufacturers, the silk merchants, the physicians and apothecaries, and the furriers. Each of these guilds was governed by an elective committee, usually chosen to serve for six months. This seems to be a democratic system until it is realized that only the masters, strictly limited in numbers, were permitted to participate in the guild elections. The remainder of the working force belonged nominally to the association but had no voice in its affairs. The management of the group, consequently, rested firmly in the hands of the wealthiest, and the guild policies reflected their interests. Since the leaders of the guilds selected the board of priors (the executive committee of the whole city), who controlled the government of Florence, it can be readily understood that the policies of the government were aimed at protecting the merchants and producers of textiles, the bankers, and the other four groups represented.

A considerable number of other economic groups existed in the city. Five others—shoemakers, blacksmiths, builders (masons and carpenters), secondhand dealers, and butchers—were sufficiently powerful to constrain the *arti maggiore* to give them some share in the government. These so-called *arti medie*, or middle crafts, would have been too dangerous to the government if in opposition and were therefore allowed some voice.

As for the other guilds, they were omitted altogether. There were eventually nine of them, including such groups as bakers, innkeepers, armorers, and sellers of salt, oil, and cheese. Quite naturally, they also wanted representation among those who determined the affairs of the city. They had to wait until a financial debacle temporarily weakened the greater guilds, and they then struck for power. A new apportionment of power was agreed upon: the greater guilds to choose two priors, the middle group three, and the lesser guilds to select three. This arrangement lasted until near the end of the century, when the great guilds again were successful in regaining mastery.

Let it not be forgotten, however, that even when all the regular guilds were represented, the interests of the masters remained paramount. The vastly larger number of workers still had no voice in affairs. These *popolo minuto* were poorly housed and suffered severely from high prices set by the guilds and from periodic unemployment during business depressions. During the century, attempts to organize were initiated by them also, and such efforts were repeatedly suppressed.

What we see, then, in Florence is that the economic forces of the city had produced definite groups or associations, each the result of the mutual economic interests of its members. Each association was, to some degree, in competition with all the others. The officials of a guild were always alert to advance the well-being of their own group. For purposes of government, certain of these groups had formed a permanent alliance and were thus able to dominate the policies of the state. A constant pressure was maintained by those not in the alliance to be permitted to share in its power and benefits. Finally, the economic force of the workers was also manifesting itself and seeking the same sort of organization as the others.

Beyond and above these various economic forces was a fundamental loyalty to the city as a whole. Patriotism, usually overriding internal dissensions of the diverse elements, imbued the citizens with the will to make and keep Florence independent of all neighbors. We ought to take note of this as a different type of social force, institutional or political in nature. We might also observe, for future reference, that the economic force of the guild, in governing the city, was perforce partially transformed into an institutional or political guise also. That is, political and economic motives became intermingled.

The chronic state of warfare with other city-states nurtured another form of social force. A military establishment was necessary, both to keep subjugated towns subservient and to ward off outside attacks. A citizens' militia served the purpose originally, but military duty was an onerous one which citizens preferred to avoid. Growth of military proficiency eventually necessitated the use of professionals. Out of this situation grew the bands of mercenaries who hired themselves to cities in need of armies. They soon discovered their own strength and the possibility of extracting blackmail or even of obtaining political control of the city by physical force. Here was an entirely different social force, the *military,* thrown into the struggles between factions. Even some of the stronger cities of Renaissance Italy succumbed to conquest by a professional *condottiere* (leader of mercenary troops) of the time.

Other social forces were present in the city. Such religious orders as the Dominicans and Franciscans provided part of the spiritual tone for Florence. In addition to the preaching office itself, they tended the sick, did charitable work, kept a sharp eye out for heretics, and provided a considerable portion of the work of scholarship. With their churches, cloisters, and dormitories, they were part of the city, though also a distinct type of social group, as the Church was everywhere in the medieval period.

One other economic group, at one time strong in Florence, has not been mentioned because it had ceased to be of great importance by the fourteenth century. This was the landed nobility. The lesser nobles of the neighborhood had, many of them, moved into the city during the twelfth century. They carried their feudal habits with them, including their incessant feuding with one another. They built towers in or near the city, reminiscent of their castles, and from these waged wars with one another. When the guilds achieved power, they compelled the nobles to dismantle their fortresses, and the aristocracy gradually blended into the bourgeois population.

The Nobility

Although the landed nobility in Italy had declined greatly in relative importance, in Europe as a whole they remained a major force. A brief indication of the direction of their activities, so much in contrast to the urban forces just surveyed, is therefore imperative. It was the understanding of the age that the noble's role lay in the defense and governing of the community, in return for which the commoners attended to those material needs which he would not be able to provide for himself. Because the feudal lord was, first of all, a warrior, the basic values of his society were likely to center about prowess in battle. Fighting was his chief stock in trade, and the knight was therefore judged by his courage, strength, and military skill. Since he was also an administrative link in a society held together by the individual loyalties of the feudal system, loyalty was necessarily extolled as a great virtue—particularly, it must be added, for one's own subordinates.

Where the lord was relatively unchecked by superior authorities, his natural tendency would be to expand his own holdings. An appetite for territorial expansion characterized all ambitious lords. Wars with one's neighbors, grants from the king, or fortunate inheritances were possible methods of satisfying this aspiration. The third of these devices entailed contracting marriages with other noble families in such a way as to secure their lands upon expiration of their male lines of descent. While trying to build up a larger domain, the lord must endeavor to keep his own vassals obedient and to build up the productive capacities and wealth of his fiefs. Cities, however alien their ways might be, were excellent possessions to have for their financial rewards, always provided that they could be kept under proper controls.

Where the growing power of the urban elements or the increasing authority of a central government threatened the ordained sphere of activities of the nobles, they usually appear as defenders of the existent order.

The nobles are often found working together as a class against the crown. They served as a social force to prevent the absolute rule by the monarch. They insisted upon meetings of the king's council in which they had their spokesmen, and later they often supported the rise of a parliament or estates-general in order to keep watch upon the actions of their sovereigns. The Magna Carta of England is an illustration of how the nobles might take the lead in checking a would-be despotic ruler. They might demand charters of liberty forcing the king to promise not to violate their liberties. The aristocracy found it in their interest to leave the kingship elective in order that they might bargain with every prospective candidate. In such countries as Poland, Hungary, Denmark, and England, their efforts foreshadow the attempts by the later middle class to secure control of the machinery of government.

As for the serf, he was the silent partner whose labor made possible the full operation of the social forces of the nobility. There could obviously be no independent social organization on the feudal manor. Peasant movements for additional freedom had little chance of success. All that could happen were savage peasant uprisings, a product of spontaneous exasperation, which were inevitably and ferociously put down by the nobles. There were some compensations for the serf. In an age when personal safety was at a minimum, the lord was pledged to protect him, and the castle served as a refuge in case of invasion. He could not be legally moved from his land. The peasant was assured of the use of a piece of land in an age when to be landless was to be a social outcast. He was part of a community which would ensure him help in case of personal misfortune.

Speaking more broadly of the rural population as it is met throughout modern history, it may be said that the farmer is usually a conservative. Dwelling on his plot of ground, at the mercy of the weather and its various catastrophes, he is usually preoccupied with the immediate round of work. His interests will revolve primarily about the farm and his neighborhood. Historically, he has shown himself suspicious of "newfangled" ideas. In the political prism of modern democracy, he is found on the Right and usually votes for the *status quo*. His chief motivation has always been the acquisition of a piece of land and then more land, since in his environment the possession of soil brings security and social status. For the parties advocating change, the farmer or peasant vote has always seemed a dead weight and has been unfairly accounted as dictated by ignorance. In the recent past, modern education and communications have made possible the creation of political parties by the peasants which have pushed well-planned programs of their own.

The Nomads

Simply for the sake of comparison, one other group, the nomadic tribe, may be briefly described. Only as Europeans have expanded to other parts of the world does the nomad appear in modern European history, and then only to a slight extent.

The society of the nomad smelled of horses and cattle, of stables and the campfire. Usually inhabiting a harsh environment, the nomad lived in a severe world. The cattle and sheep, upon which human life depended, had to have grazing lands and water holes. Out of such considerations arose the petty warfare which makes up so much of the history of the wilderness. Such a life, much moving, much fighting, made warriors out of the tribesmen, and martial values were exalted since they were necessary for survival at all. Men had to be tough and adjustable. It is no wonder that wherever they appeared they came as fighters and that their most frequent employment in the civilized communities of Asia and Africa was as soldiers hired by the government. Nor should it surprise one if these soldiers, contemptuous of the civil population, took charge of the government altogether. The history of Western Asia seems a story of successive barbarian rulers out of the plains, who imposed their will upon the merchants of the cities and the passive peasant population.

With the great distances nomads had to travel, the horse was invaluable to them. They were the ones who originally tamed the horse and passed on the art to the sedentary peoples. It can almost be asserted that man was a parasite of the horse, using the animal as he did for transportation, the horseflesh and mare's milk for food, his hide for garments, and the dung for the campfire. Horses were wealth and property, and it is easily understandable why horse theft was punishable by death.

Land, as such, was not apt to have value for the nomad. It was simply a grazing area to him. The water hole was likely to be of more value as property for the entire tribe. The nomad's most bitter hatred was directed at the farmer, who fenced off good grazing land. The man on horseback had the utmost disdain for the plodding farmer, mired in the mud, and for the merchant, with his mercenary habits and unwarriorlike traits. Both were fair game for the nomad, both were beneath humane considerations, and raids into civilized areas served both for sport and for the acquisition of wealth. The nomad has been, throughout history, the barbarian lurking beyond the frontier of the civilized world. In times of decline or internal convulsions, an India or Iran might be conquered and come under their rule. However, it should be noted that these nomads, if they did conquer, would in a few generations themselves succumb to the more advanced culture of their subjects, and presently the cycle of barbarian attacks and conquest would be resumed.

The pastoral peoples had a strong sense of their individual places in the tribe. A tightly knit community solidarity was necessary in a society where an enemy might unexpectedly attack. They kept elaborate genealogical charts and were acutely conscious of the traditions of their ruling family. Thus, the descendants of Genghis Khan ruled over the Tartars in Mongolia, in the Crimea, and in Turkistan for five or six centuries after his death. The Arabs of the Caliphate kept the Abbassides on the throne long after these had lost all real power, and men who can trace their descent to the family of Mohammed are still honored in Islam.

When a person arrives in a strange town, the mind does not immediately grasp the details of his new environment. He sees the general pattern in a confused sort of way, plus a jumble of unassorted details. These first impressions are gradually replaced by a more precise and well-balanced mental picture. Authentic learning occurs naturally in this manner, the general first coming into focus, and the specific details being arranged later in their proper places. As more particulars are learned, the general impressions undergo further modifications and correction.

The foregoing descriptions are general. They are the first impressions of the nature of social forces. They depict the general needs and goals, the natural direction of energies among certain groups. More precise illustrations will follow.

4

Social Forces

One Sunday morning in August, 1573, the good people of Plymouth, England, were in church. The pastor had probably reached the middle of his sermon when the somnolent peace of the sanctuary was disturbed by agitation at the rear of the edifice. Someone at the door had been watching two vessels enter the harbor. Ships are always news to a seafaring town, and the natural curiosity turned to excitement when it became apparent that this was Francis Drake returning from the Spanish Main.

One can imagine the scene that followed. The observer whispered the news to other men in the back of the church, and these spread the report to the back pews. The pastor's oration was now disturbed by the whispering voices as the word spread down the church: "Drake is coming into the harbor!" Someone—probably a heavy investor in Drake's expedition—felt that he had urgent business down at the wharfs, rose in his seat, sidled out of the pew, tiptoed down the aisle, and hastened away. A second person, encouraged by the example of the first, did the same. Now several people were rising and leaving the church. Whole pews of people began pushing out of the door. The church was soon emptied, and one may suspect that the preacher hurriedly concluded his day's homily on morality to follow his congregation in an enthusiastic reception for the daring pirate.

Those who had made contributions to help float the expedition undoubtedly were well satisfied with what they found. On a later expedition, the one where Drake pillaged the Spanish on the Pacific Coast of America and then continued on around the world, his gamble brought 4,700 per cent on the original investment. The little episode at Plymouth illustrates two things: considerable enthusiasm existed among the English people for adventuring in strange waters, and some people were able and willing to place their money in those ventures.

Some Englishmen were growing wealthy in the sixteenth century. The flow of precious metals from America to Spain and from there to the rest of Western Europe had forced prices up while the more stable and customary wage rates followed more slowly. Those fortunate enough to benefit by this, the merchants among them, were able to save additional money. This extra capital, according to the philosophy of these industrious men, had to be invested in some way. Naturally the possibility of sharing directly in the wealth of the New World would appeal to them.

We must not let the remoteness of these events deceive us into seeing something abstract or mysterious. To understand this social force, one merely has to look at the life on the Main Street of an American town today. Simply take the prevalent spirit of capitalism (a person who has worked in a store knows it better), of the desire to use one's money for the acquisition of more wealth through investments, and transfer it to the men of the sixteenth century. This economic factor, with which we are all familiar, was, in part at least, responsible for the Age of Explorations.

These men lacked the wealth to launch such enterprises individually. A means had to be found whereby these individual riches could be combined, a small sum for each man so that a lost gamble would not break him, yet the total in combination would be large enough to finance distant expeditions. Societies of merchants adventurers who had united for mutual advantages and protection already existed, but each person traded his own goods directly in such an organization. A new type of arrangement now emerged whereby a group of men combined for one expedition, each person buying a certain share in the enterprise. If the venture succeeded, the profits would be divided according to proportionate investments and the company ended. A new company would be established for a new attempt. This form of company permitted greater centralization in administration, since the investors handed over the control of the venture to a few elected delegates. This type of concern soon led to the so-called "joint-stock company," in which the men owned their shares permanently and received dividends on their stocks as long as the combination thrived. Such a company bore a considerable resemblance to the modern corporation.

An important point to note is that whereas the original merchant adventurers had themselves been merchants actively engaged in trade, under the new system anyone in England with the requisite capital for at least one share could adventure his money without taking an active role himself in the actual operations of the company. Thus, capital in England was marshaled for the conquest of new trading terrain.

About two hundred London merchants formed a company in 1553, each one contributing £25 for the equipping of a small fleet and the purchase of trading materials. Three ships were dispatched to the northeast, the idea being that they should sail around the northern coast of Siberia and thus reach China! Ignorance of geography prevented a realization of how suicidal this project would be at that time. As it turned out, the crews of the two ships found the northern coast of Lapland more than enough; they were driven ashore and died of the cold. Richard Chancellor, captain of the third vessel, entered the White Sea and decided that Russia was more promising than the remote shores of Cathay. He traveled through the wilderness to Moscow and visited Ivan IV, not yet grown sufficiently cantankerous to merit his later epithet of "The Dread" or "The Terrible."

Out of this visit grew a brisk trade between Russia and England. When Chancellor returned to London, a more formal organization was established with a royal charter. Over two hundred persons joined it, including such important men as Walsingham and Cecil. A "governor" was selected to head the company and twenty-eight "assistants" were chosen. (These latter would be called a board of directors in a modern corporation.) A wharf was rented in London by this Muscovy Company, and a fleet of ships sailed for the White Sea annually. At the Russian end of the trip, an island in the White Sea was used as a base, while houses of trade were secured in Moscow and several other Russian cities. English cloth was the usual commodity taken to Russia, while rope, whale oil, wax, and caviar were among the Russian products in demand in England.

The success of the Muscovy Company stimulated other trading organizations, the names of which reflect the widespread nature of English interests. They included the Eastland Company for the Baltic region, the Company of the Levant in the eastern Mediterranean, the African, the Hudson Bay, and the East India companies. The last of these became the most famous of them all, these once humble traders ultimately conquering a vast and incredibly wealthy empire. The company was initiated in 1599, when a group of men agreed to subscribe enough money to finance an expedition to the East Indies. Some of the men were already members of the Company of the Levant. A royal charter was secured in

1600, and a governor and "assistants" were selected. When the time came to make good on their promises by providing the money, some of the men decided that they did not care, after all, to adventure their money halfway around the globe, and they reneged on their promises. A period of recriminations followed, and the backsliders were threatened with jail. Most of them finally did pay, but the members had to contribute additional sums until £72,000 had been collected.

The fleet of five ships left early in 1601. In the Indies, the men purchased cinnamon, cloves, gum-lac, and pepper—much pepper. They started back early in 1603, and spent the next six months living with vast quantities of pepper in the holds—martyrs to the modern cuisine. Arrived safely home, the huge store of pepper was divided among the happy investors, each one to derive his own profits therefrom. The consequent glut of pepper drove the price down, and there was a surfeit of it in England for a half-dozen years.

Notwithstanding this too-successful upshot of the first trip, a second fleet went out in 1604. It suffered from Dutch attacks, lost one ship which sailed for home and was never heard from again, but came back with an abundance of spices—except pepper. The investors in the East India Company secured a 95 per cent profit on the results of the first two voyages. Naturally the company continued to send fleets to the East.

Not all the ventures, by any means, were successful. One immediately thinks of the colony planted by Sir Walter Raleigh in Virginia, the "lost colony" which disappeared, leaving only the word "Croatan" carved on a tree. A half brother of Raleigh, Sir Humphrey Gilbert, encountered a heavy storm on the return from his second voyage to America, and "suddenly her lights were out. . . . For in that moment, the Frigat was devoured and swallowed up of the sea."[1] Sir Martin Frobisher, another famous explorer, returned to England from America with three ships laden with stones supposed to contain precious metals. The stones were carefully unloaded, and, despite adverse reports by assayers, were locked up in Bristol Castle for safekeeping. After a second expedition had brought 1,200 more tons of the rocks, the investors, whose mania for gold had overridden Frobisher's own skepticism, were finally compelled to accept the verdict that there were no precious metals in them. The last report, true or false, is that these rocks were used to improve a road at Dartford. If so, as someone has commented, this must have been the most expensive road in all England.

[1] See the Bibliographical Notes at end of this volume for sources of quotations.

Notwithstanding failures, such handsome profits did accrue to successful investors that a great many people were tempted to gamble. The shareholders of the East India Company in 1617 included the following: 15 dukes and earls, 13 countesses and titled ladies, 82 knights, 18 widows and maiden ladies, 26 clergymen and physicians, 313 merchants, 214 tradesmen, 25 merchant-strangers, and 248 others. Records of the Virginia Company provide similar evidence that various classes in England from the highest nobility to a variety of commoners were involved in these enterprises.

A few of these men were particularly distinguished. Sir Thomas Smith, son of a haberdasher, became the first governor of the East India Company and usually held that post until 1621. He was the treasurer of the Virginia Company in these same years and was governor of the Somers Island Company (Bermuda), besides being active in the Muscovy and French companies. His house on Philpot Lane for many years was the rendezvous for merchants, sea captains, and adventurers.

A man like him was Sir Edwin Sandys, son of an Archbishop of York. He was active in the East India Company, the Somers Island Company, and was especially involved in the Virginia Company, where he succeeded Smith as treasurer. He had a great deal to do with helping the Pilgrims get financial aid for their settlement. Sandys was a prominent member of Parliament during these years and so was Sir Thomas Smith. These were hard-boiled businessmen and persons who exercised important influence in the government.

The name of Sir Francis Walsingham catches the eye because of his advisory capacity toward Queen Elizabeth I. In this earlier period, he was a member of the Muscovy and Levant companies and helped to promote the search for the Northwest Passage. It can easily be imagined how important his enthusiasm in government circles was for the earlier period of English commercial expansion. The Privy Council of England in the days of James I included such men as the Earls of Arundel, Surrey, and Pembroke, and Sir John Coke.

It is natural for us to read the chapter in the textbook on the discoveries and, regardless of what the book may say, continue to assume that these explorers had our point of view of their activities, that they were primarily seeking fame and glory, that they were deliberately writing their names in the history books. Admitting that undoubtedly many of them did desire a famous name with posterity, one must not neglect the other factors, particularly the economic motive here illustrated. Even Christopher Columbus made certain, or thought he did, that he would gain something more substantial than glory from his first voyage. The grant to Columbus in the spring of 1492, states: "Our will is, That you, Christopher Columbus, after discovering and conquering the said Islands and Continent in the said ocean, or any of them, shall be our Admiral of the said Islands and Continent . . . and that you be our Admiral, Vice-Roy, and Governour in them, and that for the future, you may call and stile yourself, D[on] Christopher Columbus, and that your sons and successors . . . may call themselves Dons, Admirals, Vice-Roys, and Governours of them."

For Americans today, the Virginia Colony was the *first* colony, the beginning of white settlement. For those who founded it, the enterprise was an investment made by practical men who thought that they saw an opportunity to make one pound bring back several more. The Plymouth Colony, its members driven by religious zeal, was backed by men interested in the financial angle to the venture. The Puritan colony, also primarily religious in inception, nevertheless brought to America some men deeply involved in English commerce. The East India Company had no ambitions of political conquest at the outset. A time came when the collapse of the Mogul Empire in India compelled the merchants to reach a decision: they could proceed to end the growing anarchy which was ruining their trade, or they could pull out of India. Their investments were too large for the latter, a whole class of people in England had a vested interest in the trade, and the once humble company began a gradual conquest, one step leading to another, until a group of stockholders found themselves masters of a subcontinent.

In this section we have seen individual men, each imbued with economic motivations, combine their efforts in order to further their mutual interests. Social forces are human energies which, originating in individual motivations, coalesce into a collective manifestation of power. Although this social force was generated by what were, after all, only small groups of men, the power which radiated from these nuclei wrought a transformation in the world of that day.

The Religious Social Force

Among the early settlers in the first Spanish colony of Hispaniola was a man by the name of Bartolomé de las Casas. His father had sailed with Columbus on his second voyage. Las Casas inherited his father's adventuring spirit, came to Hispaniola, and there received an allotment of land and sufficient Indians to work it. For a time, he seemed well on the way toward becoming a successful planter.

Gentlemen of Spain were warriors and did not work with their hands. True, not all of these adventurers had been gentlemen in the old country; that was precisely the reason why many a poor man found his way to the Indies, where pedigrees were not so important. On the island there was seemingly an ample supply of Indians, probably only semi-human anyway (in the eyes of the settlers), and these furnished a providential source of hands for the fields. The natives were speedily put to productive labor in a manner that caused a fearful mortality rate. The settlers were men who were frequently at odds with the moral code back home, the conquest would have a naturally brutalizing effect, and the old compulsions of conscience and Church lost most of their effectiveness in the wilderness. The result was an inhumanity which was the reverse of the noble sentiments originally uttered by Queen Isabella and Columbus in regard to the Christian duty of saving souls.

Almost from the beginning, some persons were horrified by the colonial practices. The first Dominican monks on Hispaniola were courageous enough to speak bluntly about the new slavery. Conscious of their lonely stand and the hostility to them, one preached a sermon on the theme "I am the voice of one crying in the wilderness," wherein he told the irate congregation that if these abominations did not cease, he would not give them the sacraments. He went back to Spain and straight to King Ferdinand. (Queen Isabella was no longer alive.) His narrative of atrocities shook even that cynical old monarch. The monk asked him if he had ever ordered such deeds. The sovereign responded, "No, by God, never on my life." The upshot was the issuance of laws for the protection of the Indians. But the Indies were remote and enforcement impossible.

Meanwhile, Bartolomé de las Casas had been stirred by the spectacle. In spite of persuasions by others, he could no longer endure to be a part of such a system. He gave up his holding and his slaves and carried his indignation back to Spain. There he divulged the true situation to Cardinal Ximenes, the potent primate of the Spanish Church. That stern paladin of the Church, already somewhat aware of what was going on, stirred up the wrath of King Ferdinand to the point where new, and equally futile, gestures were made in defense of the natives. Las Casas was appointed Protector-General of the Indians.

It would be pleasant to record his success. Such was not to be, could not be, under the social and economic conditions of Spanish America.

Las Casas spent his life traveling in Mexico, Central America, and Peru, always exhorting the hostile settlers, needling the officials to obey the royal orders, and meeting the failure of the religious man who tries to make society square with the professed moral code. The natives, however, gave him an almost idolatrous worship, the first genuine Christian that many had met. In these natives, he and his kind won one type of victory, for by their work they brought to the Indians the religious teachings of the Old World and began a centuries-long process of civilizing them. Also, by their preaching and their constant moral pressure on the officials and on the Crown, they began to tame the conquistadores and their sons. The real question is not if men like Las Casas saved the Indians from the conquerors' wrongdoing, but rather how much further human nature would have relapsed into the habits of savagery if this restraint had not been asserted from the beginning.

Another great representative of the Christian missionary spirit, Francis Xavier, traveled in the opposite direction, to the Orient. He had originally gone to the university at Paris with no intention whatsoever of becoming a missionary. At the university he encountered Ignatius Loyola, then beginning his career as the founder of the Jesuits. Loyola changed Xavier's whole outlook on life by his persuasive eloquence. Xavier set out to rival the earthly empires won by Spain and Portugal with a spiritual empire. He won such astounding success that he has been called the Alexander the Great of the Church.

He traveled from one Portuguese colony to another on the way to the Orient, stopping at each to preach for a while. Arriving in Goa, India, the capital of the Portuguese commercial empire, Xavier went to work to lift the tenor of life there. He scourged the local iniquities and caused the dismissal of a Viceroy whose immorality he found repugnant. At Malacca and in the Indonesian islands he also worked, establishing and strengthening churches. In 1549 he landed in Japan, the country where he won his greatest victory. Within about thirty years after his arrival, it was estimated that there were 150,000 Christians in the country. The total number of missionaries was only about fifty in 1580. Long before that date, Xavier had tried to gain admission to China. He died on a small island while waiting for permission to enter. It was claimed that he converted a million souls in his lifetime.

The Christians in Japan were not left alone, however, by the government. The officials became fearful that the missionaries were only the forerunners of foreign political penetration. A bloody persecution began in which the Christians were compelled to trample on a cross as a sign of renunciation of the Western faith. Those who refused died of decapitation, fire, hanging, or crucifixion. The city of Nagasaki, a Christian center, was particularly suspect, and even in the later eighteenth century all its inhabitants were required to tread on a cross in an annual ceremony. Despite the rigorous persecution, something of an underground church did survice and once again emerged to freedom in the nineteenth century to become the nucleus for a modern church. It was the final irony of fate that nowhere in that Oriental empire could an atomic bomb from Christian America kill as many Christians at once as at Nagasaki.

Bartolomé de las Casas and Francis Xavier are two illuminating examples of the many thousands who participated in the expansion of European political control and European civilization in the Age of Discoveries. As a matter of fact, men driven by spiritual impulses had helped to maintain contact with further Asia throughout the Middle Ages. The Nestorian Christians of Syria and Mesopotamia had followed the trade routes to India and China. In the medieval period there were Christian bishops in Iran, India, Tartary, at Samarkand, Kashgar, and Khan Balagh or Peking. There were assuredly more Christians in inner Asia at that time than now.

Before Marco Polo, Christian friars traveled from Europe to the court of the great Mongol Khakhan. John of Plano Carpini made the ten-month journey in 1245–46. His suggestion to the Mongol "Emperor of Mankind," who ruled from the Pacific to the borders of Poland and Syria, that he accept the crucified God of the contemptible Europeans was received with sarcasm. In less than a decade, another European missionary made the seven-thousand-mile journey. His interview with the emperor was rendered difficult by the fact that the local interpreter had consumed too much *kourmiss,* the Mongol version of firewater made out of mare's milk.

The religious spirit awakened in various people—soldiers, nobles, scholars—and brought them to the work of the Church. This was another type of social force altogether different from the economic, one possessed of tremendous vitality, and one which carried the better part of European civilization to the New World, Africa, and the Orient. These men were the other and redeeming aspect of European conquest. They left the pomp and power of the mother church far behind and came, usually dressed in the most humble garments, relying only on their power of human personality and the Word of God.

Those people who read all events in only economic terms undervalue the power of ideas. To assume that the religious expressions of the Age of Discoveries were purely a cloak for other purposes is to misunderstand the age completely. In some cases, it is true, pious sentiments were sheer hypocrisy. In many more, they were the same sort of rationalizations that we all indulge in, whereby we put a lovely name on less lovely motives and even convince ourselves. Beyond all this, however, there remains the mood of an age that believed that the salvation of the soul was all-important. It drew many thousand devout men to the far corners of the earth, into the wilderness, and among savage tribes at extreme self-sacrifice and danger.

They were not always successful. The lands of Islam remained impervious to the message, as they have to this day, for the religion of Mohammed provided an equally aggressive spiritual motive. In the age of Xavier, in fact, the Moslems were converting Indonesia and portions of Africa. The African natives were not ready for Christianity and could perceive little more than the outward ceremony. Temporary successes were won in Africa only to melt away later. In Latin America the conquest was permanent, although the native backwardness weakened the quality of the Church for many generations. In China, the Christians encountered a sophisticated civilization more than a match for themselves.

The Technological Social Force

In 1588, as we all know, the English defeated the Spanish Armada. We also know that this victory is commonly regarded as the beginning of British sea power, as the initial assertion of that strength which was to raise England to an empire. This battle, however, has another significance also, and to understand this we must backtrack a little into the story of the development of the ocean-going vessel.

The basic principles of the ships used by the Mediterranean trading states such as Venice, Genoa, and Catalonia, had altered very little since the days of the Greeks and Romans. The galley, propelled by oars, remained the customary means of transportation. Especially was this true of the war vessel. The galley was capable of rapid movement regardless of winds and could be maneuvered quickly as conditions of battle required. It possessed an iron beak in the prow, with which to ram the enemy, and battles were fought by boarding the enemy and defeating the ship-borne soldiers. Basically, the naval battle was fought by soldiers, once the initial stage was over.

For purposes of commerce, the Venetians developed a three-masted vessel, which relied primarily or entirely on wind. These galleons could be built larger, hence carry more goods, and were cheaper because fewer crew members were required. They were, however, at the mercy of the swift-moving galley in times of war. For this reason, the galley continued to carry most of the commerce during the thirteenth to fifteenth centuries.

As the Portuguese, and then the Spanish, ventured down the coast of Africa and into the Atlantic, a drastic change was in order. The ocean-going ship had to make long journeys in which the crew must depend on food carried on shipboard. The galley could not carry enough food for the large numbers of rowers required. The explorers therefore had to depend on the sailing vessel exclusively. The Portuguese developed the caravel, a vessel capable of making headway against adverse winds and of maintaining a brisk speed.

While the Spanish used the large sailing ship on the Atlantic, they continued to use galleys for war in the Mediterranean. The famous Battle of Lepanto in 1571 was fought by galleys on both sides with the traditional maneuvering, ramming, and boarding. When the Spanish Armada was dispatched against England, the bulk of the fleet consisted of the large and imposing merchant galleons customarily used for the Atlantic trade. But the *ideas* of the Spanish commanders were those of the Mediterranean galley warfare. They expected to fight another Lepanto, if it came to a battle, in which the clash would be won by the redoubtable Spanish infantry carrying the English ships by direct assault.

The English, on the other hand, had never been great users of the galley. When they became interested in seafaring on a large scale in the sixteenth century, they used the sailing ship exclusively. The ships that came out to meet the Spanish were smaller, faster, and more maneuverable than the bulky Spaniard. What was of more importance, the English had grasped the importance of artillery. Their ships were able to pour deadly firepower into their opponents far more rapidly than the Spanish.

The battle was fought the English way. The Spanish were never able to come to grips with the English, who remained at a distance while inflicting havoc on the Spanish decks. Driven into the North Sea, the Spanish preferred to go around the British Isles rather than force their way through the English in a second battle. Two concepts of naval warfare had met, the traditional Mediterranean galley tactics and the new oceanic ship equipped to fight chiefly with gunpowder, and the latter had won.

This is an illustration of a third type of social force, that of technical development. Changing conditions compelled men to adjust to them by new devices, or inventions, or ways of doing things. The new situation in this case was the problem of travel on the wide oceans which were now being opened up. Added to this was the increasing use of gunpowder, which completely revolutionized warfare. That country which, by accident or design, had best adjusted to these changing circumstances would have a decided advantage over its rivals.

The preceding two centuries had seen a notable evolution in land warfare. Early in the fourteenth century, the feudal nobility, whose very existence stemmed from their success as mounted, armored knights over any other type of armed force, was defeated at Courtrai, at Bannockburn, and at Morgarten, by commoners with pikes. These pikes were 22 feet long and were extended in front of a square of soldiers in such a fashion that a charge by the mounted knights amounted to mass murder—no longer of the peasantry but of the knights. Then the English developed their famed longbow, which wreaked more damage. The change which finally ruined the nobility as *the* fighting force, however, was the use of gunpowder. The field gun was used effectively by the French by 1450. The Ottoman Turks used it in their final assault on Constantinople in 1453. (Splendid symbolism this, the venerable capital of Roman empire, never before taken by Asiatic invaders, fell when the Turks employed a modern tool of war against the ancient walls. Much of the success of the Turks in their conquests over Christians may be attributed to their more modern means of warfare.)

The handgun was also being developed in the fifteenth century and was first used extensively in the Hussite wars. The appearance of the pikemen and the musketeers meant the creation of new professional armies drawn from various classes of society. They were expensive and only the well-to-do territorial lord or monarch could afford them. A notable increase in the power of the national kings followed.

The European of the time of the Crusades had been unable to make any appreciable advance against the Moslems. The Russians had been crushed by the Tartar hordes of Asia. The Vikings had not dared to settle the New World because their small numbers could not prevail against the Indians. A few centuries later, ridiculously small numbers of Spaniards reduced the Indians of Mexico and Peru, the Russians speedily advanced across Siberia, and the Portuguese smashed the Arab commercial domination of the Indian Ocean. What made the difference? Surely there had been no sudden improvement in the physical stock of the Europeans.

What happened to make the initial military advance so successful was the tremendous working of this social force, this development of technology, of which one feature was the more advanced military weapons. With gunpowder and the military organization required for its use, a few white men were more than a match for native hordes. One almost might say that the Europeans had ascended, during the Renaissance, to a new plane of existence. They were now *modern* men, in weapons at least, fighting against men of medieval and ancient times.

Social forces of economic, religious, and technological natures have now been illustrated. Institutional, ideological, and military forces will be examined later. The institutional factor, put very briefly, manifests itself in the tendency of all institutions to expand their power. The ideological deals, as the word indicates, with the influence of ideas, and the military originates in the necessities of armed defense. These are six social forces which generate dynamic energies in society; they furnish the power for the loom of history.

5

Causation

Sooner or later in a course dealing with European history, the question "What caused the Reformation?" is almost certain to appear. Confronted with this crisis, some people have been known to profane their bluebooks with the assertion "Martin Luther—he did it," in whatever verbose lengths they are able to contrive. Another popular aphorism that is frequently used is "The Church was corrupt," followed by a similar plethora of words. The old favorite (for certain questions), "The king was weak," is less frequently attempted here, probably because the person who can see how this one applies to the Reformation is already capable of a more intelligent type of answer.

Consider the situation in the time of Luther. There must have been at least eighty million people upon the Continent at this time. Perhaps as many as fifty kings, lords, and bishops wielded sufficient power to exercise strategic influence in the direction of affairs. A proud and assertive nobility, a growing middle class in the cities, a numerous clergy with centuries of established prestige behind it, all of these crowd the scene. A number of social forces were in operation, among them those indicated in the preceding two chapters. Yet—Luther did it! Although educated people do not anticipate miracles in nature, the same individuals may blithely announce miracles repeatedly as they examine various historical episodes!

The lowliest freshman can know more about the causes of the Reformation than could the great reformer himself. Luther blamed the events on the sinful nature of his opponents and on deliberate oppression by the Church. He believed that his opponents were pawns of the satanic power which was working for the destruction of man's salvation. His antagonists considered Luther a willful troublemaker, whose conceit caused him to exalt his own notions above the wisdom of the ages. His break with the old Church was often attributed to his inability to control his passions, the marriage of the former friar to a former nun seeming to provide ample proof of this.

In the heat of conflict, the temptation to ascribe malignant characters and purposes to one's adversaries is often irresistible. This is as true now as in the time of Luther. The political party finds it a highly useful technique to blame all the misfortunes of the time upon the other party or its leaders. Herbert Hoover thus received full credit for the Great Depression. Franklin D. Roosevelt was pictured as being personally responsible for the New Deal and as deliberately dragging his country into the Second World War. In the First World War, the Allies based their propaganda upon the principle that the German war lords were entirely to blame, and many people were quite content to limit the causes of the Second World War to Hitler and his lieutenants. Even in those cases where there may be a kernel of truth to the charges, these explanations are all vastly oversimplified. Men in public office and men who lead a popular movement must deal with certain sets of circumstances, the prevailing ideas and values, the pressure groups, and individual personalities that surround them, and, finally, with the crisis that confronts them. No man in a public movement is a free agent or can act entirely according to his own free will. Although he seeks certain objectives and will strive toward them, he must take into consideration other forces or speedily come to an impasse. All the factors in his time condition the way in which he shapes his destinies and help to determine the success of his policies.

The same criticism applies to all attempts to elevate any single person to the level of a superman or a political savior. A political party may consider it expedient to create an aura of greatness about a public figure, for the public normally feels the need of strong leadership. This device, which has been carried to an extreme by fascist movements, and by other dictatorships, should always be suspect, inasmuch as the real person, who is so trapped out in the external manifestations of genius, is highly unlikely to be more than an ordinary mortal. In general, excessive attention to the person of a leader is typical of countries whose citizens lack political sophistication.

The well-known classroom formulas, such as "Martin Luther—he did it" and "The Church was corrupt," are undergraduate samples of a type of reasoning which is, unfortunately, all too prevalent in adult circles also. Attributing major developments to one single cause, often with a connotation of great good or great evil, is typical of rudimentary political thinking. The second quotation above exemplifies the truism that if one can prove the attacked institution or party guilty of evil, the argument is more than half-won, regardless of the virtue of one's own ideas. Both approaches are based purely on superficial observation, on the tendency of the public to see history (or politics) only in terms of men, parties, and institutions, without troubling themselves with an examination of the deeper forces at work.

Another type of error is committed by persons who overrate one single social force in a situation at the expense of other factors. While this may win temporary political advantage, in the long run serious damage may flow from such a misconception of causation. Prior to the Second World War a group of people became convinced that the United States had entered the First World War primarily because of the activities of the munitions makers; some of these zealots argued that the economic interests of the "merchants of death" were the chief cause of war. This argument, reinforced by isolationist feelings, became so popular that Congress passed laws to prevent our shipment of munitions overseas in case of hostilities. Subsequent events proved that the munitions factor was a relatively inconsequential fragment of the whole picture. Meantime, the focusing of attention on a minor cause, to the exclusion of more potent factors, weakened the American position in time of crisis.

One more instance of an inadequate conception of causation may be mentioned at this time. Very often the *immediate* cause—whether seen in terms of a person or of an event—receives greater emphasis than it deserves. Recognition of the event (or person) which precipitated the larger sequence of happenings does not in itself explain why the chain of development occurred. Most of us have, as children, placed a set of dominoes on end in such a way that each falling domino would trip the next one. Although the pushing of the first domino was the immediate cause for all of them toppling, the sequence would not have been possible if the set had not first been placed on end. The more remote causes in history establish the particular situation which makes the whole historical sequence possible.

No single cause ever adequately explains a historical episode. A "cause" is a convenient figure of speech for any one of a number of factors which helps to explain why a historical event happened. The analogy of the dominoes is misleading to the extent that we may think of the events as following mechanically upon the original act. The direction that the medley of causes will precipitate events can never be precisely gauged while the event is occurring.

The problem of causation is inextricably connected with the whole question of movement and change in history, and some facility in dealing with it is indispensable for an understanding of the course of events. While studying several such historical episodes as the Reformation, the student should be training himself to see the various factors, the multiple causation, that enter into these situations until he learns to use this approach with present-day problems also. When a more advanced student is confronted with a question of causation, he can frequently hazard a fairly good response, even though he may not yet have learned the accepted explanation. He can do so because he has met somewhat similar instances before and will have a general idea of what the possibilities are. He has a certain fund of wisdom, a certain know-how in selecting pertinent factors, and will know which possibilities are likely, which unlikely, and which totally irrelevant. The purpose of this chapter is to provide an outline of causation in a major historical development, the beginnings of the Reformation, as an example of the type of reasoning which must go into the analysis of any such phenomenon. The same sort of approach should be used in connection with the Puritan Revolution and the French Revolution, as well as with lesser, and more simple, developments.

The Causes of the Reformation

Quite obviously the immediate cause for the Reformation is to be found in the activity of Luther between 1517 and 1521, although the selection of a specific event may bring differences of opinion; the most likely choices would be the nailing of the ninety-five theses, the Diet of Worms, or the famous disputation with Eck, in which Luther first clearly crossed the line between Catholicism and heresy. Identifying the initial spark, however, by no means explains the enormous extent of the conflagration which followed.

Luther's ninety-five theses immediately became the best seller of that day. Great crowds gathered to applaud him as he went to the Diet of Worms. If we can decide why he suddenly experienced this popularity, we may also gain some idea of the reason for his success. First of all, anyone who champions a cause and defies authority will attract a crowd of supporters, if only for the sake of the show. Luther had been denouncing the outrageous methods used in the sale of indulgences, an issue everyone could understand far better than discussions of abstruse theology. He was hitting out at unpopular figures, always a good way to attract a following. The friar of Wittenberg was a German, a son of the people, courageously talking up to pope and emperor, speaking for the common people and expressing what many of them felt.

Could any deeper reasons be at work that produced the quick acclaim for Luther's stand? Could it be that such a sudden blaze was generated because the inflammable materials had already been gathered by others? Had there been any earlier instances of men who had preached the same viewpoint as this reformer? (Remember that the mind of the historian inevitably gravitates in the direction of the past, seeking origins, relationships, and comparisons.) If so, this must indicate a general trend of the time in the direction of the reform which the Protestants were to take.

The career of John Hus of Prague is apt to come to mind. His life story bears several marked resemblances to that of Luther, and his proposals were very similar to those of his successors; there was a major difference however—he was burned for his temerity. A whole century before the Lutheran Reformation some of its principles were already widely approved, as witness the obstinate refusal of the Bohemians to give up the reforms of Hus. (Note, also, that Bohemia borders on Saxony, Luther's home district.) Other reformers had also preceded Luther: Peter Waldo, Wyclif, Savonarola, to mention the most prominent. Nor should the criticism of the Church by such writers as Erasmus and Valla be forgotten. Evidences of Protestant ideas appear everywhere in Western Europe during the preceding century. The monasteries were fair game for many of the leading writers of the time, the papal control of the Church roused voices in protest, and the financial dues were found irksome. Consequently, the historian may fairly assume that whatever the reasons for the Reformation were, they were operative to a considerable degree long before Luther. The Reformation could, conceivably, have begun in 1415, and it might have been postponed beyond 1520.

One point to note is that the criticism of the Church usually did not carry with it a threat to leave the institution. It was criticized, its officials castigated, its practices and policies assailed in the same spirit in which Americans treat their governmental institutions. The object was reform, not separation, the attacks representing no more a desire to destroy the Church than we expect to abolish Congress. Some people might dislike papal authority in much the same way as some Americans suspect the power of a strong President. When Luther appeared at Worms, he had no expectation of founding a separate church, and in fact he may have gone to the diet with a lurking hope of converting Charles V to his own viewpoint. Had this happened, a sweeping reform within the Church could have resulted and the universal Church remained united at least for a longer time. Even after the break had occurred, the Lutheran and Anglican churches insisted that it was the Roman Catholics who had abandoned the original idea of the Church, while they themselves were simply purifying it of impure accretions.

Luther dared to go to Worms. Powerful reasons must have driven him to risk the fate of Hus by making this journey. The assurance that his own prince, the Elector of Saxony, was on his side and the boisterous plaudits of the multitudes undoubtedly emboldened him, but beyond all this was an inner necessity, a personal conviction of a spiritual mission, that forced him to speak his mind. Luther's actions were indubitably born of motives other than personal ambition or opportunism: biographies of the reformer fully document the gradual development of his convictions from the time he became a friar until he stood in full defiance against the existent ecclesiastical authorities. This must be accounted as an instance where spiritual force acted as a primary impulse in history.

Only a rugged, roughhewn, obstinate man could have shouldered his way to success in the circumstances—the looming figure of Luther makes the personal factor important in the causation of the Reformation. Unless the odds are too great, the victory is likely to go to the side inspired by genuine zeal for a cause. Historical movements, however much they are impelled by economic and social factors, after all are carried through by men. Their states of mind are important. Even Luther, however, could have accomplished little more than propagate his ideas if he had not found many others in the same mood. Had Luther alone, or a small circle of disciples only, held Protestant ideas, no social force of sufficient magnitude to create historical events would have existed. When tens of thousands, however, were possessed of the same general outlook, the scene was set for action, and it took only Luther's words and actions to precipitate the formation of a spiritual force of enormous extent and potency. We are dealing with a large-scale example of a social force of a spiritual nature such as was described in the preceding chapter. In time, also, the Reformation stimulated an equally powerful reaction to it in Catholicism, a renewed spiritual vigor on the Catholic side sufficient to halt the European expansion of Protestantism.

The circumstances were ready for the man, and his religious zeal furnished a focal point for the hitherto diffused causes for the Reformation. One may legitimately question if any one single force, albeit as powerful as this one, could in itself have altered the course of history. From our perspective, at least, a number of social forces seem to converge upon the developing events and carry them forward.

We have seen gunpowder and the better ocean-going vessels make possible the expansion of the European into other parts of the world. The printing press, another technological advance, served as a tool of incalculable importance in the Reformation. Someone might argue very plausibly that no Reformation could have occurred had it not been for the invention of the printing press. Without this method of spreading ideas, the Lutheran doctrines could not have been disseminated so rapidly, and, if support had not quickly manifested itself, the emperor and Church might have succeeded in suppressing the movement. The press also aided the reformers by undermining the claim of the Church to pose as the custodian of final truth, since it was now becoming possible for more persons to acquire a copy of the Bible.

Social forces emerging from economic motives, powerful as they were, must have exercised an important influence on these events. The kind of merchant that we encountered in Florence or in sixteenth-century England, and who was also active in Germany, would deplore the constant flow of money to Rome. Most people, indeed, would feel indignation at this continual drain on the national wealth, and any rebel against papal authority would find useful ammunition here. The incessant sniping at the wealth of the bishops and the monasteries was partly due to the unfortunate contrast with the early ideal of the Church, but the criticisms were also likely to remind people that their contributions were not always usefully applied. Especially would the growing middle class deplore the drag on productivity caused by the clerical possession of land, the numerous church festivals, and the presumed idleness of the monks. With their ideals of thrift and industry, the middle class found many church habits irritating. Luther appealed to these feelings, with violent and exaggerated words, in his *Address to the Christian Nobility of the German Nation:* "What has brought us Germans to such a pass that we have to suffer this robbery and this destruction of our property by the pope? . . . Do we still wonder why princes, cities, foundations, convents, and people grow poor? We should rather wonder that we have anything left to eat."

We know that the nobles were always eager to expand their holdings. They had long eyed the lands of the Church, and the Reformation, with its expropriation of clerical wealth, offered the awaited opportunity. Many of England's noble families had their origin in grants of this kind, and these were likely to remain Protestant, since any reversion to the old order would jeopardize their new acquisitions. The princes of Germany likewise benefitted in this fashion, and the Crown in England and the Scandinavian countries added to its wealth at the expense of the Church.

After this brief survey of the impact of social forces studied earlier, let us see what other factors were influential in the situation. For instance, the thought must occur to one that the incipient restlessness should have been crushed by the imperial regime. Why did Luther "get away with it" when others before him had failed? The truth is that Charles V was in a dilemma. New on the throne, he was uncertain of his support and would hesitate before alienating his German subjects. Luther's own prince, the Elector of Saxony, was friendly to the reformers and possessed the force and prestige to raise a rebellion. The loud acclaim of the friar must have alarmed Charles and dissuaded him from a highly unpopular move. He undoubtedly underestimated the potentialities of the movement, the more so since he had grave political problems to grapple with elsewhere. The Ottoman Turks were approaching the far-flung borders of his realm, and Charles needed German unity in order to meet this threat. All in all, "the king *was* weak," not so much because of his own personality as in his inheritance of an enfeebled government from his predecessors.

The Crown was one of the institutions which should have suppressed the rebellion. The other was the Church itself. After many centuries as the universal Church of Western Europe, it had undergone both a loss of positive vitality and a diminishing strength in comparison with new emerging forces. It had failed to suppress the Hussite heretics. The internecine struggle between two organs of the Church, the papacy and the council, in the conciliar movement might be seen as a portent of disruption. Perhaps most significant of all, the Renaissance was having a debilitating spiritual effect upon the papacy; popes who were using spiritual resources for temporal ends were blunting their own swords. Having centralized the Church, they failed to live up to their responsibilities. By making the papacy synonymous with the Church, they drew upon the Church itself a shower of invective. The fact that many believed the Church to be corrupt shook the all-important allegiance of the great masses of the people.

The Church no longer possessed as much power, proportionately, either. New forces were rising which had long challenged the Church and which now overwhelmed it. One of these was the national state. Even at the height of the Middle Ages potent secular authorities had challenged the papacy. A king might possess the men and swords, the brute force, which could humiliate a pope, as Philip IV's men did Boniface VIII.

Inasmuch as the Church of itself could not muster a physical force to resist the state, the king's chief anxiety in such a conflict concerned the question whether his men would follow him against the Bishop of Western Christendom. As long as men were, in the last analysis, more loyal to the Church than to the Crown, the universal Church retained its power. The medieval sovereigns who defied the papacy were not attempting to rebel against the Church for the purpose of setting up a separate one. They continued to work within the framework of the older institutions.

During the fourteenth and fifteenth centuries, national kings continued to add to their power, and in France, England, and Spain these rulers arrogated to themselves increasing control over the national churches. Seen in the light of later events, the rivalry of nations during the Avignon period, the schism, and the conciliar movement betoken a growing national feeling which would burst asunder the ancient bonds. The Catholic Church was faced with its perennial problem, how to keep its international character although threatened by national feelings and provincial attachments. The Church, after all, was essentially an institution of the southland. From thence it had come, there it had matured and built up its customs and symbols. At one time, the cultural inferiority of the north caused these peoples to accept southern leadership as natural; as the northern peoples developed, however, the subservience to the south began to rankle.

In the northern countries, a sense of nationalism was a strong factor in the break with Rome. In Germany, where other national aspirations went unsatisfied, this was particularly true. The Reformation passed into effect in Sweden coincident with the overthrow of Danish rule. The English struggle against Spain would tend to associate the state church with national existence in that country. The native language was substituted for Latin in the churches of these regions. In nearly all instances, the advent of the Reformation brought added power and wealth to the kings or territorial princes. The institutional factor is a powerful one in the causation of the Reformation; one institution, the Church, was losing ground to another institution, the national monarchy, and the spiritual crisis precipitated by Luther offered the territorial princes of Germany and the kings of northern Europe a splendid opportunity to establish state control over the Church.

The foregoing outline, which by no means exhausts the possibilities of causation in the Reformation, does provide a check list of factors likely to be important in such a phenomenon. When a student is faced with a problem of this nature, a few general questions are of great assistance in analyzing the situation. When these are "tried on for size," some will immediately suggest causes, while others may have little relevance. The following nine should prove helpful: (1) What was the immediate cause for the event? (2) Had there been a background of agitation for the principles victorious during this episode? (3) Were personalities involved on either side whose strengths or weaknesses may have helped to determine the outcome of the struggle? (4) Were any new and potent ideas stimulating the loyalty of a considerable number of people? (5) How did the economic groups line up on the issue? (6) Were religious forces active? (7) Did any new technological developments influence the situation? (8) Can the events be partially explained by weakened or strengthened institutions? (9) Was the physical environment itself a factor in the situation? (It will be noticed that questions four through eight relate to various social forces already enumerated.) A systematic analysis of a problem of causation with the aid of these questions will ensure that all the major historical factors have been taken into consideration.

"Actual Origins Elude Us"

The factors in the above list obviously do not carry equal weight in the causation of the Reformation. Nor will they do so when applied to other historical events. Attempting to assess their proportionate importance, in any given case, is an excellent exercise in reasoning for the beginning student. Some individuals, reading the textual account of the theology, are apt to regard this as unimportant and will assert that the real reasons lie in the social and economic sphere. Others, of a more religious nature, are likely to take the religious ideas seriously, and in so doing probably better appreciate the motives by which the reformers believed themselves guided. Some will feel that the personality of the leading reformers bulk large in the outcome; others regard them as the puppets of more impersonal forces. Geographical influences will receive greater emphasis from some than from others. Unfortunately, no method exists for measuring these causes or for attaining a final verifiable evaluation. One possible empirical test which may help to weigh the respective merits of each cause is to imagine the Reformation with that specific factor omitted; would its absence have changed the course of events? It is in the interpretation of history that perplexity begins, but also much of the fascination.

Some perspicacious individuals may decide that the proportionate values of the factors vary with the country. Certain reasons may not apply at all in England or the Netherlands. Then, too, how account for Italy and Spain, where the Reformation made little headway? Were the factors listed above too weak in these countries, or did still other considerations enter the picture in these regions? The same causes may have different effects in different circumstances. In certain states with relatively strong central governments, such as England, Sweden, and Denmark, the Crown itself took the lead in severing relations with Rome, while in others, France, Spain, and Austria, the ruling dynasties opposed the religious changes. Ideas of the Renaissance undoubtedly helped to stimulate Protestant ideas in Germany, yet the Renaissance equally surely was a factor militating against the success of the Reformation in France.

One cause may stimulate other causes. The spiritual struggle of Luther brought economic and political influences to bear in his favor; their previous tendencies may have been in the direction which they took in the Reformation, but his deeds were the catalyst which caused positive action along these lines. Political action was an effect of the first phase of the religious controversy, and this effect in turn became a cause for the success of the movement. The revolt of the peasants in 1525 was an effect of the previous agitation; one set of causes released new and unexpected social forces, which in turn, by driving other groups into reaction, helped to deflect the Lutheran movement into more conservative channels. Although the city elements in northern Europe tended to support the Lutheran Reformation, the halfway measures adopted failed to satisfy some, and these same elements remained a strong factor in the appearance of Calvinism. In a large-scale episode, such as the Reformation, one cause may unleash other causes, a development which is originally an effect in turn causing further effects in a sequence of reactions.

When causes are traced into the background, the same never-ending sequence becomes apparent. One must arbitrarily cut the strands of causation at some point, for, as Cheyney says in *Law in History*, "Actual origins elude us; everything is the outcome of something preceding. . . ." The remainder of his sentence is equally pertinent to the chapter as a whole: ". . . the immediate, sudden appearance of something, its creation by an individual or a group at some one moment of time, is unknown in history."

We may perhaps have reached the limits of useful discussion of the subject. Until additional practice in analyzing causation has taken place, any further elaboration of the more complex relationships may be more confusing than helpful.

One warning needs to be added. The foregoing represents an attempt to provide a systematic approach to causation for the beginner. Reasoning, however, cannot be effective without the facts. A student is using facts from a textbook, class notes, and whatever other reading is provided. The historian, while using a basically similar approach, cannot be satisfied until he finds genuine evidence upon which to base his conclusions. There is only one way to achieve this: go to the evidence itself, which is made up of the records of that age. A reading of a few of Luther's pamphlets is apt to be revealing. The historian will want to read the opinions of many people who were contemporaries of Luther and Calvin. He will examine the declarations from the Roman Catholic side of the controversy. Other factors must be investigated. If he carefully examines the record in a spirit of humility, prepared to recognize tenacious reality rather than what he wishes to find, he is then prepared to formulate a worthwhile interpretation of the events.

6

Change and Continuity

Having devoted the preceding three chapters to a survey of forces which are dynamic in society and then to an examination of how several of these may combine in multiple causation for an event, we must now shift our attention to the forms of society themselves. Subjected to the incessant pressure of ever-changing social forces, these forms undergo a constant process of alteration. One of the principal characteristics of history is the grouping of our facts in terms of *growth* and *development*, of *continuity* and *change*.

We need not look far afield for simple illustrations of this seemingly abstract concept: the automobile and the game of football both display continuity and change in their development. Every autumn the automobile industry floods the country with ecstatic advertisements of the models for the following year. New names are frequently coined in order to emphasize the changes which are claimed for the new car. The new models make their appearance, changes are indeed visible, yet the car remains fundamentally the same; while the modifications from one year to another are perceptible, the car manufacturers are usually careful not to make genuinely revolutionary alterations, regardless of their advertising claims. Viewed over a ten-year period, however, the changes are likely to be dramatic, two cars of the same make, built ten years apart, often displaying few recognizable similarities. The additional streamlining of one year, a new type of shift another year, a different carburetor a third, ultimately add up to a very different automobile in appearance and performance. The automobile has been undergoing a process of evolution ever since its invention, always changing, yet displaying a great deal of continuity with the past. Even the first invention represented no complete break with the past. Its appearance was that of a "horseless carriage," and it was in fact a carriage equipped with a new means of propulsion.

Football, as a game of organized mayhem, had been played in England for centuries, albeit under the strong royal displeasure of kings who, as someone has put it, entertained the sensible notion that their subjects' lives were better sacrificed on the battlefield. Various forms of football existed, the feature in common being that it was a kicking game like present-day soccer. With similar variations, the game was also being played in America.

Americans showed a decided preference for the version of football known as Rugby, which differed from most other forms in two particulars that foreshadowed the modern game: an oval, rather than round, ball was used, and running with the ball was permissible. The first college game, as is well known, was played in 1869 between Rutgers and Princeton, with twenty-five men to a side. Yale first fielded a team with eleven men in 1876, a number which soon became standard. The main purpose of the game was to make a goal, which was worth four times as much as a touchdown; a touchdown, however, gave the privilege of trying for a goal, one feature which still survives in the modern game. Most of the game was spent in "scrummage" where a mass of men kicked at the ball—and each others' shins—until the pigskin finally popped out and someone could run with it. When he was tackled, another carnage began.

The bruises led, in about 1880, to the adoption of the first protecting uniforms. The numerous arguments compelled the appointment of a supposedly neutral referee, and by 1887 employment of an umpire became necessary for the detection of slugging and kindred forms of villainy. In 1883 a definite scoring system was established: a field goal counted five points, a goal after touchdown four, and a touchdown only two. A safety was worth one point but was raised to two in the following year.

Partly because of loud complaints from the baffled spectators, scrummage was abolished in 1880, and the more visible pass of the ball by the center to his backs was substituted. The center, be it noted, had to *kick* the ball, but the centers soon learned the trick of using their hands with only a perfunctory touch of the ball to their foot before passing. By 1890 the necessity of foot contact was abolished. The change from scrummage posed a problem of how the ball was to change hands, except by fumbles, and in 1882 it was decided that if a team could not make five yards in three plays, it would lose possession. In this way another fundamental feature of our game of football had its inception.

As the running game superseded kicking, the point values changed. A touchdown was valued at four points in 1884, was later raised to five, and in 1912 to six. The field goal was lowered to four in 1904 and to three in 1909. The goal after touchdown was reduced to two in 1883 and to one in 1897.

The game remained so much one of mass play, of numerous injuries, that early in this century football officials legalized the forward pass and added a fourth down, meantime raising to 10 yards the distance to be covered. A neutral zone was also provided between the teams before the ball was snapped. By 1912 the game had taken on its approximate later character. It continues to change from year to year in its use of certain types of line-ups, of emphasis on an aerial game, of increased substitution and specialization, and so on. This is so true that any written description of the game of twenty years ago will appear outdated to a fan. Stagg, the famous coach, wrote, "We still call it football, though everything but the name and the ball have changed."

Although football has undergone constant *change*, continuity has been maintained throughout its development. Note how comparatively slowly the scoring changes were made as the emphasis in the game altered. Many men and many experiences contributed to the making of the game. Each change, far from being purely arbitrary, resulted from a definite problem which had to be faced. Each modification, in turn, upset the game elsewhere and brought renewed demands for a revision at that point. In a general way, our political and social institutions develop in this fashion also.

Change and Continuity: Parliament

It is a long jump from the American game of football to the venerable institution known as Parliament, yet the pattern of its evolution has some resemblance to the foregoing. The American variety of football did not exist in 1870, it did exist in 1912, but no exact date of origin and no single place or group of men can be named. Parliament, in the sense that we use the word, did not exist in 1250, something like it came upon the scene in the following decades, and it was exercising considerable influence by 1300 or soon thereafter.

The reasons for its creation can be found, partially at least, in the new social forces appearing at that time. The powerful nobles had been accustomed to meet at the summons of the king to discuss affairs, to give him advice, and to function as a law court; no king could accomplish much unless he was assured of their good will, regardless of what power he might legally seem to exercise. In thirteenth-century England a great many lesser gentry, holders of land and influential locally, did not attend the Great Council of the nobles. As a group, however, they were growing in numbers and were apt to prove troublesome if ignored. For practical reasons, they could not be expected to attend the court, nor would most of them care to take the time and trouble for the journey. One possible solution was for the king to journey from shire to shire, meeting each group in turn, yet this, too, would obviously be impractical. The alternative would be for representatives of the local gentry to travel to the king and, being empowered by their fellows, speak and act for them in matters of common concern.

Another social group, the town dwellers, was also making its presence felt. These men possessed a wealth worthy of respect, especially in times when the king needed money. Their particular needs and demands had already attracted royal attention to the extent that charters were granted the larger towns allowing these the right of self-government. The king would be wise to listen to their petitions and advice also.

The gentry or knights had already been utilized, upon occasion, in such local business as collecting certain special taxes and carrying them to the royal treasury. The men who performed this duty were elected by their neighbors, and these local elections tended to become somewhat of an established practice. When the king now encountered an emergency in which he felt a need for the support of gentry and burgesses, the natural procedure would be to request each county and city to elect a few of the men, by the method already used in the localities, to go and confer with the king. (Usually they came with the voted consent of their local gathering for some requested royal levy.) Sessions of this kind were held several times during the second half of the thirteenth century, and numerous partial meetings of a like nature also occurred. These elected men would scarcely feel themselves a corporate body or conceive of their assembly as a definite political institution as yet; only over the course of many sessions would they begin to regard themselves as a political entity.

There was at this time no conception of a two-house Parliament; in a meeting of 1295 there were three houses, clergy, higher nobility plus gentry, and the representatives of the towns. This division coincided with the medieval concept of a society made up of three classes, clergy, nobles, and commoners, and the arrangement could well have continued, since we find it still in effect in the French Estates-General in 1789. The gentry or knights of England might even conceivably have formed a separate house, as in Sweden, where the Riksdag was composed of four houses until 1864. In England, however, the clergy presently ceased to attend the national assemblies, with the exception of bishops and abbots who henceforth sat with the nobility. The knights found the burgesses closer to their own viewpoint, and the two tended to gravitate together into what was eventually called the House of Commons. The nobility continued to meet together as one house, in a sense a continuation of the Great Council which had existed before the commoners were ever summoned.

The major forms of the modern Parliament had thus come into existence by about the middle of the fourteenth century. In functions, it was still far from the modern type of legislature. It is difficult for us to visualize a Congress or Parliament without legislative powers, yet the specific practice of legislation did not exist when Parliament first came into being. In the Middle Ages law was regarded as eternal, as a part of the natural order. Kings did not promulgate new law, they only mended or applied to new circumstances the law "as it was in the days of King Edward the Confessor," to quote old documents. As society became more complicated and new problems arose, the king and his council began to issue statutes which had the appearance of modern legislation.

The practice of legislation in the House of Commons came about in a gradual and perfectly natural fashion. The right of petition to the Crown having always been recognized, individual members of the lower house, from the earliest days, added their petitions to the vast numbers of appeals addressed to the king by his subjects. The members soon recognized that many appeals were similar in nature and that their time and that of the king would be saved by merging their petitions, while at the same time the king would be made to feel more pressure to act upon them. These combined petitions, agreed upon by Parliament and signed by the king, took on the attributes that we associate with legislation.

Frequently the king would refuse the petitions or amend them in an unacceptable manner. In order to curb this irksome royal habit, the delegates resorted to a kind of blackmail in the granting of taxes. According to medieval theory, the king was supposed to run the government from the income of his own abundant estates, and only in the case of a war or other emergency that required more money could the king secure additional revenue by requesting an extra contribution. An extraordinary tax required the consent of those who were being asked to donate, whether these were nobles or commoners. A king who attempted to wrest grants from his subjects without consent would not long remain healthy. The gentry and the burgesses soon learned the trick of withholding the vote for the requested revenues until *after* their demands in the petitions had been satisfactorily acceded to by the Crown. Parliament henceforth had the right of legislation, a share in a power possessed by the king and his council. As the commoners gained cohesion and experience, the lower house rose in relative importance among the governing institutions of the realm. (In these affairs, the men of Parliament were operating according to practical considerations, displaying a perfectly normal attribute, a businesslike attitude of protection for their possessions against royal seizure. They were not dealing with abstract notions of human freedom or deliberately creating a weapon to safeguard human liberty, at least not in the first stages.)

As time passed, Parliament acquired other rights. It began to impeach the king's ministers as a means of checking the king's actions. To overturn a king required a bit of doing, but to put the onus on his henchmen was relatively easy. The members of Parliament found necessary the protection of their own persons also. In about 1400 they secured the promise of the king that they could debate in freedom, although over another century had elapsed before the principle of freedom of speech in Parliament was recognized as a traditional right. (Not until 1688 was it confirmed by statute.) Members were also claiming that they could not be arrested while in session or while coming or going. They also took measures to ensure reasonable freedom from royal interference in elections in order that the winner would be allowed to take his seat regardless of the king's personal preferences.

To the modern mind, accustomed to see with precision, to demarcate spheres of activity among governmental organs, to have the powers written in black and white, the government that resulted in England is apt to be confusing. Precision is lacking: precedence and custom governed the conduct of affairs; the king, his ministers, and the Parliament shared the government jointly.

The lesson in the foregoing is that Parliament *grew,* it developed without coherent planning beyond the immediate future and without any conception of what its final form would be. It evolved out of the pragmatic handling of English affairs. Each step led to the next one. The materials for each were at hand when needed and were homely devices adopted without undue oratory. The purposes of the innumerable actors in the evolution were, at first, not concerned with the establishment of a parliament at all, but rather to achieve certain aims in their personal and collective life. Parliamentary practices were handy devices to achieve them, and as each functioned effectively it became a permanent practice. The citizens of England had developed a way of making themselves heard and of operating their polity. It was in the afterevent that later generations were to impute purposes to their ancestors in order to steel themselves to keep these now-appreciated institutions.

Parliamentary institutions of one sort or another came into existence between the thirteenth and sixteenth centuries in all the countries of Western Europe, a development so universal as to constitute ample proof that they were the product of deep and powerful social forces and that they were fulfilling genuine need. Even in Russia a national assembly met occasionally in the sixteenth and seventeenth centuries. By the latter century, however, the trend was in the other direction, and in France and Spain the royal power had increased to such an extent that parliaments could be elbowed aside. Under the Tudors, in England, the Parliament was normally acquiescent to the royal will, although the Tudors made no attempt to abolish the institution.

The Prevalence of Gradual Change

This, in a simplified form, is how Parliament evolved. The history of England provides particularly good cases for a study of such developments because its evolution has long continued without foreign invasions and consequent disruption of native institutions.

Each historical event is conditioned, as we know, by a background composed of various social forces. These, in turn, usually emerge gradually. It can be expected that an institution will develop as gradually as the social forces which are responsible for its establishment. That is, the usual occurrence, the expected process of social creation, is one of *evolution*, rather than of abrupt change. This is so universally true that the historian immediately becomes suspicious if an interpretation of the establishment of an institution is not described in terms of growth and development.

A novice in the study of history, on the contrary, will normally expect an institution or political practice to have an abrupt beginning; he will attribute a change to a certain ruler, to a constitutional convention, or to a specific law. A change may indeed have been formalized or legalized by one of these, but when the event is more closely examined, the immediate enactment will be found to be a culminating step in a chain of development. Even as changing emphases in football caused changes in scoring and rules, so the growth and decline of social forces alter the emphases in the functioning of society and require changes in the rules or in the forms of society. The process of causation, described in the preceding chapter, is at work in each change that occurs in social forms; the never-ending sequence of causes that we glimpsed is paralleled by a never-ending sequence of changes under the impact of social forces.

Occasionally, as in the Reformation, the normal equilibrium of forces is destroyed and many pressures, hitherto diffused, are galvanized into unusual overt action. Their influence is speedily reflected in a rapid series of formal changes in government. Those comparatively sudden, cataclysmic revolutions that have occurred must not be allowed to overshadow or distort the obvious fact that most changes occur almost imperceptibly, so much so that they are scarcely visible from year to year, sometimes not for decades. Politics is the art of the practical. Statesmen can effect permanent changes only as hard realities make them feasible. They are likely to be compromises between old and new, only a partial step forward. The truth is that most men are afraid of drastic innovations, partly because men prefer the familiar, and partly because the vested interests of most people are normally bound up with the existing setup. Added to the weight against change is what might be called an institutional inertia, a proneness to keep the machinery running as in the past unless strong pressure for change materializes.

No man or group of men can completely alter an existing society; it has been tried repeatedly, with invariable suffering for the people and ultimate failure for the radicals. On the other hand, no man or group of men can indefinitely prevent change. One of the principal sources of evil in this world is those extremists on both the radical and reactionary sides who are too zealous and too naïve to learn these first principles of social science.

Where revolutions do seem to transform the political face of a country, the appearances are deceptive; less visible developments nearly always led up to the climactic events. Where institutions and constitutions are suddenly introduced without this background, in a sudden upsurge of the few, their existence is apt to be perverted or destroyed within a few years. Frequently this occurs in more backward countries where modern institutions are suddenly introduced without sufficient preparation. Unless the existent social forces of a country are adequately given expression in the new institutions, the latter are doomed to failure.

A period of preparation may slowly develop on the economic and social levels before the trend breaks into the political sphere. Major changes in the structure of government and law usually occur in a period of crisis. The reason for this is that unless a considerable massing of public opinion occurs, institutional inertia and those who benefit by the older setup will prevent any alteration. In democratic countries, changes tend to come in cycles, a few years of reform being followed by two or three decades of consolidation and absorption of the innovations, this in turn being followed by a new period of change.

The history of the United States is a record of these cycles, of these pulsations of democratic change with intervening periods of comparative quiet. During the periods of normalcy, social and economic change continues, inevitably necessitating further adjustments in a new era of reform. The situation can be likened to an earthquake zone where the rocks gradually build up tension until a sharp adjustment abruptly occurs in a new earthquake.

Change and Continuity: The Seventeenth Century

The example of Parliament illustrates the general outline of evolution. The succession of crises which led to each change were not sketched. The time has now come to examine one such crisis, the greatest of them all, the period of the Puritan Revolution. Out of this period came a very great increase in the powers of Parliament, but—again—the change was not so planned originally.

James I, the "wisest fool in Christendom," was only wise in his own theories of divine right and was extremely foolish in his dealings with Parliament. Filled with his own conception of kingly power, he saw no legal rights in the English traditions of the popular assembly as it had developed in the preceding centuries. He proceeded, as best he could, to act like a divine-right sovereign. Parliament began by simply demanding those traditional rights won before the age of the Tudors; its members would scarcely have dreamed of asserting the power which they actually were to have by the end of the century.

The list of controversies between James I (and Charles I) and his parliaments constitutes an excellent check list of those fields where the king's abstract ideas and the customs of England clashed. The king claimed the right to decide controversies over elections; Parliament denied it. The king believed himself the highest judge in England. Parliament and the judiciary asserted that the courts were independent of the king and Parliament. James I claimed that Parliament derived its powers from royal grant; Parliament felt that his knowledge of English history was weak. The king tried to levy certain taxes; Parliament explained that it alone had the right to levy taxes on the people. The latter point, of course, was vital, since loss of control of revenue by the Parliament would end its ability to check the king in other directions as well. As events turned out, the chronic lack of sufficient revenue by the king gave Parliament the weapon whereby its authority was maintained. And Charles's efforts to secure revenue without parliamentary consent led directly to civil war.

Continuity in English development was temporarily broken by the sword as Cromwell's Puritans abolished the monarchy and substituted a republic. Although the ideas of the new leaders foreshadowed, in numerous respects, the England of the future, the country was not prepared for such an abrupt break with the past. Despite his own wish to rule by parliamentary means, Cromwell became a dictator when he faced the dilemma that the people, if allowed to express themselves, would vote back the monarchy. Although the English were ready for a degree of change, Cromwell's actions went too far, and the Puritan regime fell of its own unpopularity. England reverted to the status of the pre-Stuart period when the king and Parliament had governed jointly.

A quarter of a century later James II resumed the Stuart policy of weakening Parliament and enhancing the prerogatives of the Crown. The successful eighty-year defense of the parliamentary rights once more seemed endangered. The king soon learned how sturdy the underlying fabric of habit of English political life had become, for he was unseated and driven into exile. This time the victory was permanent, and the results of the Puritan and Glorious Revolutions (and of the preceding centuries of development) were put into law by a succession of statutes in and after 1688. In the denouement of the long struggle, Parliament had won an even more complete success than had been expected: the strength of the Crown had been so sapped that Parliament became supreme in the affairs of the country, and a long step had been taken in the development of modern English government. A person living in 1630, 1660, or 1685 would probably have found it difficult to believe that his government was undergoing a process of evolution; when one looks at the century as a whole, however, the several temporary victories won by each side all form a part of the larger picture, which is one of evolution until Parliament attained sovereignty in England.

Change and Continuity: The Cabinet System

Achievement of control by Parliament precipitated the development of one of the principal political institutions of our age, the English cabinet system. The cabinet system is the keystone of democratic government outside of the Americas, and since there are a number of important differences between the English and American cabinets, a preliminary survey of its characteristics is in order. In complete contrast to American practice, all English cabinet members must also be members of Parliament. They are nominally appointed by the King (or Queen), although the actual selection is made by the Prime Minister. Whereas American cabinet members serve at the President's pleasure and usually retire only when his term ends, the English cabinet continues to function until Parliament votes them down or until the majority party loses a national election. They serve as a group, being appointed at the same time and usually resigning together. They are headed by a presiding officer, on whom public usage has bestowed the title of Prime Minister.

The position of the American cabinet rather resembles that of the king's ministers *before* the victory of Parliament. Although the cabinet had been functioning for half a century when we became independent, we failed to recognize it as a permanent and valuable device of government—one proof that the evolution of the cabinet had been so unconscious and unplanned that men were not as yet cognizant of its significance. In the years after we had secured freedom, the British did recognize its value; had we become independent in 1826, rather than 1776, we might have adopted the cabinet system, as Canada did when it became self-governing.

The cabinet system was unplanned, arose out of no constitutional convention, and the men who created it were originally intent on other purposes than its creation. Not until the period of the younger William Pitt, at the end of the eighteenth century, did the politicians consciously try to follow the new practices as an ideal, while the terminology of English political practice continues to be couched in precabinet style even in the twentieth century. So strong is the habit of continuity that the King is still officially the source of law, and the title of Prime Minister was not used in official documents until recently.

If unplanned, and even scorned, as its successive features appeared, why then did it emerge at all? The answer is—necessity. It arose out of circumstances created by the victory of Parliament in the Glorious Revolution. If the king was no longer allowed or able or willing to take the lead in guiding political affairs, someone would have to do so. Parliament in itself had the whip hand, but the entire membership of the houses was too large and unwieldy to do the task. Obviously the initiative should come from those leaders in Parliament who controlled the votes and who could, with authority, speak its collective mind.

In the first years after the Glorious Revolution, King William III attempted to carry on the usual royal practice of choosing his ministers as he pleased, and, while there were complaints, the censure was aimed at the particular men chosen, not at the right of selection by the monarch. He soon saw the expediency, however, of appointing men, or the candidates of men, who could assure him a favorable vote on specific measures in Parliament. Furthermore, William III was too busy with his continental wars against Louis XIV to make a serious issue out of his own particular preferences for ministers.

William's task was complicated by the existence of two bodies of opinion (they can scarcely be called political parties), the Tories and the Whigs. William appointed men from both groups for a time, and then, since Parliament was dominated by the Whigs, in 1696 he selected an all-Whig cabinet. When this Parliament came up for election and the Tories gained a majority in 1698, however, William did not dismiss all his Whig ministers; he simply restored some Tories to the group.

These men had no conception of what was developing; they even disliked the trend. In the words of G. B. Adams, "Scarcely anything was intended in advance or deliberately attempted." The cabinet suffered from its association, in the public mind, with an original group of intimate advisers to Charles II, to which the name of cabinet (and also "cabal") had been given. The policies of these men had been highly suspect, their activities and advice to the king were difficult to check, and something of a sinister connotation continued to cling to the name of the cabinet for a long time afterward.

In the reign of Queen Anne the cabinet tended to be made up of men whose party was in power, although not necessarily so, since Anne was Tory in sympathy. The country was at war, the consent and cooperation of Parliament was a necessity, and hence Anne at times accepted ministers whose views she disliked but who could assure this cooperation.

The practice of appointing the cabinet from the majority party in the House of Commons was becoming habitual. By the end of her reign, the existence of the cabinet was accepted, yet the idea of all of its members as a single group with one will, who must be appointed and resign jointly, had by no means been fully established. No single man headed the group, nor did Parliament as yet see how the cabinet could be completely controlled by itself. Not until the early years of the nineteenth century—if then—had these constitutional practices come into full being.

By a perfectly natural process, one man would, in time, tend to emerge as spokesman for the group. Walpole is generally regarded as the first Prime Minister of Great Britain, although he himself would have indignantly rejected the present conception of that post; by his long influence in the House of Commons and in the cabinet, he nevertheless did create a precedence for the leadership now exercised by the Prime Minister. Then, in 1742, when he lost his hold on the Commons, he resigned. Parliament gradually learned that it could control the cabinet by simply refusing to support an unpopular one.

When George III came to the throne, the survival of the cabinet system was still by no means assured. He regarded it as a temporary development caused by the weakness of his predecessors, and, with the honorable intention of being a good king and of performing his proper duty, he conscientiously tried to restore the true English government as he understood it—and as most people probably also visualized it. Party rule seemed a deviation from normal government—a consequence of temporary royal decline—rather than a new and fine development leading into one of the greatest political inventions of all time. He speedily appointed his own men to the administrative positions, as the Stuarts had done, and by bribery and pressure induced Parliament to acquiesce. For a time, reaction seemed to triumph, as had been the case also in the evolution of Parliament in the 1630's and 1680's. A strong case might be made for the argument that reaction, by challenging and threatening the destruction of emerging ideas, practices, or institutions, forces a public evaluation of their worth and thereby stimulates a strengthened resurgence of the innovating elements.

The selfsame ambitions of George III which drove him into conflict with the American colonists, however, led to the ultimate triumph of the cabinet system. The failure of the royal government in the colonies spelled the failure of personal government in England also; the resignation of

Lord North and his cabinet in 1782 proved to be a victory for the principles upon which the cabinet system rested. The position of the Prime Minister was clarified in the administration of the younger William Pitt, the Crown some time later ceased all interference in cabinet affairs, and the practice was more completely accepted that a ministry must resign when defeated in the House of Commons. Exceptions to the latter practice, however, occurred as late as 1841.

While the cabinet system reached a state of equilibrium in the nineteenth century, and, from our viewpoint seems a constant and unvarying feature of British government, the process of change has never actually ended. One trend obviously under way is the increasing control over Parliament exercised by the cabinet to the point where a ministry can usually remain in power until a general election determines the popularity of the government. The cabinet now looks much more to the public, as a whole, for support or censure than it used to do. Another possible development is the tendency for a new inner cabinet to appear as the number of portfolios have increased, and the chief persons, four or five, have sometimes met separately to discuss affairs.

Change and Continuity: The Commonwealth

At the present time, the continuing evolution of Parliament and cabinet is too slow to be observed by the casual layman. Another aspect of the British scene, however, has been in process of rapid change: the relationship between Great Britain and its colonies. Here the evolution is repeatedly of sufficient importance to be noticed in the daily newspapers.

Under the impulse of national feeling, the dominions have gradually been transformed into independent nations. The climactic stage of this came in 1931 when, by the Statute of Westminster, they were recognized as complete equals of Great Britain itself. One by one they have adopted flags of their own, established their own armed forces, and conducted their foreign affairs as they pleased. Although a Governor General continues to represent the King, the name of the appointee is now suggested by the dominion government. In recent years native sons have frequently been named to this position.

The next logical step occurred when India became a republic, although it still remained within the Commonwealth of Nations by recognizing the King (or Queen) as head of the Commonwealth. Other dominions are also likely to take this step sooner or later. Indeed, the rapid evolution in this case is well illustrated by the fact that anything written here may soon be outdated. Nor can the end of this evolution be foreseen; the Commonwealth may become a permanent device for reconciling imperial ties with independence, and then again, it may turn out to have been simply a device for the gradual and peaceful disruption of the onetime enormous British Empire.

The Pattern of Change Reveals the Trend

The examples offered in this chapter are perhaps too perfect. Development is usually not as easy to observe as in these, and the intrusion of alien elements will frequently alter the manner of growth. Nevertheless, they can serve as prototypes of something which is plainly visible throughout the world. The phenomenon is by no means limited to politics. The story of the Industrial Revolution and the modern inventions reveals, as we shall see later, a very definite process of growth, of development in the midst of continuity. The backgrounds of a business concern, a university, or a city show the same process at work. In literature and philosophy, ideas and schools of thought must be treated in a historical fashion because that is the way in which they came into being. The panorama of the world presents to view an infinite variety of social bodies in various stages of growth and decline, somewhat like a view of the natural world with its wealth of plant life.

Titles of histories often contain such words as *Rise* and *Growth* and *Decline*. There is a certain loose similarity with plant life in the growth and decay of institutions, and it may prove helpful to visualize the concept by this analogy. Some notable historians, in fact, have written in such terms. The analogy has strict limitations, however, and should not be pushed too far.

A knowledge of the historical background answers the question "How did we get to this point?" and gives a good indication of the answer to "Where do we go from here?" In a word, it shows us the *trend*. A football coach who does not watch the direction in which the game is developing is not likely to win very many contests. An automobile manufacturer must take care that his new models show progressive change yet do not break continuity to the point where the public is antagonized by a radically different appearance. A statesman who does not understand the development of the British Commonwealth of Nations will be unable to gauge its likely policies. Without an understanding of the background the German obsession with militarism remains puzzling. A foreigner finds difficult an appreciation of the feeling for "States' rights" in the United States because he is unaware of the background.

So many practices and ways of thinking are born out of past experience that unless these are known, present conduct becomes a riddle. As has been mentioned earlier, the lifetime of social and political institutions is likely to be much longer than that of a human being. Their life histories are so much reflected in their present characteristics that a superficial outline of their formal structure gives no adequate comprehension of their full nature.

It is impossible, of course, to predict specifically the precise direction that social forms will take, what obstacles they may meet, and how a conflict of forces will result. Too many variables are involved, too many human elements are present, for any ironclad calculations to be made. The most that the intelligent person can be expected to do is to be aware of the eternal process of change, know what causes it, know what direction certain social forces have taken in the past, and so be in a position to make intelligent estimates. The wise conservative reconciles himself to the necessity of positive changes, and the wise reformer refuses to adopt a fanatic faith in the virtues of change itself.

We are attempting to use history in order to understand the present. Even as we do so, we must be alert to the danger that our twentieth-century perspective may seriously distort our view of the past. Our modern viewpoint tends to overweight the element of change while underestimating the influence of continuity. Most of us, when we look into the past, inevitably scan the surroundings for that which is familiar to us, and we tend to overemphasize the role of those particular changes which introduced political forms and practices familiar to us; historical writers all too often fail to give a completely true picture of an age for this reason. In any given period, the elements of continuity were infinitely stronger in the minds of the men then living than we are likely to realize today.

7

The Institutional Factor

Social forces have thus far been described in large, general terms, the assumption being that group feeling in itself spurs social action. It will be recalled, however, that the Protestants very quickly transformed the existing ecclesiastical institutions into agencies for their own usage or created new ones, and that the English merchants speedily established commercial institutions through which they might work. The existence of any social force of any importance whatsoever is virtually certain to bring about the creation of institutions through which the interested group may express itself. These organizations range in importance from the great agencies of government down to local clubs.

The world is exceedingly well populated with formal social institutions. Each of these is a permanent organ representing a set of ideas and values, articulating the views of its following or members, and enforcing some degree of cooperation and conformity upon them. They are a stabilizing element in society, providing, as they do, organization, order, and social pattern.

The institution will naturally reflect, to some extent, the spirit of the men in control, but it also tends to develop its own policies and spirit, born out of circumstances with which it comes into contact, and which transcend the period in office of any individual. The ambitions of the servants of the establishment are bound up with its fate: by its rise, they achieve fame and power, and when it declines, they share in the decline. Some men dedicate a selfless career to the welfare of an organization in which they believe, while for others it is simply a tool for their own success. Whatever the case, the institution molds the psychology and conduct of its officials. Unfortunate as it may seem, an individual can usually not accomplish much by himself; he must associate himself with a group, rise to leadership among them, and in this way secure a seat among the mighty.

Once established, an institution is certain to seek to better its position in its environment. The officials will feel that its social function is handicapped unless additional powers are secured, collisions with other social units will occur, the strength of other social units may be sapped until they can be absorbed, and the organization may even assume activities quite unrelated to its original purposes. Eventually, a formal institution becomes a vested interest, the first concern being its own self-preservation and aggrandizement. In order to assure vitality and well-being, an institution must ensure that it will have (1) the necessary economic support; (2) the facilities for convincing the populace of its value; (3) tools for defense, spiritual and material, in case of attack; (4) sufficient discipline within the group to avoid internal conflicts. Inasmuch as all social institutions tend to follow a similar pattern of growth of this kind, we may regard the institutional factor as a type of social force in its own right. While they continue to represent particular religious, economic, or other social forces, part of the institutional energies are directed toward the preservation of their own separate identities.

The Institutional Factor in the Church

Let us watch the institutional factor at work in the case of one of the most successful institutions of all time, the Roman Catholic Church. The Church came into existence as the bearer of an Idea, or a cluster of ideas, concerning the salvation of the soul. An Idea is not likely to survive in a hostile world without some sort of a shield; like a clam growing a shell about itself, the Idea stimulates its believers to create an institution for its protection and for more effective delivery of its message.

The marvel is that a doctrine of meekness and humility could survive at all, much less achieve a moral triumph over the invading barbarians, in the early centuries of the Christian Era. In an age when governmental protection was inadequate, the Church was forced to protect itself by means which at times had little relationship to the spiritual message, but without which the Idea itself must surely have gone under. (Such, at least, would be the judgment of most historians.) The growth of the secular power of the papacy offers a clear example of the type of circumstances which compelled the Church to assume its medieval form. As long as the emperor lived in Italy, the papacy was dependent upon his protection, and even when only a governor wielded the power for an emperor now at Constantinople, the pope still looked to the temporal for protection; by sheer necessity, the pope himself took over the direction of affairs in Rome when a political vacuum was created by the decline of secular authority. With the passage of time, this *de facto* authority became government *de jure* and was so recognized by the Carolingians. In precisely the same way, on a larger scale, the Church as a whole was forced to become self-reliant. Where it could, the Church sought princely assistance, and usually, though not always, the Church continued to favor the strengthening of royal power throughout the Middle Ages.

Provision for the economic support of church work posed problems quite different from those of our day. Taxation could afford little aid to churches, as happens in modern state churches, because there were few taxes or none. Maintenance of congregations by the propertyless serfs would scarcely be adequate. Furthermore, the work embraced more than mere local projects, for the clergy furnished the teachers of the day, converted the heathen, dispensed charity, maintained monasteries, and manned the hierarchy or the complex machinery of higher ecclesiastical government. The solution, basically, was the same as that used by the government itself in feudalism, the Church holding large tracts of land and providing for its priests, monks, and bishops with the revenues therefrom.

Part of this land came from individuals by wills and grants, some was given by the government, and other possessions grew out of the influence of the bishop in early towns, the whole process making the Church the landowner, finally, of somewhere between one-fourth and one-sixth of all the land. Within these areas were manors and feudal lords holding the land on the same terms as in the temporal state; the various dues and aids, feudal practices and revenues were exacted in the same way, the money and products going to the support of the Church. The Church was thus not dependent solely upon the congregations or upon the government. It was an independent institution, amply provided for, and firmly rooted in the medieval economy.

In these circumstances, the Church would have a vested interest in the continuation of the existent society. It tended to acquire more and more land as security, as a way of increasing its facilities and of enlarging the numbers of its clergy. Any drastic change would imperil its existence and endanger the charitable, educational, and preaching missions of the Church. It must necessarily view with alarm any popular movement in the cities which would challenge the position of the bishops. Peasant up-risings were to be discouraged, since they would surely spread to ecclesias-tical lands. The Church would be sensitive to attempts by the nobility to nibble off land belonging to itself and successfully prevented this develop-ment until the Reformation in northern Europe, when the nobles won a complete victory. In southern Europe, not until the French Revolution were the ecclesiastical holdings endangered.

The Church, also, for the safety of the institution as well as for the spiritual mission, needed to protect its right to propagate the faith. The struggle against paganism had left deep traces in the minds of churchmen, and survivals of heathen religious practices were still visible in the customs of the folk—the struggle against the dark forces of the past must be relent-lessly maintained. The challenge of Islam, the faith of Mohammed, formed another menace; it claimed to be the successor to Judaism and Christianity, acknowledged the Old Testament prophets, and accepted the Messiahship of Christ, but the Moslems insisted that Mohammed was come to replace the preceding messages of the prophets. Islam had won over many of the oldest Christian centers and must have seemed a terrible perversion of the Truth to the Christians. Against the underground forces of paganism and the external threat in the East, the Christians, in order to survive, must be united. In this way, sociological necessity added to the theological insistence that Christian doctrines should be preserved invio-late and that "heresies" must be ruthlessly destroyed. The temper of the times, the feeling that there could be only one faith, is hard for us to comprehend except as we realize the danger facing the Church at the time.

The Church became the official custodian of Truth. In this way a fairly uniform body of beliefs was imposed upon the diverse language groups and cultures, and a very valuable contribution to the molding of European civilization it was. In the ignorance of the times, the medley of pagan residues, the sheer irreligious passions of a warrior society, only this approach could have saved the Church. Even in the Reformation, the chief churches, Lutheran, Calvinist, and Anglican, felt called upon to stamp out the smaller groups of the so-called lunatic fringe in order to preserve the unity of society.

Some other practices of the Church, disliked by later Protestants, had very substantial reasons for existence when one realizes the conditions in which they developed. The limiting of the Bible to the clergy is an exam-ple of this. Until printing was invented, few persons could afford to own books. To the illiterate masses, a book seemed sacrosanct and surrounded with magical qualities. Reading, when done at all, was apt to be before a whole circle of people by one who had already memorized the contents. Knowledge was largely a matter of accumulating wisdom by memory without the possibility of using a reference book. In such an age, *the* Book, the Bible, must be precious, must be restricted to those trained to use it correctly. Faulty and ignorant interpretations, multiplying in these conditions according to the theologians, would soon lead to divisions, and so it would be judicious for the larger sake of church unity and ultimate work of the Church to limit the spread of the Bible. The Protestant complaint against the restriction of Bible reading by the old Church was justified after the invention of printing and the spread of literacy, but during the Middle Ages possession of the Bible by members of the congregations was not only a physical but also a religious impossibility.

The seven sacraments could serve as a great weapon in controlling the conduct of the people because through denial of the sacraments the Church could prevent entry into heaven. A person might be excommunicated, that is, not allowed to partake of the Eucharist. If a ruler was disobedient, an entire country might be excommunicated by an act known as the interdict; this also nullified the oaths of allegiance of subjects and constituted an open invitation to rebellion against the secular authority. Since only baptism, penance, and extreme unction were permitted, the interdict was indeed a potent instrument in an age when salvation was the final goal of life. The confessional and the duty of penance were other means of control. In extreme cases, a person might be tried on charges of heresy. Out of the latter grew the dreaded court, the Inquisition, which came into existence in order to suppress the dissenters of the thirteenth century, but which became notorious when it dealt with the reformers of the later period.

Secular tools might also be employed, the Church possessing enough of the weapons of a feudal lord to cope with minor offenders. Not least of the defenses was the strong position of the bishops and abbots as advisers of the king and the presence of clergy at the court in those roles where educated persons were required; in both instances, the influence upon the secular government was certain to be very great.

So far, the problem has been dealt with as a question of defense in an alien world. All of the above weapons would have been worth little if the officials themselves were not organized into a disciplined group whose loyalty to the Church exceeded all other interests. Undoubtedly the rule of celibacy was aimed at safeguarding the Church, since those priests with families would be distracted from their spiritual work. Just as dangerous, priests and bishops would be interested in passing their temporary charge over to their sons. In such a case, the practice of inheritance would have wreaked as great a disintegrative blow upon the Church as it did upon some feudal kingdoms.

Church offices needed to be protected from control by the secular authorities; even in the history of the papacy itself, instances can be found where the pope had been practically appointed by a secular lord. To provide a clerical method of election, the College of Cardinals was created. Although these Princes of the Church frequently also tended to speak for various lords, the autonomy of the Church was nevertheless more likely to be safeguarded. On the episcopal level, the local chapter, the officials of the cathedral, were supposed to elect the bishop. The system was never entirely free from temporal interference, yet the principle certainly exercised a salutary influence.

The officials had to be capable men, and men who could command. Quite naturally, the nobility would provide most of the persons able to fulfill this requisite. An exceptional son of a peasant could, and on occasion did, rise to high position, but the noble class manned most of the positions. After all, the episcopal office was, physically, a governmental as well as a religious office, and men of executive ability were required. The practice also cemented an alliance with the noble class; it gave the nobles a vested interest in the Church and, in a sense, allowed the nobility to hold control of ecclesiastical territory without obtaining permanent possession.

In the rough world of the day, feudal justice scarcely accorded with the clerical position. Priests and clerks could hardly accept ordeals, torture, and duels as proper means of justice, and therefore the Church created its own courts and laws and judges, a sort of extraterritoriality of the Middle Ages.

It might be said that the Church was the response of humanity to the conditions of the age, those whose sensitive temperaments were shocked by its roughness escaping something of it by going into the ecclesiastical foundations. Here, then, gathered those most apt to spread culture —music, philosophy, the arts. Unmarried women found a refuge as nuns. As a group, the clergy would exert influence, forcing a compromise with the barbarian elements of their society.

Recall how the middle class also had felt itself endangered by the feudal world; each social group felt the need for self-defense in a sharply competitive world where individual safety and property were not assured. An army which expects to win battles must maintain obedience in the ranks, possess a definite order of command from top to bottom, and be directed by a supreme commander of unquestioned authority. Fundamentally, the Church built up the position of the bishops and the pope for the same reason; from the historical point of view there were other reasons also, but these are subsidiary. Unless the Church could keep discipline, it would fail. In moments when it seemed to approach dissolution, men of discernment came forward to demand a strong Church—a wave of reform would rejuvenate it once again. The answer to the threat of the Reformation was a further strengthening of the papal position within the Church. The response to the nineteenth-century threat of the French Revolution, nationalism, and materialistic Marxism was the doctrine of papal infallibility.

The Institutional Factor in the Monarchy

During the seventeenth and eighteenth centuries, the strongest institution on the continent of Europe was the Crown. A brief sketch of its development will provide a second illustration of the institutional factor in history. Like the Catholic Church, it had to solve the necessary problems of procuring economic support, of building up tools and defense, of creating an efficient and loyal officialdom, and of winning popular approval. The monarchy became, like other successful institutions, a point of gravitation, drawing to itself social energies and influencing the orbits of other institutions. While performing its assigned functions in society, it automatically grew in power and splendor.

The medieval kingship derived in part from the Germanic kings, who were leaders of warriors and high priests of the folk religion. The early kings were elected from a royal family claiming sacrosanct position by reason of descent from the gods. Unlike the succession in modern times, no law of primogeniture existed, and an able adult of the family who was also a warrior would be most likely of election. Christian influences added the concept of kings as regents placed upon earth by God to maintain order: the ultimate purpose of the regime, according to the Church, was to provide physical circumstances—law and order—wherein true Christian conduct by the people was possible.

We have learned that a medieval country included several divergent classes, almost separate worlds, each defending its own particular position against the others. In such a situation, there could be no question of absolute rule by the king. His authority was hemmed in by the Church, the feudal lords, the cities, the local and national assemblies, and by ancient customs and laws. The king was the anointed leader, but he was by no means an absolute sovereign. It was the logic of his position as nominal lord of the realm that he would seek to increase his power—economic, political, and military—in order to fulfill the necessary duties of the Crown.

The monarchy required the economic resources which would make possible the maintenance of officials and armies. In the medieval period, as mentioned in the preceding chapter, the king was supposed to "live of his own." The king possessed crown lands, whose produce and dues and revenues played exactly the same role in supporting the royal establishment as the feudal manors for the lords and the ecclesiastical lands for the Church. As we know, he could summon the nobility for special services in return for the fiefs they held, while in cases of extraordinary expenses, as in a war, he might ask for special monetary levies. For ordinary expenses, however, "his own" was expected to suffice. With the return of a money economy, this arrangement became embarrassingly inadequate, and the king was driven to amplify the yield of his revenues. In countries where the nobility remained strong, the king could usually count upon support from cities and the Church, both of which disliked the violence of the upper classes as much as did the king. The good will of these sectors of society would greatly strengthen the king and aid him financially.

Once a parliament came into existence, semiregular grants of money might supplement the royal revenue. It was a hazardous source, however, since members of parliament might grant too little, refuse altogether, or, perhaps worst of all, bargain for additional rights in return for money. Two institutions, each seeking to aggrandize its own position at the expense of the other, engaged in more or less constant sparring for advantage. The ultimate objective of the Crown would be to secure from parliament a permanent grant of revenue which would not have to be renewed at each session. Such a concession, however, would destroy the single strongest weapon in possession of parliament. On the Continent, the constant peril of foreign wars and the obvious need for a stronger central authority worked in favor of the king; in one country after another, he had his way and thus opened the road to an era of absolute monarchy.

Other advantages were required in order to enhance the royal position. The succession to the throne would have to become hereditary. The king would need recognition of his legal right to promulgate the law; with this right he could mold society to his will, providing he used discretion in application. He would desire the power to make peace and war, in order that he could be free to carry on foreign policy with success.

Control of ample revenues enabled the monarch to bulwark his regime with other means of defense. The single strongest weapon of the king, his army, reinforced royal persuasion by the threat of force. Unless stupid enough to alienate numerous sections of subjects, the king should be able to deal with the rebellion of a province, a social class, or a city. Once the kings had the financial prerequisite, they built up armies independent of the feudal lords, mercenaries being hired who had no allegiance except to the man who paid them. The nature of international politics helped the king here, inasmuch as it was to the advantage of all sections of the populace that a sufficiently strong army should exist to protect the country from invasion. Such an army, of course, could serve against the native dissidents as well as against foreign foes. The necessity of protecting France ultimately redounded to the advantage of the king in the Hundred Years' War. A rising Brandenburg-Prussia, with its open frontiers, needed a strong army, and, once created, it was the guarantee of royal power. The English Parliament was defending English liberties when it bitterly fought the attempt by the Stuarts to create a standing army; one must conclude that if England had been in the geographical position of France or Prussia, however, the controversy would have ended differently.

A successful institution must maintain loyalty and discipline within its ranks. It will constantly seek to enlarge the numbers of those subject to its orders and, as this is achieved, to intensify the degree of control. The Crown would naturally strive for dominance over nobles, Church, and cities. Once the king had destroyed actual territorial rule by the nobles in their feudal states, he would try to put them to work in his service in such a way that they would be subservient: in Prussia, the noble families were forced to provide the army officers, a position where they were at the king's command, while in Bourbon France, the aristocrats became courtiers, dependent upon the king's grace in giving offices and wealth. The royal campaign to assert control of the Church, or at least to influence the appointment of bishops and abbots, had progressed by the time of the Reformation, to the point where the kings of France,

England, and Spain had acquired considerable authority over appointments and policies of the Church within their borders. In the countries
which became Protestant, the creation of state churches assured royal
dominance over the Church.

Within the central machinery of government, complete loyalty was
necessary. The administrative officials grew constantly in numbers as the
royal duties and prerogatives broadened and as the Crown assumed the
former functions of the nobility in government, administration, and law
courts. To keep their loyalty, the king tended to appoint his officials from
the nonnoble classes, inasmuch as these would owe their elevation to the
king and would be completely dependent upon his favor. The middle class
of the cities had had experience in dealing with business matters and was
more able to cope with the complex problems of running a kingdom. In
time, this bureaucracy would become a vested interest, a social force rein-
forcing the institutional power drive, the privileges and positions of the
officials being associated with those of the king; they would be as eager as
the sovereign for further aggrandizement by royal authority.

To win and to keep popular approval, the Crown needed theoretical
justifications of some sort for the constant extension of royal power. In
the very nature of things, many persons would see the necessity of law
and order, which could come only from centralization under the king. The
growth of commerce and the increasing amount of private property had
brought into existence a large class whose primary interest was protection
of these rights—whose interests coincided broadly with the growth of royal
power, and who would support the king against the vested interests of the
medieval period.

Other factors helped the absolute monarchy to win the argument.
Growing national feeling of the people would be most likely to find a
focus in the person of the king as the logical symbol of unity. The pulpit
was the ally of the Crown in its constant emphasis on the prince as the
viceregent of God upon earth. The spread of Roman law helped to provide
rationalizations for royal power, since according to Roman law, power was
derived from the emperor or central authority. The failure of the republican states to maintain orderly government provided another strong point
in favor of monarchy. Finally, the divine-right theory provided an elaborate philosophy of justification for absolute sovereignty by the monarch.

The Crown became an ever more powerful magnet, drawing to itself
the energies of society, organizing them about itself, until at last the palace

at Versailles and the proud claim *"L'état, c'est moi"* (I am the State) symbolized the complete triumph of monarchy.

The Institutional Factor in the Nation-State

If newspaper editorials and letters from readers are to be believed, the actions of foreign countries are often wickedly selfish. Americans have always been disposed to regard Europeans as being irredeemably addicted to sharp diplomacy and wars of conquest. The plain fact is that the conduct of countries *is* naturally egocentric. This "selfishness" is a principal feature of the institutional factor in history that is under discussion in this chapter: the law of self-preservation and aggrandizement is deeply rooted in all organizations.

In the competition which has obtained in the international sphere, the individual country necessarily follows an egotistic policy of considering its own interests first. The state must seek to strengthen itself as over against other nations by the various means at its disposal. It must arrange for the economic well-being of its inhabitants by keeping trade routes open and by providing raw materials and supplies. Certain strategic areas must be controlled, and responsible leaders must be awake to the threat of attack from any quarter. Because self-preservation takes precedence over niceties of morality, the law of the nations has tended to be the law of the jungle, although this truth is slurred over with polite phrases.

National policies display varying degrees of selfishness. A well-entrenched, self-confident institution or country has a far greater margin of safety and can therefore practice a more benevolent policy. Associations and institutions within a democratic country are less threatened with extinction and are therefore able to introduce a more enlightened self-interest into their behavior. To such an extent is egocentric policy the rule, however, that when the United States has practiced an idealistic policy, the nationals of other countries have been prone to regard us as either incredibly naïve or else as disguising gross selfishness under a display of Christian virtues.

We can use the example of the nation or country itself in a further investigation of the behavior of institutions, for these great states, in their perpetual contention with one another, serve as a prime example of the conduct of rival institutions. The governments of these countries are large-magnitude examples of institutions in their behavior; the motives and psychology of their officials are fundamentally similar to those of lesser social organs. A major difference, of course, is that the country-state uses direct military power in addition to other means. Lesser establishments grow and decline in popular following and influences, in the aggressiveness of their leaders, in their financial resources, in various ways that are difficult for us to measure. That which makes the government of the country itself useful for our study, at this point, is that the ambitions and goals, the successive gains and losses, can be seen in a concrete fashion on a map.

The various peace treaties, dull reading and tedious memorization, can be used for this purpose because, when studied in their proper relationships, they permit one to gather valuable hints as to the policies of the various states. Most of the terms of the treaties between 1648 and 1763 in which France is involved show changes along the northeastern frontier of that country; it can be deduced from this that the French found their greatest peril in this region and that they were trying to remedy the situation. The French, with a very long frontier to defend, would attempt to gain possession of any natural easily defended border. France was rather fortunate in some of these, for the Pyrenees in the south and the Alps in the east were of great assistance, once the French kings had spread their domains thus far. The northeast, where invasions could more easily be successful, remained a source of grave anxiety, and hence the importance of Alsace-Lorraine and the Rhine for the diplomats and soldiers of the country. Differing ideologies of French statesmen do not matter much here; they all, whether the despotic Louis XIV or the republican Danton, believed that the natural frontier of France was the Rhine. The seemingly interminable wars of Louis XIV were fought, above all, in the hope of attaining this objective.

Other means might be used in the defense of the French frontier. Alliances might be contracted with one or more of the neighbors—the most successful of these was the achievement of Louis XIV when he placed his own grandson on the throne of Spain and thus tied French and Spanish policies together for nearly a century. Still another method of rendering a potentially hostile country innocuous was by keeping it divided, as was done in the Treaty of Westphalia: the various states of Germany were made virtually independent states, none being henceforth strong enough to threaten or to gain dominance in Germany. France remained the greatest power in Europe as long as Germany was kept divided, and it was the constant care of the French rulers to keep her in that condition.

Territorial aggrandizements may be on a different plane from expansion by lesser institutions, but they are also examples of the institutional factor in history. It might be possible to prepare a "map" or cartogram of the growth of power by the French crown showing the various powers of the Estates-General, the nobility, the Church, the local authorities. Then a series of cartograms for different years would reveal how the Crown made successive advances, smashing in turn each potential competitor. The destruction of nobles' castles by Richelieu and the loss of fortified towns by the Huguenots, on such a map, would be the equivalent of a conquered province on a territorial map. These diagrams would look rather like a series of maps showing the expansion of the Hapsburgs (in the fifteenth and sixteenth centuries), Prussia, or Russia.

Successive maps of European Russia show its frontiers creeping, step by step, toward the Caspian, Baltic, and Black seas. The original Muscovite state was continental and possessed no good access to the sea. Consequently, the "drive to the sea" long remained, and perhaps still is, a dominant theme in Russian history. The wars of Peter the Great and the founding of St. Petersburg are to be interpreted in this way, for Russia secured a sure outlet to the sea on the Baltic and thereby to Western Europe. The wars against the Turks are to be seen in the same light as regards the Black Sea—first to secure a seacoast on the Black Sea and then, finding it locked at the other end, to gain egress at Constantinople. A second consideration also determined Russian policies. Russia, threatened and invaded from the west on several occasions by Swedes, Poles, French, and Germans, would do all in her power to keep such possible rivals harmless. During the eighteenth century the Russian rulers sought to keep Poland paralyzed and finally succeeded in annexing large segments of Polish territory.

Parenthetically, one ought to observe at this point that when we are dealing with territorial states, geographical circumstances are almost certain to exercise considerable—perhaps even predominant—influence. The presence or absence of mountains, important river valleys, large bodies of water, or mineral resources act as major determinants in the direction of national policies.

The territories acquired by the British were remarkably scattered over the face of the earth, and no single policy would, at first glance, seem likely to embrace them all. A study of maps centered upon the land masses of individual continents will not solve the puzzle in this case; the dominant geographical influence for modern Britain was the sea, and British expansion, to be understood, must be viewed through this medium.

Once surveyed in its proper oceanic setting, British policies are clear enough; although they eventually acquired possession of huge land areas, in original intent the English were primarily concerned in securing ports of call, way stations, from whence trading might be carried on and vessels enabled to revictual. When internal disturbances later threatened loss of trade, or another country seemed interested in the hinterland, they might extend their control into the interior. Meantime, the exigencies of maintaining the defenses of a maritime empire had resulted in the creation of "sea power"—of an adequate navy and facilities for its proper support. The original creation and subsequent maintenance of sea power is one of the principal keys to an understanding of the modern history of Great Britain.

Gibraltar was formally obtained in the Treaty of Utrecht. Taken almost by accident originally, before its worth was recognized, this pin-prick on the map was worthless as land area, but as a strategic location for control of Mediterranean trade it was invaluable. Acquisition of Minorca (in the Balearic group), at this same time, permitted the extension of English sea power further into the Mediterranean. If one knows that Toulon, north of Minorca on the French coast, was the French naval base then as now, another reason for the seizure of this small island becomes clear, since possession of Minorca permitted a constant watch by the British over their principal rival. At the Congress of Vienna, the island of Malta was added, a new steppingstone in the Mediterranean and, for good measure, the Ionian Islands off the coast of Greece. The British advance into the eastern portion of the Great Sea was virtually completed in 1878 when Disraeli procured Cyprus, a base which has now become the chief British holding in the area. A few years earlier, control of the Suez Canal had been obtained, a master stroke inasmuch as it gave Britain command over the short route to the Indian Ocean.

The British might well desire authority over the Suez waterway, the Indian Ocean being the real center of their empire in the nineteenth century. The best way to grasp the true scope of their interests in this region is to study a map, not merely of Asia or Africa, but one of the Indian Ocean itself, with the continental coasts bordering this body of water. South Africa and Australia then appear as the bases of an arch of empire, Malaya and Burma on the east and British East Africa and the southern Arabian coast on the west as the sides of the arch, and India as the keystone. Once given a vital interest in India, as happened in the eighteenth century, the British were compelled to build up a safe route to their Eastern possessions; British colonists on the western hump of

Africa, at St. Helena, at the tip of South Africa, and at Mauritius would serve as ports of call for ships traveling to and from the East. The acquisition of South Africa, Ceylon, and Mauritius, during the Napoleonic Wars, fits into this picture. Some years later Singapore and Hong Kong were added, in another extension of British sea power into the East.

The Balance of Power

Out of the competitive international life of Europe emerged a concept known as the "balance of power." An understanding of this idea is necessary for any comprehension of international affairs, especially since it continues to operate in the twentieth century.

The subject can perhaps best be introduced from the English point of view. This country, in modern times, had no particular desire to acquire European continental territories, inasmuch as she was fully occupied with her colonial ventures. The English Channel afforded protection against sudden attacks. She did fear, however, the emergence of a single great state upon the Continent which might unite Europe against her and which might, in the long run, bring such economic might to bear that England would cease to be independent of foreign control. British policy as regards Europe, over several centuries, is to be interpreted in this perspective. When no single great state in Europe threatened war, England remained in "splendid isolation." When a powerful France under Louis XIV appeared and seemed to threaten control of the Atlantic coast, Great Britain gave assistance to the threatened countries and helped to form a coalition or alliance against France. When the French Bourbons secured the throne of Spain, England again felt threatened and managed to balk the larger program by fighting the War of the Spanish Succession.

Napoleon's unification of large areas of Europe forced Britain to fight him during his many years of power, since Britain could not afford to allow him to consolidate his position. Although Napoleon smashed the successive coalitions of Britain and Continental countries, he could not reach Britain because he lacked control of the seas; eventually, the winning combination was found and Napoleon fell. Again in 1914, Britain joined the alliance against a powerful German drive which threatened to dominate the Continent. In summary, Great Britain fought in turn each of the strongest powers on the Continent, Spain, France several times, and Germany twice, by maintaining the balance of power over against the strongest Continental state.

One may visualize the balance of power as a scale, with the sides of the scale filled with weights of various kinds representing the different states and their strength. Should one side tip too far, another state will jump on the scale on the opposite side to balance it again. Over several centuries, England was able to use the scale for her own interests, to keep the scale from tipping too far—and, incidentally, to prevent the unification of Europe.

Why should the small states be willing to serve as minor weights in this bloody pastime? As has been said, the final axiomatic principle of each state must be to preserve itself. Should one great power emerge to threaten the freedom of several weaker ones, it would be merely sensible for these to combine against the greater; for example, the Dutch, endangered by French ambitions in the Low Countries, would look for support to other neighboring countries. Where no international unity existed, the only possible defense lay in contracting alliances, which would at least assure a balance of power over against the aggressor. It also follows that there was nothing sacred about the line-up of any one war; should circumstances change, the line-up for the next war was certain to be different from the preceding one.

The balance of power was also operative in the building up of alliances before the First World War and the Second World War. In the latter instance, the process was a haphazard affair. The English and French joined in the alliance to defend Poland, thereby presumably establishing a new balance of power. When the Germans upset this, the ultimate consequence was the placing of Russian and American weight on the other side until the German weight (plus allies) was more than balanced.

The involvement of the United States in the First World War may to some degree be attributed to the same reason. Although other factors were obviously also present, the fact was that we could not afford to allow Germany to gain permanent control in Europe, and we consequently threw our weight on the other side. The same reasoning prevailed in the Second World War with even greater cogency.

To summarize: The nation-state illustrates the operation of the institutional factor, inasmuch as it displays the characteristic qualities of self-preservation and aggrandizement. If the expansive momentum of a country is not checked by the enlightened self-interest of its own people, its aggressiveness is ultimately contained by the emergence of a balance of power.

The balance of power is also constantly at work, in a sense, among institutions and associations within a country. There, too, it operates to limit the overly successful group. The Founding Fathers of the United States wrote into the Constitution the concept of checks and balances between the executive, legislative, and judiciary branches of the government. The intent was to prevent any one of the three from attaining mastery over the country. Such men as Madison also expected that the associations would prevent any one of themselves from attaining undue influence.

The institutional factor is as selfish as the human personality itself; whether good or bad—and it is both—it exists and must be taken into consideration, both in historical situations and in reflections on contemporary problems. All officials of institutions need to be on constant guard against the temptation to assume that indefinite strengthening of their particular group is in itself good. Where an institutional power drive goes unchecked, it leads to either anarchy or tyranny. Under legitimate constitutional governments, this momentum is circumscribed by a growth of enlightened self-interest, by a domestic balance of power, and by law itself. During the twentieth century, even the nation-state is undergoing a slow, a painfully slow, process of limiting its own power drive in international affairs.

8

Revolution

"A revolution is caused by the misery of the people. A strong and tyrannical government persists in its misrule until the people can endure it no longer. Then, moved by spontaneous zeal and righteous indignation, the multitudes rise. They assault the citadels of power and expel the ruling class in a bloody civil war. As a consequence of the revolution, liberty is restored to the people."

One may suspect that this description—the author's phrasing based on student answers—does not stray very far from the conception of revolution held by the greater number of our citizens. This is a natural way to visualize a revolution, or, perhaps more accurately, this is the point of view we have inherited from the triumphant victors in our successful Western revolutions. When we examine the nature of such an upheaval carefully, however, every sentence in the above paragraph proves to be a gross oversimplification.

Living in a century of rapid changes which sometimes pass into actual revolution, we need to understand the nature of this deviation from normal evolution. If we turn to the historians, who being familiar with past upheavals should be able to help us, they are likely to be hesitant in providing generalizations for this complex and entangled phenomenon. They are keenly aware that each situation is unique and that any broad statement, covering numerous episodes, will inevitably be somewhat vitiated by exceptions. The problem for us, however, is to obtain a practicable picture of revolution, one which may not be completely satisfactory, but which is nevertheless of a considerably higher order of accuracy than the prevalent notions presented in the opening sentences.

First of all, the word *revolution* must be delimited to its more precise meaning. In popular usage the word is applied to any overturn of a government by force; it is also employed to indicate a fundamental transformation in nonpolitical fields, such as the Commercial Revolution or the Industrial Revolution. The phenomenon that we are about to examine, however, is one in which *a social or economic group is superseded in control of the state by another group under circumstances of violence.* The French Revolution and the Russian Revolution are examples. This definition eliminates seizures of power within the social group where one faction takes control from another, yet policy is not drastically altered; most of the Latin-American revolutions, for instance, fall into this category. One might almost call them pseudo revolutions, since the victor usually makes a pretense of mass support and genuine change while achieving power.

Why is comparatively peaceful change abandoned in favor of violent and drastic revision of a country's institutions? We may immediately offer two or three tentative suggestions, based upon certain observations from the preceding chapters. The Reformation and the Puritan Revolution, the most serious upheavals thus far studied, were shown to be the climactic phases of developments long under way—perhaps the violence and the excitement and bloodshed of the French Revolution was only the froth above the deeper flow of the current. Perhaps more continuity was maintained than is perceptible at first glance, in the sense that powerful social forces were driving French society in a certain direction and might well have achieved their goals without the more dramatic aspects of those years. It may be that, as in the other revolutions, the initial events disturbed the traditional equilibrium within the community to such a degree that some years were required for a new balance to emerge and the basic continuity to be resumed. With this much said, let us now turn to an examination of certain common errors in the popular conception of a revolution.

Error: A revolution is caused by the misery of the people

This error is more than simply another instance of oversimplified causation, for the statement itself seems to have little verity. Eyewitness accounts of the French Revolution do give an impression that the people were suffering from great want. Persons who later wished to make a case for the revolution naturally played up the misgovernment and evil conditions of the Old Regime, and a combination of factors made it possible for them to find good illustrations. Crop failures in portions of France resulted in high food prices in the cities. A commercial treaty with England had permitted English goods to flow into France, there to undersell French goods, with the consequence that French shopworkers became unemployed. A severe winter in 1788–1789 made conditions even worse. The mob scenes that followed were dramatic and eye-catching and were certainly indicative that something was fundamentally wrong. The mobs themselves furnished excellent materials for leaders intent on causing a genuine revolution or in arrogating power for them-selves.

Against the idea that the distress of 1788–1789 caused the revolution, however, several arguments can be launched. Similar distress at other times had not been followed by revolution. The general direction of the economy of France had been upward throughout the eighteenth century; if misery caused revolution, why did it not occur earlier, instead of taking place at the end of the century of relative progress? The French peasants, who were so vocal and restless in 1789 and who, it is true, had seen a worsening of their condition in the last decades, were nevertheless probably as well off as in any other country in Europe. Less than a million of the twenty million farmers were even nominally serfs, a sharp contrast to the countries farther east. If exasperation with poor circumstances were the principal cause for a revolution, the French would have been among the last to revolt.

Extreme suffering or poverty seems to induce apathy rather than rebellion, for people in these circumstances are too busy simply surviving to give much thought to government. Virtually every society in human history has had its proportion of paupers at the lower levels of society, a chronic source of revolution if the misery theory of revolution were true. This stratum of society may occasionally, in periods of weak authority, be the cause for mob scenes or of a *Jacquerie* (medieval uprising of peasants), but lack of proper leadership and planning prevents success. Exactly the same kind of episodes will occur in a genuine revolution, their impact now intensifying the trend toward radical change and even presenting the illusion that this *is* the cause for revolution.

Ah, but—was not France bankrupt? Was not this the reason that the Estates-General assembled? Careless use of words often cause confusion here: the French as a people were not—could not—be bankrupt, and in fact were growing in wealth throughout the eighteenth century, while the *government* became increasingly insolvent. The contrast between the financial condition of the government and of the people as a whole is indicative of a maladjustment so grave as to suggest a major reason for the revolution. The French government, which had undergone no fundamental revision for upwards of a century and a half, was out of date; it did not properly represent the social forces of France in 1789.

Could one measure the comparative strengths of the various social classes of France in 1600 and again in 1789 and then depict them on an ordinary graph, the picture would be clearer. In 1600 the vertical lines representing the nobility and the clergy would be quite tall, the middle class comparatively short, and the peasants and city workers even shorter; for 1789 the lines for the first two classes would be much shorter than in 1600, the workers' somewhat taller than formerly, the peasants' would have grown considerably, while the middle class line would be very much elongated. The fundamental change in the situation was the growth of economic strength and organization of the middle class, especially the upper middle class, coincident with a diminution of real power in the status of the nobility and clergy.

The structure of French politics had not been altered to accord with this gradual development. Had the evolution in the economy been paralleled by evolution in political matters, no revolution need have occurred. The years of reform, which come periodically in democratic countries, do permit the gradual shifting in the domestic balance of power to be reflected in the nation's laws and institutions without either disrupting the equilibrium or goading the losers to violence. Such had not been the case in France, the growing power of the bourgeois having insufficient political outlet. In addition, many limitations and annoyances irritated them; the clutter of tariff laws within France, the medley of laws and customs, the inaccessibility of many political offices, and, above all, the galling injustice of unequal taxation all called for drastic revision. A class whose wealth was doing much to support the country demanded a greater voice in the government. The presence of parliamentary institutions across the English Channel in Great Britain served as a constant stimulus for the French bourgeois to attempt a reform along similar lines. In 1789 the new giant suddenly snapped off the fetters that had so long restricted him. The revolution was born, not out of misery, but out of strength and hope.

In 1615 the Estates-General of France was in session. Queen Marie de Médicis dismissed its members with the ostensible plea that she needed their assembly hall to hold a ball; they went home, never dreaming that they would not meet again for one hundred and seventy-four years. There is neat symbolism here: the assembly of the people went home, and for five generations the nobles and court danced. When the Estates-General returned in 1789, there was work to be done by the industrious, sober members of the Third Estate, and they set out to do it in two years. The result was—revolution.

Error: One of the principal reasons for a revolution is the tyranny and brutality of the government

When the son of Solomon, in ancient Israel, came to the throne, he announced, "My father hath chastised you with whips, but I will chastise you with scorpions." Presently the new king encountered a rebellion.

A person almost automatically assumes that a revolution is aimed at a bad and tyrannical government. Why, otherwise, would the people rise? The natural belief has been further strengthened by the apologists for every successful revolution, who depict the overthrown government in the darkest colors. According to this line of reasoning, Louis XVI must have been a monster. He was crowned in 1774 in the traditional brilliant ceremony at the cathedral of Reims, with the nobles and higher clergy of the realm in attendance. According to reports, in the hushed and solemn moment when the archbishop placed the crown upon Louis' head, the king uttered the immortal words, "It hurts me!"

The crown of France continued to hurt this king by the grace of God, and locksmith by preference, throughout his reign. The reluctant resignation of one royal minister brought from Louis the comment, "How lucky you are! Why cannot I resign too?" One gets the impression that Louis, far from being a tyrant, was thoroughly bored with his job.

In the spring of 1789, at a crucial point, Louis XVI ordered the Three Estates to meet separately, yet when the Third Estate resisted, the king reversed his "unalterable" command. Arthur Young, an Englishman who was traveling in France in 1789, writes: ". . . the press teems with the most levelling and even seditious principles . . . and not the least step is taken by the court to restrain this extreme licentiousness of publication. . . . I am all amazement at the ministry permitting such nests and hotbeds of sedition and revolt. . . ."

The fall of the Bastille, the symbol of tyranny and absolute mon-archy, was hailed by liberals everywhere as an act of liberation. The victorious mob paraded the freed victims of oppression, the prisoners found in the Bastille, through downtown Paris. Note carefully who they were: four counterfeiters, two lunatics, and one debauchee!

The picture that emerges is not one of strength, but of such ridic-ulous weakness as to evoke derision. Someone has very aptly said that governments are not overthrown, they commit suicide. A long-established regime, due to its long habit of wielding power, fails to sense the ebbing of its authority, its leaders misinterpret the true nature of the threatening insurrection, and—perhaps most fatal of all—it displays weakness when confronted by resistance. Against a government which is strong and alert (and avoids defeat in war), the chances of a successful uprising are slight. An outbreak is most likely to occur when a government is ob-viously incompetent, when it yields concessions under pressure at the last moment, when its weaknesses raise hopes of a successful insurrection. Then the "falterings of those who hold legal powers" encourage the attempt.

Error: The transfer of power occurs when the people storm the citadels of the government in the course of a civil war

This, again, is a natural assumption. Let us, however, investigate the actual course of events in the French Revolution. The direction of affairs was taken over by the National Assembly in the early summer of 1789, when it obstinately refused to obey the king and defied the threat of the use of force. By failing to employ the loyal elements in the army to subdue the National Assembly, the king relinquished control of affairs. Although sporadic outbreaks did take place, especially the storming of the Bastille, and numerous acts of violence occurred in the countryside, these by-products of the general restlessness can scarcely be called civil war. The reformers had, to all intents and purposes, secured control of the machinery of state merely by brushing aside a show of force by the traditional authorities.

When the assembly drew up a constitution, a moderate government along English lines was provided in which the Crown would still be a respected institution. Numerous other reform measures were prepared which make up much of the constructive and permanent accomplish-ments of the French Revolution. The moderate elements in the nobility and clergy, at first, could feel that what was happening was for the best;

while individual privileges might be lost, many had been prepared for the inevitable by the prevalent ideas of the Enlightenment. Either gathered up in the contagious enthusiasm or stupefied by the alteration of the unalterable, most of the upper classes surrendered their special status in favor of a union of the nation.

In the original definition of revolution, "circumstances of violence" was noted to be an integral part of the phenomenon. This qualification is scarcely fulfilled in the phases of revolution thus far described, and if the process of change ends at this point, we are dealing with a transition of an essentially evolutionary, rather than revolutionary, character. Substantially the same process occurs repeatedly in democratic countries and may, in cumulative effect, cause changes as drastic as in an actual revolution. That which distinguishes the two, apparently, is the outbreak of armed resistance to the innovations.

Civil wars are associated, in the public mind, with revolutions, the assumption being that the reformers attempt to attain power by this method. We have discovered, however, that the virtual collapse of an old regime permits peaceful accession to power by the reformers. Those who usually start the civil war are the former ruling classes, who have been deprived of more than they had expected, and who now realize what loss of power really means. In the French Revolution, the outbreak of war with Prussia and Austria marks the real beginning of this phase. In certain other revolutions, the same order of events seems to occur. The Puritan Revolution entered its violent stage *after* the Long Parliament had taken power in 1641. Charles I saw that the only way to regain power was by an appeal to arms; he then rallied his forces and began the conflict. In the Russian Revolution, some fighting occurred when the Communists took over, but the real civil war did not begin until the following year when the Whites, the anti-Communists, began a drive to oust the Reds. Even the American Revolution fits the pattern to some extent, since the British moved armed forces to the colonies when the Americans insisted on maintaining liberties held before George III attempted to strengthen British control.

The above examples all occurred within the framework of a Western society and whether this order of events would always occur is, of course, dubious. It did so in the abortive Spanish Revolution of the 1930's, although the former ruling class in this case succeeded in winning the civil war. In order to view the Chinese Communist revolution in these terms, one would have to regard the Communist success as the Jacobin phase of the revolution which began in 1911. The Jacobin period of a revolution is the most radical stage, and is the one which must now be considered.

Error: In a revolution, the people rise spontaneously and take power

Most revolutionists of modern times have claimed to represent the interests of the people. They ascribe their actions to the popular will. When they write the histories of their successes, they like to picture themselves as leaders of a great mass movement which welled out of the populace itself and irresistibly swept away the opposition. The proponents of the *status quo*, on the other hand, normally explain the disturbances as being the work of a few agitators who lead the people into violence and resistance by their demagogy. They are prone to believe that if these few dangerous men could be removed, the revolution would quickly subside. Somewhere between these two extreme points of view lies the truth.

An examination of such an episode as the fall of the Bastille provides no clear-cut answer. At first glance, the incident may seem to have been the result of the spontaneous uprising of the people. One may ask, at this point, "What people?" Only a small proportion of the Parisians were present. The city had been in a state of excitement for several days; mobs had wandered about Paris; the usual young men about town, full of strong drink and bravado, were bent chiefly on excitement; criminal elements were doubtless present, as well as sincere and patriotic men; many persons played a passive part as spectators or were gathered up in the contagious enthusiasm; it was a heterogeneous crowd, inspired by mass psychology and probably led by men who suddenly saw their opportunity. Unfortunately for us, these men did not emerge from the mass so that we can say who they were. The court believed them, true or false, to be agents of the Duke of Orléans, and, in fact, persisted in simplifying the revolution into a plot woven by the duke in order that he might replace Louis XVI on the throne. The picture that available evidence gives us is that of a mob collected by the events of the preceding days and the anticipation of further excitement, and this was then played upon by leaders who assumed command of the enterprise. The enthusiastic approval, which greeted the deed, however, in a sense associates the whole French people in the act.

The case of the march of the women to Versailles is a little clearer. Most of these women were of the dregs of the city who would scarcely have undertaken such a march on their own volition. This looks like a case of clever organization on the part of well-disguised leaders.

Whatever the case may be in these instances, a movement such as this brings together men with similar purposes, their common enthusiasms create a sharpening sense of purpose, and revolutionary societies soon bring additional organization into their activities. The society which ultimately emerged as the guiding spirit of the radicals was the Jacobin Club. It originated as a gathering of some of the members of the National Assembly who met together to eat and to discuss political ideas. Eventually club members threshed out their ideas in meetings, decided upon their policies, and then worked, much like a modern political party, in the legislative sessions to push their measures through. Moderate in tone at first, the society finally passed into the control of the extremists, and it became the core of radical strength in the nation. Jacobin clubs were established throughout the country and drew to themselves the more radical and enthusiastic individuals; the parent organization in Paris, through the branch clubs keeping contact with the different districts, could quickly mobilize a vocal public opinion and react to threats of counterrevolution. The machinery of the Jacobin Club permitted a small minority to dominate France for a time.

Other revolutions have also produced organizations which channelized popular restlessness and supervised the "spontaneous" rebellion of the people. The Committees of Correspondence in the thirteen colonies to some extent served such a purpose early in the American Revolution. In the Russian Revolution, the Communist party played the decisive role in organizing and leading the cohorts of rebellion, its leaders having benefited from long study of the technique of previous revolutions as well as the reasons for their success or failure. The radicals will also seize or create other institutions which will give additional control; thus the French radicals used the Committee of Public Safety and the Communists the popular councils or soviets.

The salient point in all this is that the moderates are overwhelmed by the momentum of revolution and fail to stabilize the situation. The reforms already wrought are threatened with destruction by embittered and determined men; their violent challenge, of such a nature that moderate countermeasures will not avail, brings to the fore the equally determined and fanatic supporters of the changes. The centrifugal force of the crisis strengthens the extremes at the expense of the moderates until two bodies of hostile men are arrayed against one another in civil war.

The exigencies of the situation, the desperateness of conditions, impel the revolutionaries to resort to extreme measures. Suspects are arrested and summarily gotten rid of in the general hysteria. The hatred against the reactionaries and the defection of the king, in the French Revolution, prompted a movement to cut the last ties with the past, such as the monarchy, and build a new state and society based upon the ideas of the eighteenth-century philosophers. Judging from the French example, a revolution enters a violent stage due to a combination of resistance from the opposition, the presence of a well-knit revolutionary group that wishes to carry the movement to its logical conclusion, and the proximity of the mob, whose arms are ready for use when force is necessary.

A fairly good rule-of-thumb standard for thinking about the radical stage of a revolution is to assume that about 10 per cent of the people are strongly in favor of the movement and another 10 per cent are equally strongly against it. The remainder may be inclined one way or the other but not sufficiently so to work actively for their side. They may be drawn into the struggle by momentary enthusiasm, they may be molded by propaganda one way or another, or they may cherish a virulent dislike for both extremes. The momentum and the leaders emerge from a small minority; any revolution is certain to be a minority revolution after an initial swelling of popular enthusiasm.

For a time the Jacobins imposed their republic and their extremist ideas upon the country. This was followed by a period of gradual return to more normal conditions. Several reasons may be noted here for the end of the Jacobin phase in this, or any other, revolution. Sometimes the revolutionists liquidate themselves when the reign of terror is turned upon their own leaders; men, living in a state of suspicion and fear of the opposition, will inevitably focus this mood upon their colleagues also, and, having learned to use violence against others, they will not hesitate in like treatment of their fellows. Once the victory over the opposition is won and the more extreme ideas of the revolutionists fail in practical application, enthusiasm gives way to an intense longing for normalcy. The passive spirit of the vast majority of the population, prevented by fear from finding expression in vocal criticism, nevertheless,

by the very massiveness of its indifference, erodes away the determination
of the revolutionaries.

*Error: The result of a revolution is to gain greater freedom for the
people*

This usual assumption must be handled with care. Successful revolutionists naturally claim to have restored liberty to the people. The fact
obviously is, however, that the French under the Jacobins or Napoleon
were more directly affected by the government and were better controlled by it than under the Old Regime. The Communists gave the
Russians a police system far more efficient than that of the tsars. The
American government, after the establishment of the Constitution, was
stronger than the British predecessor.

Judging by these examples, one must decide that a revolution
usually replaces a decrepit authority with a vigorous one. The new
administration will exercise more effective control than its predecessor,
which is likely to result in a positive lessening of individual liberties.
At the same time, the removal of the principal abuses existent before the
insurrection will give a sense of added freedom. The presence of men,
newly risen from the ranks, in the principal offices may make the new
government popular. Finally, the social class which achieved control in
the revolution will have escaped restrictions and for it, at least, the feeling
of additional liberty will correspond to the facts. That is, if a revolution
ends the maladjustments which helped to bring on the trouble in the
first place, the entire structure will function better; even though the
government is a strong one, it will presumably be operating in the interest
of the more vocal part of society.

A word needs to be added about successful counterrevolutions. In
the event that the civil war is won by the extremist opposition, the
former ruling class takes power again amidst the massacre of the reform-
ing radicals. Does the country then go back to prerevolutionary conditions? Scarcely! The same necessities which created a tightly knit Jacobin
Club also create a disciplined and iron-willed group of conservatives.
Having learned the perils of inefficient administration, the conservatives
now install a strong government, which assumes firm control over the
populace. In the campaign to regain power, the conservatives have been
compelled to broaden their outlook in order to attract a following; in the
process, they may be compelled to accept parts of the revolutionary
program, admit to their group persons or classes not formerly aligned

with them, and sponsor broad general slogans, often based upon religious or national feeling, which will draw supporters. Consequently, the goal of complete "Restoration" of the bygone is as illusory for the conservative as the goal of complete liberty is for the revolutionary.

The Pattern of Revolution

As a final summary, a brief sketch of the probable successive stages in a revolution is in order, although we must take care to remember that the pattern can be only a tentative one because of inevitable variations.

Generally speaking, the initial indication of impending upheaval is the activity of writers in denouncing existent conditions, pointing out the worst maladjustments, satirizing and rendering ridiculous certain common practices and ideas, and destroying faith in existent institutions. These men provide new goals for humanity, coin popular slogans, and paint pictures of future utopias if suggested reforms were to occur.

In the second stage, widespread public dissatisfaction manifests itself and culminates in riots, assassinations, and other acts of violence. The ruling group is intimidated into making repeated concessions until a real transfer of power occurs—the third stage. By peaceful means, the reformers try to carry out their ideas. If the measures are of so drastic a nature as to split the nation, the ability of the moderates to maintain control is lost, and the initiative passes to the extremists. In this, the fourth stage, the former ruling group, now out of power, and experiencing the disabilities of this position, attempts to regain control of the machinery of government: civil war follows. The struggle entrenches the radicals in power, and in the fifth stage they attempt to bring into realization their utopian dreams.

When their tenure of power has run its course, the drift to normalcy occurs, which is called the Thermidorian Reaction in the French Revolution. According to Crane Brinton, whose book *The Anatomy of Revolution* should be consulted by anyone wishing a more complete analysis of the phenomenon of revolution, Russia would seem to be undergoing a protracted Thermidorian Reaction. Some writers add a seventh stage to the pattern, that of Bonapartism or imperialism, in which the new regime embarks upon a career of conquest under the guise of liberating other countries. In that case, one might be inclined to believe the Russian Revolution to be in the imperialist stage, even though a specific general or Bonaparte has not assumed control of the country.

9

The Bases of Loyalty

According to Voltaire, "History is but a picture of crimes and misfortunes." It must have been chronicles of this kind that another eighteenth-century writer, Beccaria, had in mind when he proclaimed that nation happiest which is without a history. Although the annals of mankind *are* filled with the sound of wars and civil strife—the focus of attention has been, and cannot help but be, on the dramatic—one must admit that this emphasis presents a distorted picture of the actual circumstances.

The outline of history may be compared to the front page of a newspaper. News is found in the sensational, the unexpected, the criminal event, rather than in the fact that millions of people lived peaceably during a particular day. In the same way, the history that is reported to later generations is the extraordinary rather than the ordinary.

When one is aware of the potential strength of social forces, of the explosive qualities of human ambitions and emotions, of the tensions and frustrations that permeate every society, law and order in the community seems a miraculous blessing. One single political community will include a number of groups with different economic motivations. It may contain groups that worship different gods or at least worship the same God in different ways. Priests, warriors, farmers, merchants, manufacturers, and laborers usually manage to work together and to solve their problems without open recourse to violence. Wars have followed wars, and yet, century after century, certain countries continue to exist as if each were held together by gravity. Certain galaxies of states in various parts of the world maintain their courses and relative international positions for hundreds of years.

Such a gravity does exist, partly spontaneous and inherent in all social groups and partly artificially inspired by the government of these countries. We are likely, perhaps, to assume that *force* is the element which holds the state together, for that is what seems most in evidence in our reading. Force is the ultimate resort, it is true, but even a dictatorial regime, by the volume of its domestic propaganda, admits that physical power alone does not suffice. Although every town has a police, most people do not conform to laws merely because they fear the police. The ties that bind, in the last analysis, are moral and spiritual rather than physical, and the successful community exercises control over the mind as well as the body. Its members are taught certain beliefs in common over and beyond the ideals and goals of the various groups within the community; they believe themselves associated together by reasons that transcend those of the individual and they revere certain symbols as indications of this.

On a small and familiar scale, the fabric of loyalty can be discerned in the functioning of a fraternity or sorority. The members of one such group have a common "we-ness" as over against the rest of the campus. In order to further the feeling that their particular group has some special distinction, setting it apart from and elevated above the others, the members cherish secret rites and mysteries known only to themselves. Each social group has a special coat of arms and other symbols conveying secret meanings. Each has its own history, its heroes, its valiant deeds, which enhance pride in the organization. Rivalry for athletic trophies and campus offices stimulates loyalty, and the very sacrifices demanded are intended to engender a feeling of a personal stake and share in the organization. The advantages conferred give a certain vested interest in it; a member's prestige and standing is enhanced or jeopardized by the fortunes of his own group. He merges part of his individuality in the group and derives a certain satisfaction in finding himself a part of something greater than himself.

Every successful social institution follows this same pattern to some degree. The fabric of loyalties of an entire country, the same type of thing on a much larger scale, is the gravity that holds the individuals and social groups of a country close to the direction and interest of the commonwealth itself. The country evokes emotional associations and beliefs in ideals sufficiently strong to override various conflicting elements.

Monarchism

In the period of Restoration, two sets of loyalties were in conflict in Western Europe. The one looked back to the traditional viewpoint toward government of the eighteenth century. The other had found expression in some of the writers of the eighteenth century, had come into dramatic but temporary victory in the French Revolution, and was the fighting creed of a vocal minority in a dozen European countries after 1815. It was in France that the clash between the two was most apparent in the fifteen years after the Congress of Vienna.

One group of people, a portion of the returning *émigrés*, hoped for a "Restoration" of society as it had been before 1789. They believed that the king derived unlimited power from God and that a hierarchy is the natural and divinely ordained form of society. The idea that men were created equal and that they could, of their own will, contract together to form a government seemed a blasphemous presumption to them.

King Louis XVIII was endowed with too much common sense to yield entirely to this group, at least not until near the end of his reign. He did, however, do his best to cover up his concessions to the Liberals by restoring the old symbols of faith and by clothing his actions in the phraseology of the Old Regime. Louis XVIII, in announcing the Charter or constitution, made quite clear that he was *giving* it to the people rather than the people framing it themselves in true constitutional fashion. He dated the Charter in the nineteenth year of his reign, although he had just ascended the throne, and thereby emphasized the legitimist claim that he had been legal ruler of France since the disappearance (and presumed death) of the dauphin, the son of Louis XVI. The white flag of the Bourbons replaced the tricolor of the Revolution. Even when again driven into exile during Napoleon's Hundred Days, Louis held daily meetings with his ministers and maintained a pretense of reigning.

When Louis XVIII addressed the representatives of the people, he talked of *his* policies; the ministers were *his*, rather than responsible to the parliament; the king was taking the advice of his people, but he was not obeying their will. All this was mostly fiction, of course, for the ministers were tending to become subject to the will of parliament, and the deputies, more than the king, made the decisions. The French were well on the way to the English method, whereby parliament rules while the official proclamations are still couched in language reminiscent of the seventeenth and eighteenth centuries.

The Ultras and Charles X refused to be satisfied with the forms of divine right and clung stubbornly to the substance of the old loyalties. In true eighteenth-century style, they focused their devotion on the dynasty itself, found a martyr in the Duc de Berri when he was murdered, rejoiced in the seemingly miraculous posthumous birth of his son and heir, and went on crusade for their ideals in a campaign to restore divine right in neighboring Spain. Conversely, an original sympathy for the Greek rebels melted away among the Ultras when the Greeks declared for sovereignty of the people.

Charles X went even further in restoring the old symbols. He arranged for himself a medieval coronation at Reims, restored the title of dauphin to the heir, and acted out the ancient monarchical pose of the all-wise, benevolent, God-ordained father of the people. Unfortunately for Charles X, France had grown beyond this, the more sophisticated part of the population finding the old symbols and practices ridiculous. Faith in divine right was ebbing, and a new faith was replacing it. After the 1830 revolution, Chateaubriand put this neatly when he declared: "Monarchy is no longer a religion."

In other parts of Europe, this particular symbol maintained its function longer. Monarchy, over the ages, has been one of the most successful devices for stimulating and holding the allegiance of the people. The keystone of this set of ideas and symbols was the Crown, and the court of Louis XIV at Versailles was the perfected expression of this type of belief. Complex rituals and ornate manners were developed to express the proper reverence for the Crown. A class of courtiers served the king with great ostentation and ceremony, all governmental appointments were made in his name, all decrees or legislation were issued as if from him, the army of the country was a royal army, and the country's flag was the banner of the dynasty. All men were king's men, and all highways were "King's Highways." A wide variety of honors and titles were at the disposal of the Crown and could be used to bind to the throne all men worthy of such distinction. For the benefit of the people, the king was portrayed as the father of all his country, benevolent and kind, seeking the welfare of his people and willing to listen to their petitions. In this fashion, all residents of the country were bound together in a common allegiance as subjects of the same king and were geared to work for common purposes.

One of the principal rites of the monarchic system and one which presents a great many facets of kingship in a single scene is the coronation. The enthronement of a British sovereign, which takes place in Westminster Abbey, is filled with practices developed over the centuries which reveal to the men of the twentieth century something of the spirit of monarchy. In 1953 Churchill and the Conservative ministry obviously arranged the magnificently staged coronation of Queen Elizabeth II as an opportune method of stimulating British patriotism and of strengthening imperial ties.

The pageantry begins with a colorful processional into the abbey. When the participants are in their places, the Archbishop of Canterbury presents the new king to the assembled populace in the formula known as The Recognition. This ceremony, evidently a survival of the time when the kings were elected, consists in the archbishop asking the multitude four times, in the four directions of the compass, if they will serve the king. Each time they respond, "God save King George" (or whatever the name may be), and trumpets are blown. (The somewhat abbreviated description given here is for the coronation of a king, rather than, as occurred in 1953, of a queen.) When this gesture of election is completed, the king prepares to take an oath to rule according to the laws and customs of Britain. In one form or another, kings of England have always taken some such oath, but the present one dates from the time of the Glorious Revolution. After making his promises, he goes to the altar and takes the oath with his right hand on the open Bible.

The remainder of the ceremony takes place within the setting of the Communion Service of the Church of England; this service continues until the saying of the Creed, at which point the archbishop resumes the ceremonies of the coronation by anointing the monarch. A small amount of holy oil is poured from an ampulla, a sacred vessel, into a golden spoon. The archbishop dips his finger into the oil and makes the sign of the cross on the king's head, breast, and palms. After the king is given a sword and spurs, a ring, an orb, and scepters, as visible emblems of his dominion, the climactic moment arrives: after the archbishop has blessed the crown at the altar, it is placed upon the head of the king while he remains seated in a chair. The crowd again shouts, "God save King George. Long live King George. May the King live for ever."

The king now descends from his chair near the altar and is lifted into the throne. His being literally lifted in this fashion is believed to be a survival of the Teutonic practice of raising a new king on a shield and his being acclaimed while on the shield. Certain men then come forward and do homage to the new ruler. First, the Archbishop of Canterbury, representing the lords spiritual, kneels and takes the oath of allegiance. He is followed by a representative of each of the noble orders, the dukes, marquesses, earls, viscounts, and barons, each coming in turn to declare himself the king's "liege man of life and limb." In this performance, straight out of the medieval feudal practice, the commoners have no part. This section of the ritual is concluded by a final exhortation from the Archbishop of Canterbury.

His queen is then anointed, crowned, and enthroned. The royal pair receive the Holy Communion, the service is completed, and, after the singing of the national anthem, the participants file in procession out of the abbey.

In this service are mingled vestiges of pagan Teutonic practice, the majestic ritual of the church, the feudal pledge of homage, and the business of pledging the king to abide by the will of the people and the restraints of law. The coronation is essentially a sacrament which, as *The Illustrated London News* says, "binds together not only the living of a nation with one another, but the living both with the dead and those still to be born." The king becomes, in an act of faith, a mystic bond with the supernatural and with the ages. The full authority of the Church of England is brought into the ceremony in the religious char-acter of the rite and in the chief role being taken by the Archbishop of Canterbury, Primate of All England.

Legend and symbolism reinforce the emotional impact. The sacred ampulla, the small vessel which contains the holy oil for the anointing, according to one old version, was given to Thomas à Becket, famed and sainted twelfth-century Archbishop of Canterbury, by Mary, mother of Jesus, who appeared to him in a vision. (The French believed that their ampulla had been brought for the original consecration of King Clovis, first Christian king of the Franks.) The Stone of Scone, which lies under the coronation chair, has an even longer tradition. The English took it from the Scots, the latter having long used it as the coronation stone for their own kings. The Scots claimed that the stone was origi-nally the same stone that Jacob rested his head upon when he saw the heavenly ladder. That some Scots still regard the Stone of Scone as a symbol of their nation was proved by the brash act of some young Scottish Nationalists who stole it temporarily from Westminster Abbey in 1950.

The swords and spur represent the military aspect of the kingship. One of the swords is blunted as a sign of mercy. The orb bears a cross on top, indicating that the world is subject to Christ. (Portraits of medieval monarchs of various countries show the king or emperor bearing such an orb.) One of the scepters has a dove at the top, the symbol of the Holy Spirit, whose inspiration directs the action of the king.

The British obviously have maintained the pageantry, and some of the spirit as well, of monarchy. They have reconciled the two seemingly alien types of loyalties, and the same is true in a limited number of other lands. Something of this process was under way to a greater or lesser extent in all of the Continental countries during the nineteenth century. The continuing strength of the older attitudes was retained, while the more recent sense of national association and of social contract was permitted to secure a place in the creed of the various countries.

It will have been noticed that belief in monarchism is expressed by various devices: a creed or pledge expressing the essentials of the faith; symbols evocative of deeper meanings, such as the crown and scepter; rituals or courtly etiquette as a mean of portraying reverence and obedience; a history in which is narrated the heroic acts and sacrificial martyrdoms inspired by so worthy a cause. Similar devices form a part of all great beliefs, including the two conquering faiths of the nineteenth century, liberalism and nationalism.

Monarchy and the Nation

Over against the Ultras, during the Restoration in France, stood the Liberals. To the cries of "Long live the king," they responded "Long live the Charter!" In opposition to the Ultras, they organized societies with such names as "Friends of the Truth," "Friends of the Press," and "Chevaliers of Liberty." The Liberals rejected the white banner of the Bourbons and, when they ousted Charles X, enthusiastically restored the tricolor as the emblem of France. The heroic death of Marshal Ney before a firing squad gave the Liberals a martyr to revere; his crime had consisted in going over to Napoleon, when sent to arrest him upon his return from Elba. Later, other men such as the famous four sergeants of La Rochelle, who were suspected of plotting against the royalist government, suffered for their faith and gave renewed emotional strength to the Liberal cause.

The Liberals believed in the nation and the sovereignty of the people. When they obtained in Louis Philippe a king of their own choosing, they called him the "citizen king" and were delighted that he behaved like a member of the bourgeois. He took the title of King of the French People, rather than King of France, and was ruler by the "will of the people" rather than by the "grace of God."

These beliefs and practices were representative of middle-class feeling in the nineteenth century, when the distant symbol of the Crown no longer sufficed as an adequate emblem of unity. The conception of a superior king and court did not accord with the egalitarian sentiments of the middle class, and the increasing literacy and knowledge of the people resulted in a greater need for personal identification with the government. The citizens set up a new symbol alongside of the Crown, the nation, thus substituting a feeling of commonalty for *all* the people as members of the nation. The individual was prepared to look upon himself as part of a greater whole, of which each one was an active member, and in which each had a personal stake. The slogan of the French Revolution, "Liberty, Equality, Fraternity," summed up the new conception of the community.

While the Ultras tried their best to forget the Napoleonic era, the Liberals tended increasingly to look back to it with nostalgia. In those years French armies had carried Liberal ideas all over Europe, and France had been the master of the Continent. The years of victory were glorious ones for any French nationalist.

Even in the period of the Restoration and in the reign of Louis Philippe, one can see that a belief in the nation might lead to emphasis in one of two directions. The stress might be placed upon the importance of individual liberty, thereby leading to a gradual growth of genuine democracy. On the other hand, the people might become imbued with zeal for their own particular nation as over against other nations, the result being intense nationalism. The two were ingredients of the same movement in the earlier nineteenth century, but in the twentieth century extreme nationalism sometimes became a threat to democracy.

Nationalism

Nationalism is the principal cement which holds the modern country together. It assumed its modern form, roughly speaking, in the period of the French Revolution. By the end of the eighteenth century the growth of transportation and communications, gradually widening the intercourse between different parts of the same country, had created the physical bases for the conception of a broader loyalty, while at the same time weakening some of the appeal of the prevalent provincial sentiments. The middle class, long irritated by what was to them senseless tariffs and barriers between provinces, leveled these and made the country economically one when they came into power. The larger practicable unit above the provincial quite naturally would be the confines of a territory in which people spoke the same language.

The most reliable criterion of the existence of an actual nationality is the presence of a large number of people living in a contiguous area who speak a common language. While usually true, some important exceptions can be found to this normal situation: Belgium, Switzerland, and Canada, for instance, each has more than one language group but is nevertheless regarded as a nation. Although the German-speaking part of the Swiss live next to Germany, they are not commonly regarded as part of the German nation. In South America the inhabitants of a large part of the continent are Spanish-speaking, yet there are nine separate Spanish-speaking nations. Nearly all Irishmen speak English but persisted in long opposition to absorption into the English nation. Even within such a country as Italy, the dialects may be so different as to render communication difficult between a Sicilian and someone from Turin.

Other factors help to determine nationhood. In the case of the Irish, the fact that they were mostly Roman Catholic caused a constant feeling of difference from the British to persist. Unquestionably the Poles, a Roman Catholic salient between Protestant Prussia and Greek Orthodox Russia, were encouraged by the religious factor to regard themselves as a separate people. Lebanon, with a Christian majority, has separated from Syria for reasons of religion. The subcontinent of India was split in two, when the British withdrew, by the existence of two principal religious groups, although India is geographically one and had possessed a single government for over a century.

In some cases a very definite geographical entity will become a nation despite considerable differences within the area which otherwise might lead to a split. Italy is an example and so is Spain. Within the latter country, the Catalans and Basques tend to regard themselves as nations different from Spain, yet the very definite boundary constituted by the Pyrenees has helped to keep the country united.

Existence of a strong government and a brilliant history in the days before the emergence of modern nationalism, as was true of Spain, has sometimes helped to mold a nation. The French included in their nation the Bretons (of the peninsula of Brittany), the Provençals of the south, and the Alsatians, and have succeeded in making them French even though native dialects or languages may persist in these areas. A limited number of Africans of much more alien origin have also been absorbed into the French cultural and political nation.

Someone has defined the nation in these terms: "Any group of people which regards itself as a nation *is* a nation." This does not tell all the story, but it does emphasize the factor of popular will which may override differences in language, customs, and religion.

Nationalism is by no means spontaneous, although its root, the love of home locality and of one's kinsfolk, is. The patriotic fervor of individuals varies greatly, reaching all the way from those who are completely indifferent and irresponsible to those who are equally completely narrow-minded fanatics and who insist that all others shall be the same way.

Even as monarchy ceased to be a religion, national feeling was taking on religious qualities. Like any strong pattern of loyalty, nationalism has symbols which serve as focuses of reverence and as reminders of the deeper meanings of the faith; rituals, anthems, shrines, and special holidays serve purposes very much like those of a church.

The flag is to nationalism what the cross is to Christianity. The flag of the country, in its design and colors, carries certain meanings that designate that particular country. Some type of emblem has been used by governments to distinguish themselves since ancient times; the Persians of Cyrus and Darius used a golden eagle on a white flag; the owl was the symbol of Athens and appeared on its coins; the symbols were usually carved on plaques and carried on standards as in the well-known case of the Roman legions. The most usual device for the modern nation's flag is the use of two or three bars, either vertical or horizontal, with certain colors traditional to the country. Other frequent emblems include the cross or crescent, stars, and the sun. Beyond these fairly common symbols are a number of more distinctive figures such as the elephant of Thailand, the mosque of Afghanistan, and the hammer and sickle of the Soviet Union. The old imperial flag of China portrayed a dragon.

The most peculiar flags in existence today, incidentally, are those of colonies or states. Among the American flags are the famous Bear Flag of California, the buffalo of Wyoming, the palmetto tree of South Carolina, and the pelican of Louisiana. The banner of New Mexico, appropriately enough, carries an Indian symbol for the sun, while some Southern states include St. Andrew's cross, reminiscent of the Confederacy. The flags of various foreign colonies and states include such interesting devices as ships in sail, an ax and saw, bulls, swans, snakes, salt, the piping crow shrike (a bird), the dodo, the heron, the kudu (an antelope), thistles, giraffe, and cranes. Most peculiar of all, perhaps, is the three-legged apparition of the Isle of Man.

A whole ritual has been developed for expressing reverence for the flag, for its raising and lowering, for proper ways of hanging it, all of these too well known to Americans to need any further elaboration here. Every country has a national anthem which is solemnly sung on important occasions. National holidays exist in all countries and are devoted to the remembrance of past glories, the anniversary of independence usually being the principal one. A day dedicated to war heroes, such as Memorial Day in the United States, will bring the ritual of nationalism into full play. Certain birthdays of the greatest men of a nation's history are sometimes also national holidays. The cult of the Unknown Soldier has grown up since the First World War. National shrines, such as Arlington and Westminster Abbey, are significant centers of reverence and so are monuments or tombs of national heroes.

A natural tendency exists for the history of a country to be written in terms of the noble deeds of its own sons and the wickedness of its enemies. Where the peoples of two countries like France and Germany assiduously nourish the memory of wars of aggression, atrocities, and treacheries of the other, the necessary community loyalty may indeed be nourished, but at the price of continued distrust and discord among neighboring states. Bolstering the national ego by engendering hatred of other countries among its own citizens is a well-worn device of most nations. In Latin-American countries, the Yankee is frequently made the butt for such dislike. The new nations of Asia quite naturally use the memory of imperialism as part of their appeal to the emotions. Even Americans can never quite forget the ancient antipathy for the British created by the War of Independence.

Each nationality tends to omit from its history those episodes that do not reflect credit upon itself. The Germans after the First World War were more excited and embittered by the war-guilt clause of the Versailles Treaty than by the more tangible loss of territory, and even after the Second World War they were reluctant to admit any responsibility for that conflict, war crimes, or concentration camps. The British and French have been proud of their colonial empires, while tending to overlook the seamier sides of their policies there. Americans would rather ignore the real reasons for the War of 1812 and our weak conduct in that conflict. A comparison of the brief account of the American Revolution in British textbooks with the long American description of the same revolution would be revealing. Russian and American descriptions of the Second World War scarcely seem to be dealing with the same conflict.

Each nation ascribes to itself a special mission, which usually takes the form of believing itself to be a defender of civilization. The French tend, and with some reason, to believe that the Rhine is the frontier of liberty and that they represent European culture against the "barbarism" of the Germans to the east. The Germans, in turn, regard themselves as the custodians of culture against the Slavs and the "decadent" French. The Israeli see in themselves the vanguard of Western civilization and techniques in the Near East. India, under the guidance of Nehru, views itself as the custodian of special virtues derived from its religions. Russia, under tsar and under Soviets, looks upon the West as decadent and due to collapse in the near future.

Most countries, especially the newer ones, have irredenta or areas in which their nationals live but which are under a foreign flag. The persecution of these people, played up in the national press, serves to remind everyone of the distinctiveness of their nation, of martyrdom to the cause, and provides national cause for armament and war. When describing policies or actions of countries, we often fall into a mode of expression wherein we write as if the country actually had a will and feeling—a very revealing indication of our actual conception of a nation. Cartoonists, of course, show England as John Bull or a lion, Russia as a bear, and the United States as Uncle Sam or an eagle.

The intensity of national feeling varies considerably from country to country, ranging all the way from a nationalism which is merely cultural to the extreme racialism of the Nazis. In general, a newly founded nation or one in an extremely precarious position will possess a more violent form than countries long established and secure. American nationalism, except in time of war, is a mild version of it.

Human societies, since the earliest recorded history, have relied on patterns of loyalty as a means of integrating the energies of the community. In the ancient monarchies and in the Orient, the ruler was usually regarded as a living god; church and state combined to serve him. The established religions have frequently, in themselves, provided the foundations for a unified society, as in the medieval Church and in Islam. Even today, the entire Moslem population, regardless of country, tends to join in a common allegiance to Islam and its hero-prophet, Mohammed. In recent decades, the adherents of Marxism have been possessed of the bold ambition to make of socialism a new and universal basis of loyalty for all mankind.

However different the actual content of the various political philosophies may be, a distinct and comparable pattern is visible in all of them. It is roughly analogous to the elements met in a church, and these political forms, in fact, have frequently been borrowed from genuine religious organizations. A focus of reverence is provided, whether a god, a human being, or an abstract entity like the nation; a set of symbols, such as the crown, the flag, and the scepter, evoke mystical meanings in the minds of believers; greater emotional overtones are stimulated by such solemn rites as a coronation; invocations, creeds, and songs vocalize the faith. A special history tells the story of the valiant struggle of good against evil, this particular loyalty being equated with righteousness, and tales of heroes and martyrs awaken ambition and self-sacrifice. Out of these elements is designed a pattern of loyalty which serves as a "gravity" binding the anarchic individual to the community.

10

The Individual in History

The chapters so far have dealt mostly with the impersonal factors that help to determine the course of history. Individual persons have usually appeared to be little more than pawns of powerful social forces. Most of us prefer, however, to believe in man's free will, in his capacity to make decisions both as a private individual and as a public figure. We like to think of history as an arena where the heroic emerge victorious by reason of a righteous cause and by superior personal qualities. We cannot help but distribute praise and blame for men's actions as we encounter them.

There are two extremes of interpretation in regard to the amount of influence which the individual may have in deciding historical issues, determinism and the so-called "Great Man theory."

The proponents of the Great Man theory would have us believe that the major developments of human history are accounted for by the great men who sometimes seem to exert an almost superhuman control over the fate of their generation. Human progress is regarded as being primarily due to the work of these geniuses, who may be generals, statesmen, saints, or men of ideas, but who seem to tower over the men of the times in their vision and ability to lead others. They frequently are so gifted—according to this point of view—that ordinary rules of behavior do not apply to them. They have been able to master the circumstances of their times and remold them according to their own ideas.

The Great Man theory, in a somewhat more limited form, comes naturally to us. Historical figures evoke our interest, sympathy, or hate far more than the impersonal functioning of government machinery or the abstract interplay of economic forces. History consists of stories, and stories must have heroes and villains. The men and the women are easier to remember; they force themselves upon our attention. We study the history of our country in the lower schools in terms of the lives of men who have helped to make it great. The modern dictatorships have accentuated the tendency to personalize history by their emphasis on the leader, by their insistence that he possesses qualities of a special nature and some sacred mission or destiny. Hero worship appears to be an essential part of all patterns of loyalty.

In contrast to this conception of "supermen" are the various theories of the determinists. These often leave little more room for individual choice than the possibility of gauging correctly the direction in which history is moving and then "leading" in that direction. Their proponents hold that leadership is more apparent than real. They believe that history is a record of a constant process of evolution toward a predetermined goal in which interruptions may occur, and there may be unforeseen delays and detours, but the ultimate result is foreordained. If a certain historical figure had not emerged to take command at a given moment, the movement would nevertheless have continued and another man would unquestionably have appeared instead. If a leader fails to assess correctly the inevitable direction and the implications of a given situation, he will fail. Some determinists would say that the so-called leader is merely the voice of his group and can achieve anything only as he acts according to their will. They assume that any man in authority is the prisoner of his situation and will be successful according to his skill in maneuvering according to the maximum social pressure. At most, the determinists would admit that a truly great man can influence events only if the times are ripe for him.

Each side has something to offer. The Great Man theory at least points up the fact that the role of an individual in certain crises can be decisive, and it does emphasize the character and personality of the history-making person. It leaves room for free will and makes of history a genuine struggle whose issue remains in doubt. The other side emphasizes the dependence of a person upon outside factors; he must have the tools to work with, in the form of a crisis, social forces, social machinery, and certain ideas.

Influence of Historical Figures upon Events

One can immediately call to mind certain persons who definitely seem to have changed the course of history in their own countries. All the instances that follow are debatable, and the reader is very likely to have his own ideas of the truth in each case. This, in itself, illustrates the nature of the problem.

Napoleon Bonaparte was a willful man carving out a career and fame in a fashion that no other general of his time could or would have done. On the other hand, he did have the strange new France back of him, a France that had already aggressively crossed its frontiers in its revolutionary fervor and had broken with its old traditions. There was Napoleon's statesman, Talleyrand, a schemer of the first order. Surely his intriguing activity made a difference, considering his primary responsibility for the restoration of the Bourbons and his work at the Congress of Vienna in alleviating the conditions imposed upon France. Still—the man changed his ideas and loyalties repeatedly with an unerring instinct for what was coming next. Perhaps this man who was, in turn, priest, revolutionist, Bonapartist, Legitimist, and Orleanist was merely more acute in his perceptions of the trend and what was coming next, and by his actions made himself appear to be a leader.

The instance of Louis Napoleon might be raised. It could be asserted that he is an example of a man who came into power due to his own perseverance against handicaps and who managed to change history in spite of them. On the other side of the picture is the argument that he represented certain nationalist forces that were asserting themselves in one form or another regardless of who was in power. In this same period, the abrupt end of the reign of Louis Philippe seems an instance of the personal element affecting history: if he had not lost his nerve at the critical moment, he might have died as king of the French.

King Henry VIII of England assuredly changed the religious history of his country and for what seems a trivial reason. He established a Church of England free of foreign control and seems to have made England Protestant at a time when, in comparison with Germany, little occasion existed for it. A wider look at the question changes the perspective considerably, for Henry VIII, after all, made little change in essentials. The Church of England remains Catholic to this day in some respects. The papacy had long been unpopular in England before Henry

VIII formally abolished its control in that country. The real Protestant Reformation in England scarcely makes its appearance until later, in the form of the Puritans, and, like the Huguenots of France, they failed to take permanent control of the country.

Perhaps the man who made the most drastic changes in his own country was Peter the Great of Russia. Here we certainly have an instance of the force of a single personality. Even for him, however, we could point out many instances where his policies, far from being a break with the past, represented a continuation of the past, such as the continued centralization of government, the strengthening of autocracy, the completion of the drift toward serfdom of the peasantry, and the expansion to the sea. Some of his reforms remained little more than paper decrees. After his death, furthermore, a conservative reaction nullified still other changes. What was left was principally a tendency toward Westernization among the upper classes, and it might be argued that this would have come anyhow.

Among the more obvious examples of the capacity of the individual will to affect changes are the Hohenzollerns of Brandenburg-Prussia. The two Frederick Williams and Frederick the Great followed a consistent policy of militarization of their country to a point where it was able to exert a power far above its normal physical capacities. The determinists would say that this policy was inherent in the situation; intelligent rulers of Prussia, dedicated to defense of the land without natural frontiers, had to follow such a policy or perish. A similar case is that of the Vasa dynasty of Sweden, where a succession of able monarchs elevated Sweden to an influence beyond its genuine powers. Eventually a ruler appeared who stretched this power too far—Charles XII—and Sweden collapsed. The rulers of Sweden were able to transcend natural resources quite far, but finally the realities of the situation caught up with them.

Even more flagrant cases where a man tried to reverse the tide of history can readily be discovered. Charles X of France was a man who even before the French Revolution hated the intellectual harbinger of the new era and refused to accept the new outlook. He obstinately defied the new forces, obviously trying to deflect the course of history with all his power. When he became king, he held the throne for only six years, then was catapulted from power in a vivid and dramatic example of how active social forces can overwhelm even the determined individual.

Two other men who fought the good fight for the wrong cause were Charles I and George III of England. Had either of these men won, they would have been regarded as heroes. History is the story of the successful, or better, the successful write the history. One might also consider the case of Joseph II of Austria, who, attempting reforms in the direction in which events were moving, made a mistake in timing, and pushed his reforms too rapidly and too far. The net result was that his reforms were canceled after his death because he had aroused the passionate opposition of too many social forces of the old order that were still strong enough to fight back effectively.

Instances might be mentioned where the influence has been exerted by sheer incapacity. What would have happened if Louis XVI had possessed a strong personality and great political wisdom? He could, conceivably, have permitted Turgot to carry out his reforms, thus warding off greater changes, or, later, he might have controlled the Estates-General by proper leadership, and thus minimized the movement. He could by no possible means have kept the Old Regime intact—the trend was too strong in the other direction—but he could have kept the changes in the pathway of evolution. France would have suffered less, although the history of the period would have been far less spectacular. No person could have withstood the social pressures of the time; he might have channelized them differently.

Speaking of the French Revolution reminds one of the roles of Mirabeau, Lafayette, and Robespierre. Mirabeau influenced the radical course of the revolution because he was not there. He died in 1791, and it has been suggested that he alone could have directed the revolution into more quiet waters after the initial period of reforms. There was a place for a strong man in 1791–1792, and he did not make his appearance; it was the right time and place, but the right man was not there. Lafayette, active in the same period as Mirabeau, commanded the National Guard and had enormous prestige at one time. At least one of his biographers has suggested that he never did know what was going on, in the sense that he had no conception of the deeper forces causing the revolution and driving it into a more radical manifestation. The long Reign of Terror coincided with the ascendancy of Robespierre. It ended with his death. Are we, then, to attribute the Terror to Robespierre? Or were Robespierre, Danton, Saint-Just, and the others attempting to control forces and movements that, once unchained, were too immense for any one man?

Many historical figures, one is tempted to say most of them, did not know in which direction they were actually headed. Posterity has known it far better with the advantage of hindsight and attributes a greater rational decision than the original men themselves possessed. Some small part of their work has been significant for the future development and has received attention, while the remainder of their labors, including what they themselves often thought most important, has been forgotten.

History is often made by the right man at the right time. William Pitt the Elder came to power in England when the English were losing the Seven Years' War. By his strategy of control of the seas, he transformed the conflict into one of Britain's greatest victories, whereas another man in his place might well have followed a different course, or no course at all, and so lost the war. Pitt was astute enough to see where the English strength lay and used this knowledge. Richelieu built up the power of the central government of France at a time when circumstances called for it. The Hohenzollerns militarized Prussia when the need was obvious.

Winston Churchill in 1940 was assuredly the right man at the right time. Too brilliant to be entrusted with power in normal times, he was the man of the hour in 1940, and by his rugged heroism prevented the fascist "wave of the future" from washing over England. This same Churchill, however, in 1915 sponsored the ill-fated Gallipoli campaign. If successful, it would presumably have saved Russia from defeat in the First World War and incidentally prevented a Communist revolution in that country, yet Churchill at that time was not able to muster enough support among the British and French to push the campaign to a successful conclusion. He was the right man and the time seemed ripe, but still the scheme did not come off properly.

One of the most peculiar cases of the right man at the right time was Peter III of Russia. An ardent admirer of Prussian militarism and of Frederick the Great, he became tsar just in time to take Russia out of the coalition against Frederick at a moment when the latter was facing catastrophe. Peter III, soon thereafter killed, was on the throne just long enough to save Prussian militarism. A nincompoop himself, a man who certainly had no conception of the importance of his act, he nevertheless indirectly played an important part in the molding of modern Europe.

Someone once wrote a short story in which a traveler in France in 1776 meets a French army officer who fancied himself a military genius and devoted his time to planning battles. As the narrative unfolds, the officer, sick and on the point of death, begins to seem familiar.

Finally it dawns upon the reader that this is Napoleon Bonaparte—but a Napoleon born too early! In the story, Napoleon died in obscurity, a genius without opportunity.

A large element of "if" prevails in history. The play *If Booth Had Missed* is based upon this. Abraham Lincoln became a martyr because he was killed at the right time. It is dubious if Lincoln would have become an immortal had he lived to cope with the problems and hatreds of the Reconstruction era.

The book *If: Or History Rewritten* contains a series of essays by different men on what might have happened *if* a certain factor had been different. One essay deals with the possibilities of what might have happened if Louis XVI had made good his escape from France instead of being captured near the border. Another writer imagines the consequences if Napoleon had possessed steam vessels with which to invade England. Churchill, incidentally, wrote one of these tales, based upon the supposition that Lee had won the Battle of Gettysburg. The reader may be highly dubious that the results would have been anywhere as radically different as these writers suggest, but there is little doubt that the details would have varied considerably from what did happen. Such reading is at least to be recommended for stirring the imagination, for seeing the possible factor of the accidental and the human factor amid the great movements of history. It is a good antidote to determinism.

A historical episode might perhaps be compared with a game of poker. No man can win consistently without fairly good cards. A historical figure in any situation is also dealt "cards" in the form of social groups that back or oppose him, problems he must cope with, the condition of the institution he must depend upon, the lieutenants he must work with, and other factors. In historical instances, many men have been unable to read their cards right, for these are far more complex than aces, jacks, and deuces. A very great perception is required in social situations for a leader to see what type of hand he is holding. Many men have won by the good fortune of having a good hand, without possessing enough skill and luck to appraise it properly. To push the analogy further, skill and luck are necessary in knowing whether to throw in the hand or bid. The historical figure must have the cards, he must know his opponents and have some ideas of their cards, and he needs to have skill if he is to be consistently successful.

Sidney Hook, in his volume *The Hero in History*, distinguishes between what he calls the "eventful man" and the "event-making man."

The eventful man is one who happens to be at the right place at the right time and, due to his position, makes important decisions or appears to make them. He comes into the limelight because he is part of larger events which are important. He may be borne to power by forces beyond his control, his conduct may be determined by pressures about him, yet it was he who was obliged to make the decision. The event-making man, on the contrary, is actually able to control the events to a degree and drives society in the direction which he wishes it to go. He is a genius, one who by his outstanding characteristics of intelligence, will, and ability to influence other people, has an actual capacity to accomplish his purposes. He is much more than a pawn in the game.

We may sum up this section with a few general characteristics on the ability of the individual to influence historical events: (1) some social forces are too powerful for any man; (2) the details of a single historical episode are determined largely by the work of the actors concerned; (3) the actual long-term trends are far less likely to be determined by the individual hero; (4) cases of obvious great influence are usually actually cases of the "right man at the right time"; (5) an occasional genius, by extremely dexterous and willful actions, may achieve a historical mutation; (6) every instance must be judged in its own particular context, for no universal formula will cover all cases.

Leadership

The ambition, intelligence, and exertion of the countless individuals making up society is, of course, the basic source of the energies in social forces. A powerful component of this is the specific struggle of the individual for power over his fellow men, for a position of authority over others. Desire for personal aggrandizement is probably the most explosive of all social forces, Marxist emphasis on economic factors notwithstanding. Individual ambitions furnish the brains, the personal leadership so necessary for success, and frequently spearhead movements otherwise economic or religious in origins.

The constant osmosis of the competent up the social scale is generally healthy for society. It prevents the social structure from becoming static, and it brings high intelligence and vitality to leading positions. That leadership can become a peril to society, however, is testified to by the numerous devices adopted in various countries to prevent one person from acquiring too much power. This in itself, incidentally, is testimony from experience that the individual certainly can influence the development of history. Such measures have often failed, an indication that greater forces than that of individual ambitions were at work.

As has been mentioned before, a man in a position of authority will almost inevitably seek to enhance his own power. He seems to feel that he lacks enough power to accomplish his purposes. He may be completely honest in his feeling and believe that he has no personal desire for it. The problems that face the conscientious official and the constant pressures that assail him from every direction seem such that his goals cannot be attained without additional power. The temptation, where the republican tradition is not strongly engrained in a people, is to step outside the slow, cumbersome processes of popular government altogether the more readily to achieve his goals.

All democratic governments must be on their guard against such dangers. The French, twice burned by their experiences with the Napoleons, have hobbled their leaders to such a degree that the French goverment is notoriously inefficient. The French President occupies little more than a nominal post, and strong men have little chance to be elected to the office, while the Premier, who is responsible to the parliament, very seldom holds office for even a single year. European countries have followed the French example. The Swiss limit their President to a position little more than that of a chairman of an executive committee and curtail his term to a single year and also specify that he cannot be immediately reelected. The Latin-American republics often have constitutional provisions that the President, who there wields a great deal of power, cannot be immediately reelected. (It may be added that this provision is frequently overridden by ambitious men.) The ancient Romans, during the republic, entrusted authority to the office of consul, but established two of them so that each would check the other. The classical Greeks and the Italians of the Renaissance city-states went to great lengths and to peculiar constitutional devices in order to prevent too great concentration of power in the hands of one person. In the United States the President was traditionally limited to two terms; but Franklin D. Roosevelt broke this rule and was elected four times. After his death an amendment was written into the Constitution limiting the presidency to two terms.

It is, of course, impossible for a man to become a leader simply by dreaming about it or even by dedicating himself to a world-saving task. Society, as has been noted earlier, is composed of many social groups or associations, various interest groups, weak and strong institutional machinery, other ambitious or jealous persons, and social forces that keep a constant pressure on all forms of leadership. A leader must have someone to lead. Either by deliberate intent or by adoption by a group, he must come into a position to influence some association or institution in order to have enough power to make his will felt on a broader plane. An association or institution permits the voice of the single individual to be magnified to the point of being heard by a wide audience. *The association or institution is the lever, a very powerful lever, whereby the individual may transform his own personal will into social action.*

Roughly speaking, a man attains such a position by one of four processes: (1) by inheritance; (2) by institutional selection; (3) by organizing his own association; (4) through influence of ideas.

A rather large proportion of the men mentioned in modern history have attained their status by the easiest method, by inheritance. They did not first have to surmount the problem of getting into power; they found themselves in such a position whether they wanted to or not. It was very commonly believed that persons of upper-class background were born with a special capacity for leadership not possessed by commoners. The crowned heads were not the only ones to inherit positions, it should be noticed, since the aristocracy, which produced most of the other important political figures, were themselves born into positions of some leadership. They were trained for leadership and grew up in an atmosphere where such qualities were constantly present; their social environment itself tended to create the habit of command. To some extent, the same atmosphere is likely to prevail in upper-middle-class families in democratic countries today.

In the second type of leadership, by institutional selection, the leader also steps into a position of power which has already been formalized by his predecessors. Earlier leaders had developed the position, created the controls which went with it, the area over which these controls were held, and the methods used to maintain the controls. The difference from the first type of leadership lies in the method of coming into power. Those leaders have most usually come up through the institution, holding lesser offices in successively more responsible positions until their obvious qualifications make them eligible for the top positions. Because such a person has been trained in the service and proved himself well adjusted to the values and practices of the institution by successive promotions, he normally makes a true representative of the institution in society as a whole. This sort of person is usually a good organizer, the "boss" type of person, rather than one of daring adventure.

The latter sort of individual is less likely to prove acceptable to the controlling elements of an institution or association, for his obvious ambition evokes the jealousy of his peers, and his policies are likely to be daring to the point where he may seem to jeopardize the well-being of the whole group. Because he cannot endure the hampering restrictions of traditional practices, such a person is very likely to ruin his own chances long before he reaches the top. If he does achieve power, he is most likely to do so in a time of crisis. In more normal periods, he is apt to react, in his frustration, in rebellion. His unsatisfied ambition reveals itself in scoffing at established practices and values, in conscious refusal to go along with policies of the association, and eventual secession from the group if he is able to do so. This sort of person may become a leader by capitalizing on some new movement, on some popular element, and organizing a new association where he can make the rules himself.

(The fourth type of leadership, that of ideas, belongs to a separate discussion on the role of ideas in history and will be discussed in Chapter 12.)

The qualities of leadership differ with different groups and different situations. One can list certain probable traits of good leaders, such as energy and thoroughness, complete devotion to work and accomplishment, persistence, courage, a capacity and willingness to assume responsibility, self-confidence, will power, an ability to get along with people. In community affairs, as surveys have shown, the persons who become leaders are frequently characterized by constant activity, by an ability to understand and appreciate the position of another person, a self-disciplined personality, and willingness to fight for what they believe. Superior intelligence may be important, but if that intelligence is greatly superior to the group, such a person is apt to be suspect and hence not permitted to lead.

One can scarcely talk of traits of leadership without knowing what type of group is in question. On the community level, very different men will emerge to leadership in a business firm, a university, a sports organization, and the local political machine. All types of personalities are to be found, and, fortunately, differing kinds of associations or social groups give them all an opportunity if the person has some intelligence, some social graces, and a willingness to work hard in some particular calling.

Looking at it in another way, there are bosses, experts, saints, and prophets. The boss emerges as a leader because he has a talent for making people do things for him and for organizing activities. The expert rises because he has superior knowledge that gains him prestige and standing in the community and skills that are valuable to it. The saint and the prophet each have their appeal, including the conscience of man and the wish to emulate those who are admired.

The boss, the man who usually makes political history, may achieve his position through one set of qualities and keep it through another set. He may ride into power through popularity with his fellows and then keep it by superior organizing ability and judicious granting of favors and arousal of fear. Historically, the person has frequently taken power because he has become the spokesman for certain ideas, has become identified with them, and the masses have favored them. Instances will occur where a man rises to rulership with the support of certain groups and, once in command, finds it necessary to shift the bases for his own power by transferring his own leadership to another group. Many historical figures have failed, once they were in authority, because their capacities for rising to power were greater than their ability in governing. On the other hand, the ambitious person who pushes to the top and there employs his energies in the aggrandizement of the institution thereby gives renewed vitality to that institution.

The leader-group relationship is reciprocal, and each acts upon the other. The man who emerges to leadership is likely to fit the group to begin with; he is likely to have been molded during his earlier membership into a certain type of person by the social environment of this group. As the top man, he may be little more than a symbol of the group, the person who vocalizes what the rank and file or at least the subleaders are thinking. Far from actually guiding, the leader is often the servant of his followers, bound in his word and conduct by what the followers want, regardless of what he himself may feel. If he launches out on an independent course, he will soon cease of acceptance as nominal pilot of the group. In other instances, the key figure may be the servant of his machine and completely further its interests, yet at the same time use that machine for his own interests and ambitions in a larger sphere. Any major political figure is almost certain to operate in this fashion. A really astute master of politics, business, or any other pursuit knows how to manipulate his machine in such a way as to keep control. He maintains a balance of power among his lieutenants, keeps their hopes of reward or fear of punishment always alive, plays one against another, and always wins enough success for the machine to keep himself in power.

Individualism

Undoubtedly the idea of individualism itself should be mentioned in connection with the topic of this chapter. Americans recognize the freedom of every person to make history in his local community or, if he is sufficiently competent, on the wider state and national level. This attitude has emerged from the long and often painful odyssey in search of liberty by modern man.

Whereas it was once thought that people of a certain class were born with qualities of leadership, Americans firmly believe that anyone can become a leader. Sociologists have ceased to accept the concept of the "mindless masses" who are simply tools for an elite. Nearly every person of sound mind has strong opinions in certain matters where he is directly involved, and he is entitled to cast his due weight there. A surprisingly large number of people become leaders in some field in their own locale. Any public poll reveals a rich diversity of opinion, albeit frequently of considerable crudeness in thought and expression.

Because American students have, fortunately, had no opportunity to experience its opposite, the concept of individualism is apt to remain vague for them. We can gain some idea of its nature by a brief comparison with collectivist societies. One might, as an example, contrast the American family with a typical peasant family of almost any country before the triumph of individualism.

The individual was firmly bound to the family, a name for a group often including uncles and aunts, in-laws, and cousins, all living under one roof and all participating in the village economy as a unit. The primary concern was for the welfare of the whole household, of which the single person was a member in virtually the same literal way as an arm or a leg is a member of the body. Even if an individual gained permission to leave the village and go to the city, he was still expected to send his earnings home. The wife or husband was selected by the family or its head. Except for an audacious few, individuals were irrevocably attached to their own social group, a person followed his father's occupation as a matter of course, and by his birth he was labeled for life. There could be no privacy in these surroundings, little opportunity for personal talents, or incentive for development of personality. This type of family-individual relationship is typical, is the norm, in the history of most human societies.

In these circumstances, personal property scarcely existed. Even the temporary use of land was in the hands of the whole family. In most cases the land and forests and grazing lands belonged to the village (or tribe) as a whole, and each family had a right to a share in its use. The method of achieving leadership by building up personal property or wealth of one's own simply did not exist.

Or consider the mental world in which the person lived: some essential ideas drilled into the individual, a set of customs and traditions perhaps wise in themselves, yet leaving very little room for individual conceptions. The intellectual atmosphere was as firmly fixed as the physical environment about the village, and any novel ideas might prove positively dangerous to anyone creative or imaginative enough to entertain them.

The individual belonged to four groups: his kin, his caste or class, his neighborhood (the village or clan), and a church accepted by the whole community. His individuality was obscured by his rigid classification as a member of particular groups with certain clearly understood duties and allegiances. The contrast between this situation and our own offers some indication of the growth of freedom in modern times.

Modern individualism is, above all, the consequence of the emphasis of Christianity on the worth of the individual. This was reemphasized in the Reformation as the priesthood of all believers. The emergence of modern capitalism was another factor. The bourgeois, emerging as self-made men—living examples of the assertion of individuality in economic matters—felt themselves to be masters of their own fate and tended to show a disregard for established traditions and customs and authority. The rise of modern science, by encouraging faith in rational thought rather than in tradition, strengthened individual self-confidence.

A word more needs to be said about the relationship of the middle class to individual liberty, for there is a remarkable parallel between the existence of a bourgeois and the prevalence of human liberty as we know it. The bourgeois itself invariably regards private property as the essential guarantee of freedom, and the middle class sponsored constitutions or charters, such as the French Declaration of the Rights of Man and of the Citizen, which carefully safeguard its existence. Whereas the nobility derived its security from its privileges, for the members of the Third Estate security has come from their land and their money; lose these and their whole social position is lost. Because the entire basis of liberty and dignity and position rested upon their possessions, the bourgeois would be as eager to safeguard these as the older classes have been to preserve the privileges upon which rested their authority and prestige. Without property, the bourgeois felt, the whole edifice of liberty must necessarily collapse. This feeling was of tremendous importance, for upon it was erected the society of nineteenth-century Europe and America.

On the face of it, human liberty has made less progress in the twentieth century than in the preceding one hundred years. We need not, however, be unduly pessimistic about seeming retrogression. Individual freedom in the Western countries had been developed over a long period of time until the habit of respect for the rights of the individual became engrained. Beyond a total of some twenty countries, at most, this process had never been completed or, in many cases, even started. The *idea* of liberty became popular in the nineteenth century, but the *habit* of liberty had not been established. In periods of crisis, reversion to more direct and primitive political action is likely to occur. As far as human liberty is concerned, most of the peoples of the world are in the stage of development that the West was in a century or two ago. In the meantime, conditions in police states provide us with good perspective on how far we have come.

We live in a society wherein a tradition of individual freedom has evolved. In the free modern society, the individual is presumed to be at liberty to express himself in talents and opinions unless his actions prove damaging to others. He has gained a right to autonomy, the privilege to choose, a right to be more than just a member of a certain family, caste, or association. However much social forces may continue to influence his conduct, we believe almost instinctively that he need no longer be merely a pawn of historical forces.

11

Inventors and Inventions

The man-made features of our environment have been more radically transformed in the past two centuries than they had been in the two preceding millenniums. We see these features growing and proliferating with every passing year to such a degree that we accept this phenomenon of progress as normal. The memory of the older generation goes back to a world without the airplane, the automobile, the radio, and the cinema, to mention only a few. The oldest living persons were born before the invention of the telephone, the electric-light bulb, the steam turbine, the hand camera, and the gasoline engine. Science moves ahead so rapidly that school textbooks in the sciences become obsolete very quickly.

The twentieth century, with its wars, political upheavals, and depressions, still lays claim to progress and advancement by virtue of astonishing strides in science, medicine, and technology. Part of the problems which confront us are the problems of growth, of adjustment to these new inventions, and of modifying our lives to suit changing conditions.

Various facets of the historical processes—continuity and change, cause and effect, the synthesis of factors, the role of the individual—are clearly perceptible in the panorama of technological evolution. Experience has shown, however, that students will memorize the names of inventors and their inventions, but will frequently miss the moving dynamic, the momentum which derives from the interrelationships between inventions or discoveries. Since the factual material in this chapter is largely limited to persons and inventions already familiar to anyone who has read a standard textbook, the focus of attention should be upon the relationships, the aspects of the historical processes to be seen in this field. To the extent that we study the position of the individual inventor in the midst of the entire pattern of development, we are continuing the topic of the preceding chapter, the role of the individual in history. In another sense, the picture of change and of growth that emerges in these pages makes this chapter a resumption of the earlier one dealing with continuity and change.

Continuity and Interdependence in Inventions

The period of accelerating change in industry becomes clearly perceptible by the second half of the eighteenth century in England. Several developments were under way, none of them attracting much attention, which were to lead to the Industrial Revolution. Among these were changes in the cotton industry.

Cloth had been made in the home by two successive processes, first the spinning of the cotton into thread and then the weaving of the thread into cloth. Sometimes both were carried on in the same household; otherwise the two were done at different places, an agent or entrepreneur being responsible for the distribution and collection of the materials as an enterprise from which he derived a profit. The spinning consisted in first combing the material to straighten out the threads of the fiber and then spinning the long fibers together in order to make a firm thread. This was accomplished with the old-fashioned spinning wheel. It was work done in the home after the hours in the field or on rainy or cold days as a means of earning a little additional money.

The two processes did not take an equal amount of time, for the single weaver could use up far more thread than the individual spinner could provide. In 1733 John Kay patented the fly shuttle, which made it possible for one man to operate the loom and do it more rapidly than before. The problem of securing thread then became more acute than ever. The spinners, with their product in such demand, found high prices for their work, while the weavers were, conversely, in worse straits than before. Obviously a great need existed for a better and faster way of spinning. The answer came between 1764 and 1767 when James Hargreaves invented the spinning jenny, which used a number of spindles or miniature spinning wheels.

A new problem, however, posed itself, and it was to prove typical of the Industrial Revolution as its pattern evolved. While the spinner who owned a jenny, or an improved model built by Richard Arkwright, could now do very well, what would happen to the spinner who could not afford a jenny? The price for his products dropped drastically as the volume of produce increased, yet the individual spinner could produce no more in a day than before. The machine was to ruin the individual handicraftsman.

The problem of power for larger spinning machines manifested itself, inasmuch as hand (or foot) power was insufficient. Arkwright solved the problem, after a fashion, by establishing a shop in which the machines were run with the aid of water power—a momentous step, for in it we see the beginning of the factory system. Production and the workers were transferred from the home to the factory.

Water was not a very satisfactory form of power in England, where streams were scarcely large enough or fast enough for a paddle wheel to function properly. Furthermore, insufficient rainfall would stall the machinery completely. Factory owners therefore soon turned to the steam engine and began to use it instead.

Why had not the steam engine been used before this, and why did a man like Arkwright experiment with water power first? Because the steam engine became adequate for such a purpose only as it was improved in response to the needs of the early factories. A background of development lay behind the application of steam power to factory machinery. Thomas Savery had first patented a steam engine in 1698 in answer to one of the problems of the day, how to pump out the water which seeped into mine shafts. When Savery's engine did not prove strong enough, Thomas Newcomen built an improved version. In the period of Arkwright, James Watt produced still better ones, of a type strong enough to be used for the purposes required. Thus two hitherto separate paths of technological evolution merged in the new factories.

If we look more closely, we will, in fact, find more than two, for Watt's invention was dependent upon the quality of iron. It had previously been customary to make machines out of wood, with the exception of axles, bearings, and the cutting or grinding parts. The production of pig iron before the Industrial Revolution was an expensive process requiring much labor plus large quantities of charcoal, and it was therefore made only on a small scale. Since wood, from which charcoal is made, was becoming increasingly scarce in England, the ironmasters were forced to seek a new fuel, the obvious substitute (to us) being coal. The ironmasters were reluctant to change their habits and formula, but they eventually did so. Soon the enlarged demand made coal mining an important occupation.

The adoption of coal not only solved the problem of fuel for the making of iron but was also cheaper since it entailed less labor. The so-called "cast iron" produced with coal was brittle, however, and so progress had created another problem in place of the old one. During the eighteenth century the quality of iron was gradually improved, and as this happened the use of iron spread: pipes, mortars, and boilers were among the objects manufactured. The use of blast furnaces by John Roebuck in about 1760 marked another step forward.

In 1783 "puddled iron" was discovered, this being a less brittle and stronger type of iron. Finally, iron could be made cheaply and in sufficient quantity and quality for steam engines and other machinery. Without this century-long train of development, the Industrial Revolution in other fields could not have advanced into the factory system.

Because men had to learn how to work iron with sufficient skill to make the engines, the element of human skill must also be mentioned. In Newcomen's time, an engine like that of Watt was impossible, not only because of the quality of iron, but also because the precision had not been attained. When Watt was developing his idea, the mechanics were just approaching the ability to produce such a machine.

From the foregoing, it can be seen how the Industrial Revolution had a gradual and unobtrusive beginning in several different fields. One thing led to another, one improvement stimulated the search for another. The different fields were interdependent upon each other. One train of development depended upon progress in another field, while at the same time acting as an inducement for the other fields to hasten the pace of development.

The series of inventions and discoveries just described in turn set in motion or accelerated a considerable number of other developments of fundamental importance. A rapid increase in textile manufacturing raised the demand for raw materials such as flax, hemp, wool, and cotton. The supply of cotton was greatly limited by the necessity of extracting the seed from the cotton by hand. In the 1790's Eli Whitney, a New Englander migrant to Georgia, invented the cotton gin, which separated the seeds from the cotton by a machine process. In some cases a discovery or invention lies dormant for years before its value is appreciated; in other cases the invention coincides with and is produced by a pressing need at the moment. Whitney's cotton gin was most decidedly in the latter class, for men broke into his shop and stole the machine, replicas were immediately made, and it spread quickly throughout the South. (The use of the cotton gin brought a vast expansion of cotton growing. Additional labor was needed, and slavery in the South gained a new lease on life. Thus the cotton gin influenced American history, and, it is scarcely too much to say, changed its course in the following decades.)

The new system, with its increased production, required a better means of transportation, in that raw materials and fuel had to be brought to the factory and the finished product carried to the market. The complexity of the new system, as well as the greater quantities involved, necessitated a radical revolution in the field of transportation. In America the same need was felt for an additional reason. The westward migration was well under way, and the problem of distance was becoming increasingly acute as the farm products required transportation to the centers of population and as the Western migrants needed Eastern goods. Rivers offered one solution, but only for downstream passage. The steam engine provided a better answer. A series of attempts to put this prime mover to use for river transportation produced the steamboat. The original failures did not deter further experimentation, the need being obvious and compelling. Once the river steamboat became practical, men began to expand its range by digging canals, an action in itself proof that still another invention was needed for land transportation. Frenchmen also succeeded in building steamboats in the years before their political revolution, the French seemingly had within their grasp the possibility of wresting sea power in the Channel away from the British during the Napoleonic Wars by use of the steam engine, but the opportunity—doubtless fantastic to practical men—was not recognized.

The British, living in a country of few large navigable streams, provided the locomotive. Horse-drawn vehicles, traveling on wooden rails, already existed, upon which coal or iron could be carried—even passengers had been transported from one place to another. Richard Trevithick was one of the first to apply the steam engine to a vehicle, and George Stephenson developed it into an actual locomotive, upon which further improvements were soon made. In the case of the steamship, further progress was facilitated by the introduction of the screw propeller in 1836. The chain of evolution continued, new ramifications appeared, and still other necessary improvements became pressing in this self-perpetuating process.

Although the Age of Discoveries had, much earlier, created a need for swifter and safer ocean travel, and increased trade within the European states called for some such invention as the locomotive, the inventions did not appear until the early years of the nineteenth century. Why had they not come earlier, inasmuch as the need was there? Surely there were men intelligent enough and imaginative enough to conceive of them? A brilliant mind was not enough, of course, because the inventor also had to have the possibilities, the proper materials with which to work. He required good iron, the widespread use of coal, a fairly powerful steam engine, and men with mechanical skills to handle the iron. The locomotive and the steamboat were not feasible earlier, and once the above factors existed, men quickly saw the possibilities and produced both of them.

Another factor should be added, the intellectual curiosity which started the modern age of science in the persons of men like Copernicus, Galileo, and Newton. Science had largely remained on the theoretical plane until near the end of the eighteenth century, but in the period of the beginning of the Industrial Revolution, scientific thought was going increasingly into solving the problems of production. The emerging manufacturing class was discovering the benefits of science and to some degree further stimulating its progress.

Other aspects of modern production arose in the period following the appearance of the factory. One of the major developments of the time, seemingly insignificant, yet of such paramount importance that industry could not have progressed far without it, was standardized screws and bolts. Henry Maudslay, one of the unsung heroes of science and technology, was able to create machinery proper for this purpose. Prior to this time, screws were cut individually by hand, with the result that no two were precisely identical. The improvement was made possible by the increasingly accurate machinery that was being produced. Once machines had been created whose gauges could be depended upon to ensure identical parts, something an artisan himself would find exceedingly difficult, the trick was accomplished. Maudslay's work initiated that indispensable part of the modern industrial system, the replaceable part. The assembly line became feasible.

Under the new system, each group in a factory could continue uninterruptedly turning out one particular part, which meant much faster work and greater efficiency per man, the use of less skilled workers, and the production of goods at less expense. That particularly American development, mass production, had begun. Eli Whitney again enters the picture here, for it was in his gun factory that an assembly line of sorts first made its appearance. Some decades later, Samuel Colt began to produce the Colt revolver by a method copied and improved upon from Whitney.

The wide, open acres of the Middle West required new methods of farming—of sowing and reaping. The machine age came to the farm with the invention of reapers by Cyrus McCormick and Obed Hussey. These were built by the methods of mass production and had full interchangeability of parts. The sewing machine, in the same period just before the Civil War, was made in the same way.

Factors Involved in Inventions

In motion pictures, the inventor or scientist is usually portrayed as a single-minded, idealistic person, determinedly pursuing a goal despite many handicaps. Eventually, after many discouragements, he succeeds in making his discovery or his invention when one of several things happens: he dreams about the correct answer, he hits upon the solution by an accident, some apparently irrelevant incident (probably involving the girl he loves) provides a clue, or some great illumination strikes in the mind of the genius. The usual portrait is that of a single person working against the scoffing of his neighbors and without material and mental assistance from others.

In the popular mind, science has never quite been disassociated from one of its parents, magic. The laboratory equipment has replaced the paraphernalia of the magician. Scientific-sounding names and complicated formulas have replaced the abracadabra of the magician.

True enough, the inventor and scientist have definitely earned the public plaudits for their original work. A long period of concentrated toil and devotion to a goal usually lies behind their accomplishments. Nevertheless, even though the portrayal of the lonely inventor may sometimes be true in a physical sense, no one knows better than the inventor himself that the picture is grossly incomplete. It is the Great Man theory applied to the history of technology, and it has the same flaws, the same oversimplifications, as in political history. Inventions that become known can no more come out of a vacuum than can political events. A man of potential genius at the wrong time will accomplish little.

Some of the most fundamental inventions, such as the steam engine, have occurred several times before they were adapted to use. Hero of Alexandria, in the classical period, understood the force of steam and how to use it. Although the late Greeks and the Romans stood on the edge of the Industrial Revolution in this one respect at least, its coming was nevertheless postponed for many, many centuries. With their slave labor, their types of industry and certain states of mind, no real demand for new types of power existed at that time. A steam engine was invented by Worcester in the seventeenth century, and Papin, a Frenchman, also invented one in the same century, though neither was put to use. The real evolution began when Savery's invention was installed in the mines and its weaknesses caused Newcomen to produce a better engine. Watt's original engine was intended for the mines; some years later it was adapted to the grinding of corn, and only about 1790 was it harnessed to textile machinery. Discoveries, often not useful when made, come into prominence when later developments open up hitherto unthought-of possibilities. One may ask the question "When is an invention really made?" Is it when the first working model is constructed? Or when it is really applied? Who invented the steam engine, Hero, Worcester, Papin, Savery, Newcomen, or Watt? There is certainly no single Great Man here.

We might recall how many later inventions were earlier sketched by Leonardo da Vinci. Yet we do not usually regard him as the inventor, although he understood the principles of many of them. His ideas were not taken advantage of at the time because the industrial and cultural level was not yet ready for them. That is, the fate of any invention is dependent upon such circumstances as whether a need happens to exist for it at the time, if agencies are available who benefit from adopting it, and whether other branches of science and technology have advanced to the point where the invention can be properly applied.

We saw this in the case of the steam engine. Further progress on the Newcomen engine awaited the production of better iron and, especially, the advance of mechanical skill to the point where workmen actually could make an engine requiring more exact measurements. Without these, any further advance on the steam engine was necessarily stalled. Hence, every invention is dependent upon technical advance in other fields, as well as upon popular demand.

The early work on electricity culminated with the invention of the dynamo in 1831, but the first power station was established only in 1882. The invention of the telephone and the electric-light bulb, shortly before the power station, spurred its construction. Only widescale practical application brought this development.

An invention has, generally speaking, one or more of five possible factors behind it. The first, of course, is the curiosity and intelligent experimentation of the men who succeed in solving the problem. The second is the exigencies of a particular line of development whereby each successive improvement promptly opens the way for another—the way in which automobiles, locomotives, and airplanes are constantly being improved; a situation poses a problem which the inventor then seeks to solve. The third factor is the appearance of a new invention in some other line of development which may later be transferred and which may even cause a radical change, as happened when the steam engine or the diesel engine was applied to transportation. The fourth is a definite need in an allied line which may stimulate inventions, such as the improvement of iron. The final factor, the one which will ultimately determine its use, is the general need in industry for such an improvement.

The demand may be of an active nature, widely felt, and the invention is thus seized upon and used immediately, as was the case with the cotton gin and also the use of steam power to pump water out of mines. The textile machinery of England seemed so desirable to the Americans that they advertised in England for the secret. Although English law forbade the export of such machinery or the emigrating of textile, iron, or steelworkers, one, Samuel Slater, an apprentice in Arkwright's factory, fled to America. Once there, he built the machine from memory, and it was immediately successful.

Sometimes a need was so great that a crude invention, by our standards, came into use before scientific development could provide a better device. The demand for rapid communications caused the French to install a network of semaphores by which messages could be transmitted from the borders to Paris in an astonishingly few minutes. So effective was this hand-operated system, so well did it fill the need, that the installation of electric telegraph lines was somewhat delayed in consequence.

Cases could be mentioned where a great demand existed, and a solution was found yet was not immediately adopted. Although Dud Dudley began to use coal in the smelting of iron early in the seventeenth century, other ironmasters were reluctant to follow him despite the shortage of charcoal. In this instance, the discovery was not delayed for lack of technical progress; it was due to the state of technical knowledge, the ironmasters believing that coal-smelted iron must necessarily be inferior, since it did not conform to the time-honored formula. A low cultural level is likely to inhibit technical progress. Printing presses were destroyed by mobs in some places when first introduced because they were believed to be of the devil. People have been prone to reject the new and better in favor of the traditional simply because it is traditional.

In many instances there was indeed a need for an invention, but only a few had the imagination or optimism to believe that age-old practices could be changed. The steamboat, the reaper, the sewing machine, the telegraph and telephone, the electric-light bulb, the automobile, the airplane all originated in the minds of a few curious or inventive minds. Once the innovations were shown to be practicable, people quickly awoke to the possibilities involved, and they speedily came into general use.

Where the cultural level is ready, an invention will come sooner or later; if one man does not discover it, another will. Henry Cort and Peter Onions independently of one another puddled iron in 1783. Dominique Arago and Humphry Davy, working separately, found that an electric current around a bar of iron converts the bar into a magnet. Michael Faraday and Joseph Henry both learned in 1831 that electricity could be generated by magnetism. Charles Darwin and Alfred Russell Wallace were both developing the idea of evolution. Several persons had noticed the effects of X rays on photographic plates before Roentgen became interested. These various discoveries were "in the air"; science had advanced to the point where someone was certain to find each of them.

The case of the X rays reveals another aspect. A new discovery may be right before a person's eyes if he will but use them; if he is too intent on following another track, he may miss it. Louis Pasteur found a proper inoculation for chicken cholera by accident, then had the curiosity to wonder about his chance discovery, and in the process of finding out he made a very important contribution to science. Alexander Fleming discovered penicillin by accident; he investigated the accident, and made an important discovery which earlier men had missed.

Many of the first inventors failed to obtain fame: Sedden, an early inventor of the automobile (there was no single inventor), is little known, and neither is Richard Trevithick, afore-mentioned predecessor of George Stephenson. Burlingame, in *Backgrounds of Power,* lists what he calls a "galaxy of genius" who worked at the end of the eighteenth century in the beginnings of the Industrial Revolution. Among these he mentions names unknown to all but a few people: Bramah, Brunel, Wilkinson, Maudslay, Roberts, and Nasmyth among others. Although not yet recognized as immortals, they, in a collective sense, probably did more to change the shape of our society than any political figure that we have studied.

Any single invention is the climax to the work of a number of men. Where a particularly complex operation is concerned, dozens of people may have provided important aid in finding the solution, and literally thousands in the background made earlier, but necessary, contributions. As Burlingame puts it, the intelligent inventor takes the reservoir of knowledge at its top level and uses the ultimate in predeveloped techniques available to him—every inventor stands on the shoulders of those who preceded him.

Inherited Knowledge as a Retarding Influence

The fact that an inventor or scientist is the inheritor of the accumulated knowledge of the past may also, in certain ways, retard advance. Ideas often display remarkable tenacity, continue to be accepted, even when more advanced ones have become feasible; these outmoded concepts may become a barrier to scientific progress inasmuch as the scientist frequently cannot escape, despite his best efforts, from evaluating his observations in terms of prevailing conceptions. We read the story of inventions from our point of view, and we see the successive improvements as *firsts*, as the crucial points where something new appeared. The other aspect of the pattern of continuity and change is that each novelty emerges out of a context of tools, techniques, and ideas that are *not* new. The original locomotive, while novel, was still made up of machinery and operated by techniques that antedated the locomotive; the original automobile was a horseless carriage. We are meeting the same phenomenon that we also saw in political evolution: each change, while significant, emerges directly out of older practices and is greatly conditioned by the continued survival of other older practices.

The story of the background for the Darwinian theory of evolution offers an example of how traditional knowledge may hamper new discoveries. Although many men had seen fossils and been puzzled by them, the then universal assumption that the opening chapters of Genesis were to be taken literally barred the way to any effective theories here; the fossils must necessarily be explained within the framework of the abrupt creation of the world rather than be used in the formulation of new generalizations based purely upon actual observation. One possible solution, for instance, was to attribute fossils to the effects of gigantic catastrophes since the divine creation some six thousand years ago. During the eighteenth century thinkers were gradually driven to the realization that the world was far more than six thousand years old and that infinite modifications within species and between species made any sudden divine creation of each type unlikely. Successive theories than began to appear, in which men tried to incorporate the new observations—without breaking away entirely from the general story as given in Genesis. The enunciation of the theory by Darwin was made possible by over a century of groping, of partial insights often obscured by the persistence of the older viewpoint.

Another example of the tenacity of older viewpoints in the midst of change is to be found in the work of Copernicus. This astronomer set out, not to make a scientific revolution, but merely to improve the existent Ptolemaic system by making certain observations square with the prevailing theory and by simplifying the extraordinarily complex notions of how the celestial machinery worked. In the course of his labors, he found that his purposes were best achieved if he assumed that the earth moved about the sun, rather than the earth being the center of the universe; aside from this, he continued to work within the elaborate Ptolemaic framework, and was prevented by his preconceptions from grasping many implications of his own hypothesis. An indication of how medieval his ideas actually were can be gained from his explanation for the rotation of the earth: he asserted that a sphere is the perfect shape, and it is in the nature of a sphere to rotate. Butterfield, in *The Origins of Modern Science, 1300–1800*, refers to the "conservatism" of Copernicus, and shows how his mental processes were characteristic of the late medieval period. One is tempted to compare his historical position to that of Luther, in that each was a conservative whose ideas were out of the medieval milieu, but whose work inadvertently opened the way to radical changes.

As a matter of fact, the problem of planetary motion, which Copernicus "solved" so naïvely (from the modern point of view), continued to hamper further progress in astronomy for a long time. In the realm of scientific thought, as with inventions, a promising development may be stunted because certain essential ingredients for additional progress are lacking. Butterfield points out that men in the fifteenth and sixteenth centuries were groping toward more modern kinds of mechanics and more modern forms of experimentation, only to run into a virtual impasse for lack of proper mathematical knowledge. The accomplishments of the age of Newton would have been impossible without the appearance of such advanced forms of mathematics as analytical geometry and infinitesimal calculus. Certain inventions—the telescope, microscope, barometer, and air pump—were also of paramount importance in preparing the way for the fundamental scientific formulations of the Newtonian period, without which, in turn, the early stages of the Industrial Revolution could not have occurred.

In view of the reference, in an earlier chapter, to the role of the printing press in making the Reformation possible, it should be of interest that Butterfield suggests the possibility that if the printing press had been invented earlier, the advance of science might have been more rapid in the later medieval period. For lack of proper communications, certain early ideas, which seem suggestive of those later accepted, were not properly transmitted to the following generations, and the sequence of evolution was retarded. By the seventeenth century the exchange of information and ideas among scientists was considerable, and the establishment of academies of science, as central organizations for this purpose, helped to accelerate the notable scientific advance of that period. Further discussion of the transmission of ideas must be deferred to the next chapter.

A few final observations remain to be made in concluding this subject. Another factor in the acceleration of development in modern science and technology, previously hinted at but not specifically stated, was the presence of intense competition. A wealthy manufacturing class, possessed of abundant capital and seeking new ways to add to it, began to support the inventors and scientists; a business company which could acquire a better device or technique thereby gained an edge over its rivals. In order to achieve such advantages, manufacturers eventually established facilities for inventors, a step which would further enhance the progress of technology. The rivalry might even extend to whole nations, since the more advanced country would be strengthened, as over against others, in both peace and war.

Speaking of political considerations, the point should be made that wars and revolutions may cause wide deviations from normal technological evolution. France was making rapid industrial progress toward the end of the eighteenth century and, in fact, seemed well on the way to her own industrial revolution. When the political events of 1789 and the following years occurred, the evolution in industry was interrupted, and not until after the overthrow of Napoleon was it resumed. Wars will also stimulate certain lines of advance, as witness the work in atomic energy in the Second World War; nothing but a national emergency would have caused the mobilization of scientists, equipment, and capital requisite for success in this enterprise.

In the event that our civilization should enter an age of decline as other cultures have done in the past, will these inventions and tools be lost? The historian can judge only by what has happened in the past, although the extreme complexity of present-day technology, as compared to earlier forms, may render any such verdict most untrustworthy. His estimate would have to be that any invention which provides additional power is not only likely to be accepted at the time but will most probably remain a permanent acquisition of humanity, in one form or another, regardless of historical vicissitudes in other fields. That is, a society is far more likely, in periods of decline, to lose its abstract knowledge or cultural insights than tools which give power to their possessor. Carl Becker stated it this way in *Progress and Power:* "Implements of power once used may become obsolete, the secret of their use may be lost for a time; but in general it is true that once possessed of a new implement of power men do not voluntarily abandon it."

Since the beginning of the Industrial Revolution, man has discovered a new world as surely as the men of a couple of centuries earlier had discovered a new geographical world. A new source for creation and exploitation of wealth has been found, although it has been the result, this time, of voyages of discovery into the nature of the physical world rather than in an extension of the geographical environment. The outburst of technological change did more than merely act as a social force in history; in this case it literally changed the plot and provided a new setting for the narrative.

12

The Role of Ideas

The zeal with which women hasten to follow the latest changes in styles causes patronizing amusement among men—who conveniently forget that the utter conventionality of their own clothing indicates an equally strong urge to conform to community opinion. The conformity in clothing is ruggedly individualistic, however, when compared to the degree of uniformity in basic ideas that exists in the average community. The minor differences, exaggerated in the course of warm discussions, serve to hide the essential sameness of the stock of ideas among most people.

In any human society a large measure of agreement prevails among its members, and, indeed, the stability of that society depends upon this condition. Our ways of thinking, our forms of explanation, our symbols and analogies, our axiomatic premises tend to be conventionalized into certain patterns familiar and acceptable to all. What the physical atmosphere is to our bodies, these ideas are to our minds. Principles and standards are to our mental health what oxygen is to our bodies; without them we lose the attributes of the human being. They give us the necessary philosophic explanations and provide us with a way of finding meaning in our environment and experiences. Taken together, ideas which are more or less common to all of us constitute what we call a culture pattern.

Ideas are obviously much more than mental reproductions of what we observe. Since no human being can even remotely attempt to assimilate all of reality, the insights are necessarily *selective* and emphasize certain features of our surroundings. They carry meanings, born out of our experiences, and they are integrated into our personalities. We are peculiarly possessive of our thoughts: each person tends to feel that he personally has created his ideas—no one else could possibly possess such an intimate insight into Truth—and he will consequently defend his opinions with a great deal of heat. No idea takes on genuine reality for us until we have undergone experiences that teach us the truth in a particular meaning. Every student has, at one time or another, encountered an idea in a book, learned it intellectually, and later, due to some specific incident, rediscovered it personally, when for the first time it conveyed a sense of reality and conviction.

The purpose of this chapter is to provide an elementary sketch of the role of ideas in social processes and to examine, in a general way, how these ideas reach the status of common usage in society. Where do these ideas, these intimate possessions of ours when accepted, originate, and how do they become universal? All through these chapters, we have been aware of the presence of ideas in the various events without focusing our attention upon their specific place in the drama. We have observed how men are motivated by various factors, and we have recorded their consequent actions, but we have taken little notice of the obvious intermediate step between the social forces and the actions of individuals, namely, the formulation of a mental picture in the minds of the actors of what the situation is and what should be done.

Instances may occur, as in mob scenes, where the action seems spurred by primitive passions, yet even here some form of thought lies at the root of conduct. Organized social movements cannot appear and institutions cannot function without ideas. *They are the threads which bind the minds of men together sufficiently for joint action to occur.* A leader cannot lead for long without positive communication between himself and the others. Ideas are the shorthand expressions for a more complex reality and enable men to picture to others the purposes which they wish to achieve.

This chapter is concerned with a certain set of ideas akin to the loyalties discussed earlier, ideas which have been involved in large-scale action. They are concepts that have been particularly successful in the last centuries in being accepted as their own convictions by very large numbers of people. Among these are the divine right of kings, democracy, socialism, progress, nationalism, liberalism, and toleration. Each one, beyond the simple definition of what it means, has become the center of gravity for a swarm of associated insights, and its mention immediately evokes, in the mind, a cluster of supporting concepts, modifications, and associations.

A Comparison with Inventions

As an introduction, recollection of the process whereby inventions were made and spread would be of value, inasmuch as some similarities can be observed. Inventions, whether spurred by a pressing need or by curiosity, take on importance as they fulfill certain needs in the existent circumstances. An idea will scarcely be widely accepted unless an active group finds that it expresses their outlook. Inventions come into being in answer to changing circumstances, and new concepts (really new applications of old concepts) become popular as changing conditions create a need for new explanations. A successful invention quickly creates a demand for an improved model; a successful principle will quickly stimulate improved versions to cover a larger area of facts or to conform to special circumstances. The history of inventions is that of a family tree of inventors, each inventor stemming from a previous one. Men of ideas tend to come in schools of thought, characterized by one or more leading insights, wherein the thinkers derive inspiration from one another. An invention or scientific discovery may occur in more than one place, that is, as parallel inventions. Similarly, certain thoughts tend to become popular as a number of persons entertain approximately the same notions in the same period because the same circumstances give rise to similar reactions. Acceptance of ideas, like the creation of inventions, is dependent upon the cultural level of a people.

There are, however, important differences between the two. Even though the exact time of appearance of an invention is often difficult to pinpoint, it is certainly *new,* since it did not exist at an earlier time. In the realm of thought, it has been asserted, very few, if any, completely new ideas have appeared since the Greeks. A certain stock of basic ideas exists, and society selects and drops them according to circumstances; ideas are not invented—they are adapted and clothed in new raiment.

The great men of ideas, hence, are persons who realize more acutely the full meaning and possibilities of certain insights and who remold and amplify them in order to make them relevant and living to their generation. While current circumstances do help to determine the popularity of certain concepts, the genius of ideas is far less dependent than is the inventor upon the immediate situation. The fundamental problems of human relations and of the relation of man to God do not, after all, vary fundamentally from one generation to another; the more the genius is able to express in an original fashion these relationships, the more enduring his fame is likely to be. If one inventor had not made his contribution, the comparatively narrow and specific problem would have determined that someone else would have produced a machine or statement of theory very much like it. The genius of ideas, on the contrary, produces a unique work, a product of his own particular personality, because the variations of the basic ideas are infinite and inexhaustible. Inventions and scientific theories are specific and controlled by physical circumstances; ideas are not like hard pellets, subject to transmission from one mind to another without being to some degree transformed in the process of transfer.

Fashions in Ideas

Quite possibly, every basic idea that ever existed is still possessed and cherished by someone somewhere on earth. There are, however, what might be called fashions in ideas, where certain concepts become popular and are widely held while others are neglected. Sometimes we refer to climates of opinion (the Germans talk of the *Zeitgeist* or the spirit of the age) which characterize each historical period. The Age of the Renaissance, the period of the Reformation, the Enlightenment, the nineteenth century, each is distinguished by a special flavor and tone, particular key words and phrases, certain convictions, that differentiate it from all other periods. Each was the product of certain distinctive conditions, changes, and prominent features of life that called for explanation and enunciation. Renaissance thought reflected, above all, the spirit of the urban community, while the Enlightenment, speaking very broadly, sprang from the popular recognition of recent successes in astronomy, mathematics, and the sciences.

The great thinkers could scarcely bring these periods into existence by the unaided force of intellect or persuasiveness. The attitudes are "in the air," there for anyone to discern and formulate more precisely. In periods of "cultural lag" (where ideas have failed to keep pace with physical progress), the maladjustment between ideology and human reality spurs the search for "new" insights. The thinkers are the sensitive antennae of society, the first to sense keenly the attitudes of an emerging age and able to express them in a period when a changing society finds the hitherto predominant sentiments, formerly satisfactory, becoming less convincing. The history of ideas, from this point of view, is that of a constant struggle to interpret human problems in the light of conditions that continue to change. A certain group of insights achieve general acceptance, remain triumphant for a time, and then begin to lose their hold, as a new school of thought appears.

By no means all the opinions of a thinker are accepted by posterity. The thumbnail sketches of a man's ideas that we read in a history of philosophy or literature course are far from a complete presentation of what he himself regarded as important. Later men picked what they wanted or were most impressed by because these conformed to their *own* attitude, while the rest were jettisoned and forgotten. Nor can any man be completely representative of an era; he is also the son of the past and can scarcely know precisely the direction of development. An author can never be certain how his ideas will be used by posterity: Rousseau would undoubtedly have been horrified at the Jacobins of 1793, Marx at the Russian Communists, and Herder, father of nationalism, at the fanatics of nationalism in the twentieth century.

The Diffusion of Nationalism

We are not so much concerned here with the genesis of the idea in the mind of the genius as we are with what happens to ideas once they become public. The genius can scarcely, in most cases, be said to *teach* others, to *place* insights in others' minds. What is more likely to be the case is that he formulates exact concepts and statements that already, in a rudimentary sense, exist in the minds of some others; if not, he is apt to be ignored, or he becomes a prophet of the future whose real significance is appreciated only by later generations. In most cases, the genius attracts a ring of disciples because he has expressed their sentiments in a more compelling fashion. One might say that the scientist-inventor formulates theories which must be proved by experimentation in physical phenomena, while the genius of thought formulates ideas that stand or fall as they ring true in the life experiences of others.

The circles of disciples may come into existence, as occurred in the origins of the great religions, by personal contact and word-of-mouth communication. These disciples then spread the word in the same fashion among others. The means of communication, however, were enormously expanded by the invention of the printing press, which permitted the spread of ideas through books and other publications, while modern inventions such as the motion picture, radio, and television have opened up new possibilities. The communication may be formal, as in the case of the scientific societies of the eighteenth century, where the academies in Paris, Berlin, London, Turin, and St. Petersburg communicated frequently with one another and shared discoveries made in any one center. It may be a more spontaneous process, such as the diffusion of the democratic ideas in Germany, Austria, and Italy which made possible the chain reaction of the 1848 revolution. Agencies like the *salons* of France or special clubs frequented by an intellectual group, and accessible to distinguished visitors from other countries, may help to determine contemporary opinion, or communication may occur through books and letters primarily. In any case, the process of diffusion will produce a number of geniuses, each elaborating upon the original ideas and exploring the possibilities and applications of them.

The development of nationalism in some specific country offers an excellent illustration of how the process works; the spread of nationalism among the Czechs in the nineteenth century will serve as an example. The Czechs had lost their rights of self-government in the Thirty Years' War and, as part of the Hapsburg domains, had been dominated by the German nobility since then. The native Czech language had ceased to be a cultural language and was now limited to peasant usage. While a certain local patriotism existed, chiefly among the nobles and in defense of local privileges, very little was remembered of the Hussite period and the age when the Czechs or Bohemians had stood off the armed might of Germany. Joseph II and Maria Theresa even attempted to Germanicize the people.

It was partly a reaction against this latter measure and partly the ideas of nationalism, originating in Germany, which reawakened the smoldering embers of local self-consciousness. The movement began among certain intellectuals who started a study of the Czech language and the history of the people. Philology, the study of languages, was the seed of nationalism. In opposition to the German domination, the Czechs began to exalt their native tongue and to prepare it for literary uses. The old masterpieces were republished and translations made into Czech of foreign works. So lacking was the Czech language in vocabulary, due to its disuse in higher circles, that many words had to be borrowed from other Slavic languages.

Along with this work went the study of the past of the country. Palacký, the principal historian and subsequently called the "Father of the Nation," recalled the sacrifices of the past, described the glorious era of the Hussite wars and the tragedy of the Thirty Years' War, and restored a sense of pride and mission to the Czech people. The history of the country was depicted as a long struggle against the Germans. Since the nobility was mostly German, the Czech national movement exalted the common people, associating national liberation and democracy as part of the same goal.

The original ideas of nationalism were diffused among the intellectuals and others who had a university education. Professors preached nationalism, and students carried it all over the country. Members of the upper middle class, as usual, were the most receptive to the idea, they being the best educated and also those who bought the most books. In other countries as well, the merchants, bankers, lawyers, physicians, and professors were the most enthusiastic over the doctrine of nationalism. These were also the people who, irritated by the anachronistic governments of central Europe, were looking for some philosophy to dignify their opposition.

Nationalism was diffused among the common people by other means. The newspapers played some part. Singing clubs were organized for the purpose of preserving native songs. The famous *Sokol* organizations, gymnastic groups, held national celebrations in which folk dances, costumes, and songs were popularized. Above all, the nationalists labored to secure control of the schools, in order that they might mold the minds of the next generation. Where the clergy joined their side, the blessing of pulpit and altar was of enormous help with the peasant population. When the nationalists triumphed, the army became another school for indoctrination of patriotism.

Once the spread of nationalism was well under way, the nationalists entered the next stage, that of mass organization of the population for liberation. This took the form of political parties, which could bring pressure to bear upon the foreign masters. In most countries, the political parties and nationalist societies were responsible for acts of resistance against the authorities. When the time inevitably came that the government lost its power to resist, as in a war, the nationalist group seized the levers of government. An idea had triumphed.

The Diffusion of Socialism

Another type of idea that was being spread in the nineteenth century was socialism. Similar concepts had appeared repeatedly among both ancient and modern writers without becoming the occasion for a great historical movement. Socialism in itself was not sufficiently compelling to attract more than an occasional idealist. If any social group did exist which might have found an expression of its own wishes in socialism, it was unorganized and incapable of giving voice to its opinions.

The appearance of the factory and the factory town raised the conceptions of socialism beyond the realm of pure speculation. A large number of men found themselves working long hours in bad conditions for poor pay, with the inevitable consequence that a certain state of mind was created among these laborers. Without benefit of a philosophy or fine rhetoric, they conceived a hatred of the employer. The thought would obviously occur to them that the factory ought to be owned by all of them and then all the profits would go to those who, in their eyes, did all the work. Furthermore, as they labored together, each worker could scarcely help but see himself as one of a large number of men with similar complaints, problems, and outlook; consciousness of themselves as a group was taking root among them. These persons were spontaneously brewing socialist thought in a rudimentary form, and they were ready to listen to anyone who could express these ideas in a more clear and forceful way.

The philosophic and intellectual exposition of socialism, undertaken by the Utopian Socialists of France, was continued in a somewhat different form by Karl Marx; the amorphous state of mind of the working class was now articulated, complete with economic and philosophic justifications. Hatred of the manufacturer and capitalist was elevated to the level of a theme of universal history in the assurance that the central plot of history was the struggle of the oppressed against the oppressor—the class struggle. For a time, at least, the loyalty of the workers to their own class was elevated above loyalty to the nation. A definite understandable goal of socialization of the means of production and distribution was presented. The laborers were told that the economic processes themselves were operating in favor of the working classes and that victory was inevitable.

The ideas of socialism continued to be elaborated by other men. Of the several types of socialist thought that were evolved, Marxism gained by far the greatest number of adherents. Within Marxism itself, factions appeared, which disputed among themselves as to the various tenets of the faith.

A good example of how the diffusion of socialism took place is to be found in the Fabian Society, which, however, was by no means completely Marxist. It was made up of some of the leading intellectuals of England and included such persons as George Bernard Shaw, H. G.

Wells, Sidney and Beatrice Webb, and Mrs. Annie Besant. In a series of brilliant essays and books, they worked out the program and possibilities which the Labor party was later to try to put into effect. On the European continent, somewhat similar groups were working on the elaboration and diffusion of socialism. The man of ideas, the agitator, the congenital rebel, and, ultimately, the man of power all found ample scope for their talents.

The idea accepted, social organization soon followed. Working-class unions, a natural development where such a social group was becoming conscious of itself, had been formed prior to the acceptance of socialist ideas in some places. In the United States labor unions were usually created in order to improve working conditions, without any thought of also socializing the economy, while in continental Europe, on the contrary, the socialists soon secured control of the trade-unions. For the first time, the socialists had a powerful tool with which to impose their ideas. Through the strike and similar devices, they could forcibly obtain a hearing for their wishes. The unions also provided the leaders with a way to control their followers. The discipline necessary for a successful institution was imposed. In Germany, in the Social Democratic trade-unions, the degree of organization passed far beyond the British or American, with the creation and almost exclusive use of their own newspapers, magazines, libraries, and even recreational facilities. Marxism, in such a case, became as possessive of a man's soul and mind as a religion.

The socialist, like the nationalist, organized political parties as another tool for achieving gains for labor. The Socialist, Social Democratic, or Labor parties (the name varied from one country to another) increased their voting power as the factory system spread, until representatives of labor were able to gain admission to the governmental ministries. Between the two world wars, they were able to take control in some countries and began to introduce their socialist measures. By this time the institutions of socialism and the working classes were taking on the attributes of other institutions, as described in an earlier chapter.

The Pattern Summarized

Although it is obvious from the foregoing that considerable correlation exists between a situation and the ideas accepted, it is less than between an invention and the circumstances that bring the latter into existence. Presumably an age of improved communications and widespread literacy would bring some form of emphasis upon a larger terri-torial domain, and this would most likely be based upon a common language. Equally probable, the employment of a large number of workers in a privately owned factory would produce some type of socialistic think-ing. There still remained a wide margin of choice as to the exact content of the philosophy in each instance. The human element and chance play a considerable role in the final selection. Sidney Hook says that the ideas that win acceptance are usually those that are the most compre-hensive, flexible, and relevant.

A suppressed group may well accept almost any doctrine that chal-lenges the dominant group and offers a rational reason for opposition. A belief that has prestige because it has been victorious elsewhere or is accepted in leading intellectual circles may sometimes be accepted re-gardless of immediate relevancy. Thus, the republicanism of Latin America at the beginning of the nineteenth century accorded badly with existing conditions. An idea may be accepted because it fringes on or duplicates, with new terminology, an idea that is already familiar: social-ism in Russia has certain aspects not unlike the older collectivism in that country. Fascism seemed a more intense form of nationalism to many people. In contrast, a concept may be accepted because of its novelty to a generation of intellectuals or simply because the possibilities of further elaboration of existent principles seem exhausted. Finally, ideas may be imposed by force, the selection being so restricted by a governing group that no real choice remains.

Even where an idea is accepted, it may be so modified as to become quite different from the original concept. The socialists of Western Europe eventually gave up the theory of violent revolution in favor of working through the democratic system. The Russian socialists were successful in revolution, and the Communist party has continued to work in this direction. While all countries became nationalistic, various types of it appeared, which Carlton Hayes has classified as Jacobin, traditional, liberal, and integral nationalism.

Inasmuch as the early proponents of an idea are likely to be zealots, convinced men who work for a cause with little intent of personal profit, their differences of opinion are likely to be serious. Each is completely convinced that his conception of the idea is the true one. Hence, any historical ideological movement is likely to be rent with factions unless strong measures are taken to prevent it.

The creation of a band of adherents inevitably brings organization. A society is created, a club established, a party formed, some type of institution emerges for the purpose of spreading the points of view of the dedicated group. In the case of the nationalists in such countries as Bohemia, political parties appeared which solicited all the possible votes and fought in the political arena for autonomy. The socialists also created their political parties, whose strength grew constantly as the Industrial Revolution created more and more urban laborers. The socialists also entered the trade-unions and used them for political purposes.

A subtle change now appears in the principal ideas. As they pass from the intelligentsia to the wider appeal of the average person they lose their atmosphere of speculation, of philosophical meditation, and tend to become dogma. They assume the form of slogans and battle cries. The emotional elements are exalted in order to gain and hold loyalties.

A new class of men emerge to leadership in the movement, these being men of action, men who are more interested in success and power than in intellectual concepts. They are likely to use the doctrines as tools for gaining personal adherents. Loyalty becomes more important than truth as institutional psychology produces a concomitant set of tenets in connection with the preservation of the institution. The basic ideas of a successful institution tend to become sacrosanct, objects of worship, as part of the fabric of loyalties.

To ask the proportionate weight of ideas in the framework of social events is to enter a long and fruitless discussion. Social forces, social action, human institutions are inconceivable without ideas. They are, as described earlier, the threads which hold men together. They are the concentrated reflections of the other social forces. Ideas are the shorthand which makes it possible for the human mind to bring a degree of order out of infinite complexity. An idea is a tool, an auxiliary, for the members of society in their task of living together, and it is a catalyst which makes possible the unleashing of social forces. We are inclined to doubt if the idea is usually the most basic factor in any great historical movement, yet, equally obviously, it cannot be omitted from any discussion of such a development.

Individual interpretation of the weight of the idea varies according to the predisposition of a person. Many people, especially those men of action who so largely make the decisions, put little faith in ideas, while others become completely imbued with conviction and are ready to sacrifice all, even become martyrs, for what is to them an abstract and idealistic cause. Any belief which is not capable of evoking such devotion is not likely to become a prime factor in human affairs. It may be that for a time a group of devotees can become a social force in their own right. Fundamentally, however, an idea which is not adopted by a group which is also motivated by other drives as well is not likely to rise to first-rate importance.

13

The Use and Misuse of History

While the bulk of the work in the average introductory history course consists in reading history that has been written by others, in most such courses the students are eventually requested to write some history themselves, which usually takes the form of preparing term papers or reports. Writing history is not quite as novel to one as it might seem at first glance, for, in a sense, we all have done some of it. A person who keeps a diary or narrates events in his daily life in letters to his friends is composing a kind of history. A writer on a school paper is describing historical events, albeit on a local scale. Any person who happened upon a student's diary or letters a century from now would be keenly interested in them for their intimate glimpse into our age. If they fell into the hands of a scholar, he might even quote that student and perpetuate his name by putting it into a footnote.

When a person produces a term paper or report, he is writing a simplified form of history. It is simplified because he is not using the special techniques of the historian, and he nearly always works with materials that have already been prepared by others. All that is required in order to find the information is a quick trip to the local depository of human knowledge, the library, and a few minutes spent looking up the selected topics in the card index.

The writing of history by undergraduates has been made easy by the establishment of libraries and the work of countless persons in collecting information and preparing it in proper form. Not so long ago, most families grew their own food, baked their own bread, and made their own clothes; now these are bought over a counter. When we want light, we simply press a button. A twist of the dial brings us music or pictures from distant places. When we want knowledge, we have the same sort of convenience, for the modern library is accessible for our use. Incredibly, enough, this service is almost free. (Perhaps this is why we take it so much for granted!) The library, as much as radio, television, light switches, or grocery stores, is a product of that modern progress which now makes available to us, quickly and directly, whatever we may need.

Complete information about all human history is, of course, not available in even the best libraries. Large portions of the story are irredeemably lost because only in recent centuries have men usually taken pains to keep detailed records. The modern Western countries have an embarrassing plenitude of information, as far as the main outline of their recent history is concerned. In some cases, as with the Romans and Greeks, a fair amount of records were left. Even here, most of our information comes from sources other than official ones, and many of the facets of life which we would like to know about were not considered worthy of description at the time. In some segments of human history, virtually no written records have survived.

Historians must therefore have recourse to all types of evidence in their reconstruction of history. Actual historical writings from an age are especially welcome if other evidence proves the accounts are trustworthy. Other surviving materials, such as personal reminiscences and letters, must be studied. Whatever government documents, records, or inscriptions are to be found, these will often furnish valuable information. Where actual written materials are not available, the historian (or archaeologist) must examine such other clues as surviving ruins of buildings, coins, pottery, tools, and articles of attire in his attempt to reconstruct the story.

Accounts by eyewitnesses or contemporaries of the events or surviving objects from the time are termed *primary sources*. To the aforementioned scholar, a diary or letters would be primary sources, and so would the report of current events in newspapers. Other historical accounts, written by persons who have studied the primary sources or who are using the works of those who have, are known as *secondary sources*. The textbook is an example. Histories of countries are usually secondary sources. In most cases, a biography is secondary, but an autobiography is primary.

Increasing Knowledge about the Past

A current textbook is the latest link in the long chain of knowledge from the original chroniclers to the present. Every sentence of it has a history of its own, a story of how this particular fragment of knowledge was preserved or rediscovered and then carried down to us. Some may be as prosaic as a chronicler jotting down happenings in the manner of a journalist recording day-by-day events. Others may have the elements of a good detective story in their background. Although a history textbook bears the name of an author, it is, in the last analysis, the work of many thousands of minds in various parts of the world and living in different ages.

Some of the adventurers in the writing of history have become famous in the annals of modern scholarship. An occasional person has had the good fortune, the enthusiasm, and the skill to become a Columbus in the world of scholarship, to discover a new world or civilization that had been completely forgotten in the intervening millenniums. Perhaps the best known of these is Heinrich Schliemann, a German merchant, who, stimulated by his interest in the Homeric legend, set out, in 1871, to prove that Troy had been more than a beautiful myth. He began to dig in a mound on the Turkish coast of the Aegean Sea, which he suspected was the location, and after two years he found enough evidence to substantiate his claims. In fact, he found too many Troys, several successive strata of ruins on top of one another within the mound, and it remained for better-trained men than himself to identify the particular layer which was the Troy of the legend.

Another Greek myth, behind which was hidden the story of a vanished people, was that of Minos and the Minotaur. Sir Arthur Evans began his excavations on the island of Crete in 1900, and he and his successors discovered an unsuspected civilization, the Minoan, that had flourished over three thousand years ago.

Another instance of a forgotten empire being rediscovered was that of the Hittites, the ruins of whose capital city were found to the east of Ankara in 1861. Much more recently, archaeologists have disinterred, in India, the ancient cities of Mohenjo-Daro and Harappa, which predated the commonly assumed time of the arrival of the Aryans in that country, and whose discovery consequently has provided some knowledge about a land whose earliest history had hitherto been a blank. The list of such discoveries could be very greatly amplified and can be found in any good history of archaeology.

A particularly fortunate discovery, in connection with the Hittites, was the finding, between 1906 and 1912, of a library of their official archives containing about 13,000 clay tablets, intact or in fragments. The language was unknown, but Friedrich Hrozný, a Czech scholar, in a few years, managed to decipher the cuneiform writing on the tablets; the inscriptions proved to be invaluable, not only for the history of the Hittites but for what they revealed about other peoples of the Near East. The Minoan script of Crete proved a more baffling puzzle, inasmuch as neither the Minoan language nor the characters of the scripts were known. In 1935 a schoolboy, Michael Ventris, listened to a lecture by Sir Arthur Evans on the Minoans, became fascinated by the problem of the unknown scripts, and determined to learn their secret. During the Second World War he served as a cryptographer, learned the techniques of deciphering codes, and subsequently applied this skill to the Minoan Linear B script, one of the three known types of ancient Minoan writing. In 1952–1953 he discovered that the language of Linear B was not Minoan, as had most usually been assumed, but Achaean, a form of Greek. With the identity of the language known, Ventris was soon able to connect the Linear B signs with Greek syllables and thus to read the script. Ventris' accomplishment, pushing the history of written Greek back from about 750 B.C. to about 1450 B.C., will result in a far more precise and factual comprehension of the most ancient Greek age, as well as causing a profound revision in the perspective on the whole period.

These archaeological finds are, of course, only one phase of the constant work of scholarship. An old document, discovered, may throw new light on some controversial topic. A vase, a brooch, a skull, a small item in an old chronicle or government document, a letter by or to a historical figure, all these and others are pieces in the jigsaw puzzle of history.

As we have just seen, one single such discovery may change an interpretation of widespread importance. It was formerly assumed—and the error still seems to have circulation in some classrooms—that the Turkish seizure of Constantinople blocked trade to the East and thereby forced the Europeans to look for new trade routes. The connection between the events of 1453 and 1492 was long universally accepted. This idea of a cause-and-effect sequence, however, was exploded when an American professor, Albert Lybyer, who had once taught at Roberts College in Constantinople, went to the primary sources. He became interested in the problem when he noticed a discrepancy: even if the Turks closed the trade routes, they did not become masters of the Syrian and Egyptian routes until nearly twenty-five years *after* the discovery of America. But did the Turks close those routes that they did control? Lybyer reasoned that any throttling of commerce would lead to a scarcity of such Eastern products as pepper and a consequent rise in prices for these commodities. An examination of pepper prices in England and France in the fifteenth century revealed no such increase; on the contrary, they showed a small general decline in the years before Western Europeans began to go directly to the East. From other sources, he then proved that far from wishing to block trade, the Ottoman Turks wanted the revenue from it and therefore encouraged the commerce. The original assertion was thus completely disproved. The Western Europeans did look for new trade routes, but for other reasons.

A second example of how the study of primary sources may compel the revision of history concerns the panic of A.D. 1000. Some old books contain the story of how frightened people were when the year 1000 approached because they expected the world to come to an end. There are vivid descriptions of the panic, how some people gave away their possessions, how others plunged into a final orgy, and how the people betook themselves to the hilltops at the end of the year to await the second coming of Christ. It made a very dramatic picture, and the Sunday supplements occasionally still retail it and thus keep the story alive.

In the nineteenth century, however, a Benedictine monk proved that the episode never happened. Although he was thoroughly familiar with the literature of the medieval period, he could recall no actual mention of this hysteria in the writings *of that time*. His suspicions aroused, he made a methodical examination of all available annals and documents from around A.D. 1000 and found no allusion to any such universal panic. Other scholars joined in the search with the same results. An investigator, working from the present backward, found that the earliest published mention of it was in 1605. It became perfectly apparent that the writer of 1605 had decided for himself that the people of A.D. 1000 *must* have been afraid. He did not realize that the Christian calendar was not widely enough in use at that time for most people to be aware that the end of a millennium was approaching. Far worse, he did not check back to see, from contemporary sources, if any proof for his statement could be found. He simply fabricated the story, and later writers took his word for it and did not check back either. Only when scholars did go back to the primary sources did they discover the falsity of the assumption.

Sometimes a piece of evidence is uncovered which goes flatly contrary to accepted belief. One famous example is the controversial case of the Kensington stone, a slab of rock which was "discovered" by a Minnesota farmer in 1898. It was covered with runes (an old Scandinavian form of writing), which, when deciphered, told of eight Goths (Swedes) and twenty-two Norwegians who had camped on the site. The date was 1362! On the face of it, the idea that the white man had reached the middle of the North American continent by that date was preposterous. The runes were long assumed to be a forgery, and no one paid any further attention to it, but in recent years, due chiefly to the persistence of one man, Hjalmar R. Holand, the authenticity of the runes has come in for considerable discussion. According to some learned philologists, certain idiosyncrasies of the runes, originally held to be proof of the clumsiness of the forgerer, are now known to be characteristic of this late period of runic writing; these men would say that the seeming evidence of forgery, now, conversely, may be proof of its validity, since no one in the last century, much less a forgerer, was aware of these changes in styles of runes. Others continue to insist that the farmer could have fabricated the runic letters with the aid of an encyclopedia known to have been in his possession. There the matter rests; some historians are caustic about the whole thing, a few are convinced of its authenticity, and the remainder are highly dubious but prefer to suspend final judgment for the time being. Quite noticeably, writers of textbooks in American history continue to avoid any mention of the Kensington stone in their accounts.

These various examples illustrate how the writing of history changes as new facts are uncovered. Historical accounts do not change as rapidly as books on science perhaps, but the discovery of new evidence, its assimilation into previously known knowledge, the checking and counterchecking in order to achieve complete authenticity goes on constantly. A textbook of today is very different in content and approach from one of 1910.

There is something about the printed word that tends to impose upon the mind a conviction of immutability and that gives to the printed statement an illusion of dogma. From the illustrations (which could be added to indefinitely), it should be obvious that this feeling does not accord with the actual state of things. A textbook, containing the truth as far as we can know it today, is always subject to future corrections.

The Writing of History

Since the historian is writing about events that *someone else* saw or heard, the writing of history is necessarily a cooperative effort. He is largely dependent upon those original witnesses for their accuracy of observation and truthful reporting. He is also indebted to those before himself who collected and worked with the information. He is one of the fraternity of scholars whose lifework is the preservation of the knowledge of the past, the uncovering of more information, and the assessing of its meaning and usefulness to the present generation. To express his indebtedness to those others, the historian uses footnotes. If every sentence has a history of its own, as was stated earlier, one might say that the footnote is a much-abbreviated résumé of that background.

The footnotes have other uses. The historian employs them to buttress his own statements. He is, in effect, saying, "If you don't believe me, here is the name of a man who has studied this particular problem very carefully, and this is what he thinks." Footnotes also permit the writer to tell the reader where he may find a more detailed account of the topic if he wishes to pursue it further. Footnotes are handy receptacles for additional information by the writer if he does not wish to cram it into the text of the article or book. Here, too, he can make some additional and more personal comments which, if inserted into the main narrative, would break the continuity of the story.

When one is referring to a source in a footnote, one should include the name of the author, the title of the work, and the page or pages where the information was obtained. If more than one volume or edition exists, the specific one must be indicated. Inasmuch as there is no single standardized form for a footnote, and practice varies somewhat, any further directions in any specific history class will have to some from the professor.

Not all information needs to be documented. A considerable portion of it is regarded as "common knowledge"; most of what appears in a textbook or encyclopedia would be classified as such. Knowing when to footnote and when not to is a tricky business and one which the novice invariably has trouble learning. It is an art which must be mastered by practice rather than by the application of a few simple rules. In general, however, any information that comes directly from primary sources should be footnoted. In using secondary sources, one must decide whether the information is common property or if the particular writer is entitled to special credit for his statements. If his opinions or interpretations are being used, a footnote is necessary. If his exact words are quoted (always in quotation marks, of course), they must be documented.

Even as the historian uses other people's information, he must always remember that they were subject to human error and prejudice; he must learn to judge their capacities for writing accurate descriptions of events. This is equally true whether it is a primary or secondary source that one is consulting. The material must be investigated and tested in all possible ways to make certain that it is authentic. We may recall the Donation of Constantine, which Lorenzo Valla proved to be a forgery after it had been regarded as authentic for centuries. The poems of Ossian in English literature is another famous example of a forgery accepted as genuine for a time. The infamous and false Protocols of Zion, apparently concocted in about 1905, is a further example.

Even though the authenticity is unquestionable, if they are written records, they must be scrutinized carefully. We are studying the accounts of those presumably in a position to know the truth. The historian must try to decide if the person actually was in such a position, and if he had any motives or bias in his writings. If possible, his work should be checked against other records of the times. Frequently the record itself can be analyzed for indications of possible falsity—use of words not current in that period, references to events that had not happened or to ideas not prevalent may be a tip-off. Thus the historian is a scientist or, better put, a detective, as he tries to establish the truth. The work is never completed, for later historians will very possibly find new evidence which will alter the verdict. The physical scientist can repeat an experiment to assure himself of the validity of a statement; to achieve the same purpose, the historian will try to find new evidence, assay it, and then see if it fits the prevalent generalization. If it does not, either the new fact or the generalization is wrong, and the historian must ascertain which.

The historian is careful to remember that the facts shall determine his conclusions; he is perpetually checking the sources of the evidence from which he is writing. He seizes upon every bit of information that is discovered to see if they bolster or weaken his own previous deductions. His "facts" range all the way from certainties (as completely so as the human senses may prove them) to those highly conjectural in quality, and he will know approximately where to grade each one. If unacquainted with a particular topic, he will hold his own judgment in abeyance and will know whom to trust for a considered opinion. *The carefully worded, tentative statement of an expert is worth far more than the positive affirmation of the novice.*

This survey has outrun the level of the term paper. These are matters which the more advanced students, especially the masters and doctors candidates, must learn. Anyone who wishes to know more about the technique of historical research and writing should consult such books as Louis Gottschalk's *Understanding History,* Allan Nevin's *The Gateway to History,* or G. J. Garraghan's *A Guide to Historical Method.*

It goes without saying that the total field of history is by now far too large for any one person to master it all. A division of labor has therefore come into being whereby the individual historian concentrates his scholarly activity on one particular field, any one of several hundred, such as the French Revolution, feudalism, the origins of the First World War, the American abolitionist movement, or the ancient Israelites. In some cases only half a dozen persons in the entire world may be busy in a particular compartment of history. The findings of these scholars are usually published in the form of monographs (learned articles replete with footnotes) in scholarly journals. Eventually someone writes a book on the whole area of investigation and incorporates what these men have discovered. Five, ten, or twenty years later, newly uncovered materials may necessitate a new book on the same subject. Sometimes one expert will take exception to the conclusions of another and a shower of controversial articles and books will enliven the scene until further evidence settles the issue. At the other end of this whole process of scholarship are the writers of textbooks, who try to select the most essential and relevant information for the use of students, and the popularizers, who make the information palatable to the general public.

Interpretations of History

Historical writing, like fiction, architecture, and painting, tends to reflect the age in which it is produced. The historian is describing a human situation, and how many different points of view does one not find for these in everyday life? A historian cannot avoid portraying history according to his personal valuations of it, and also, if he would be understood by his contemporaries, he must clothe his thoughts in the distinctive modes of expression of his own age.

The various interpretations do not disturb the beginning student for textbooks usually adhere to what is generally accepted by most scholars. Confusion is most apt to appear when reading other history, not textbooks, where the author is definitely stressing one viewpoint. It is well to be aware of their existence and to be prepared for them. Although they may be confusing to the beginner, differences of interpretation are also signs of growth, for they are an indication that historians are constantly seeking new angles from which to examine the basic facts.

What, then, are some of the broad interpretations, characteristic of different ages or of our own, which we may encounter? If one should chance to read a Greek or Roman historian, one would doubtless find that he narrated individual episodes chiefly in terms of the great men involved. If a broader causation was needed, he attributed the course of events to the gods or to a more impersonal and mysterious Fate. In the medieval period writers were naturally inclined to view history as a struggle between good and evil and as a pattern in which God manifested his plan for the salvation of mankind.

In the eighteenth century, when Reason was exalted and when traditional institutions and ideas were under attack, the historians tended, as in the case of Voltaire, to depict the past as a chronicle of crimes and misfortunes; they were quick to stigmatize those historical figures who seemed to them to have contributed to the misery and ignorance by acting according to superstitious beliefs. Acutely aware of recent successes in finding general laws in nature, the writers sought similar laws in society and in so doing studied the influences of climate, geography, and other factors upon human actions. The same Enlightenment, giving birth to the idea of progress, produced historical works based upon the optimistic belief that rational thought was now finally enabling man to ascend to a higher plane of civilization.

The romanticists, valuing the past more highly and influenced by the concept of progress, emphasized the developmental aspects of human institutions. In so doing they evolved the concept of organic evolution: an institution or idea or age contains seeds of growth within itself which will germinate and mature in their own particular patterns in very much the same way that plants do. More recent writers were to employ this idea in an extreme form to create dogmatic patterns of history along deterministic lines. If historical development follows a pattern of its own, what then becomes of individual effort? Man is simply a pawn of greater forces, and his only choice is whether to join in this inevitable movement or make a futile fight against it. This type of determinism became a social tool of great weight in the hands of Fascists and Communists. Both of these tell the people that history is moving inexorably in a certain direction, in the one case toward a victory of their race, and in the other toward a triumph by the working classes.

The emergence of nationalism quite naturally induced a great increase in histories of individual countries, many written in a spirit of such patriotism that everything about the native country was exalted and the enemy countries blackened. It led to schools of thought by national historians in which the role of the English or Germans or French were grossly exaggerated and each was made out to be the particular bearer of civilization against the iniquitous enemy. Much of the distorted history of the recent past has emanated from the ultranationalist writers.

The growth of the middle class, the coming of the Industrial Revolution and its problems, and the tremendous growth of production stimulated the appearance and growth of the economic interpretation, which is undoubtedly the most prevalent at the present time. According to it, the more important sources of causation and of human motivation are to be found in economic considerations—the greatest weight is given to those explanations for historical events which are derived from a study of what is happening in the economy.

During the nineteenth century, while science was rapidly rising in prestige, historians began to apply a scientific methodology of their own to historical materials. This movement is customarily associated with the name of Leopold von Ranke, a German historian. He insisted that the historian must describe events as they actually happened, using eyewitness accounts and documents from the time, and that the historian must never permit his own predilections to enter into the narrative. Although his followers were no more able to attain complete objectivity than their predecessors, their emphasis on reducing the personal element as much as possible was a healthy corrective in the writing of history.

Erroneous and Misleading Forms of Reasoning

In dealing with interpretations, one needs to know the obviously false, the patently distorted. The educated person knows how to read between the lines to some extent. While he may read two well-written contradictory explanations for an event and tend to agree with each in turn, he can spot the obviously colored and the crass propaganda. He can tell what is obviously *not* the truth. Although it is certainly not the task of the historian to inculcate the philosophy which a person shall possess, he can teach the student how to detect the more crude devices of propaganda. They are also worth remembering in our own writing, so that we do not fall into these pitfalls ourselves.

We have learned, in earlier chapters, that the Great Man theory is dubious. Any account which plays up any single person as the all-embracing cause, which exalts the individual beyond probable human limits, must be suspect. The causes are being oversimplified. As a corollary, let it be observed that any political propaganda of such a sort in times of election are of the same nature. The converse might also be noted: any persistent debunking of a historical figure or contemporary political personage is likely to present a lopsided and distorted picture.

We have also learned that ascribing a single cause to any event is too facile an explanation. Any piece of writing in which one single factor is overemphasized and others are ignored is suspect. A principle device of propaganda is the systematic omission of other facts or factors which go contrary to the statements being made. Unless the reader is alert and has enough knowledge to be aware of the omissions, his mind will necessarily tread the mental path that the writer intended it to follow. He will use the author's logic alone and reach the same conclusions. The reader should always be wary of undue emphasis, should always ask himself where the emphasis is and what the writer wants him to believe. Frequently students, having read a book, will remember the title but forget the name of the author. It is more important to remember the writer's name than the title, for if he has written considerably, he will have a reputation. His very name is something of a label for the book, indicative of what may be expected in its contents, its quality, and its slant, if any.

A narrative which presents one side as being purely good and the other purely evil must be suspect as a definite sign of special pleading and as a positive indication of propaganda. We should know that no historical picture is that simple. One of the factors which has fooled many people about the evils of our time, including fascism and communism, is that they are *not* completely evil, for each does carry with it elements of good, proclaimed ideals, and promised reforms. If evil were not sometimes difficult to recognize, unlike the fairy tale witch and the equally naïve Hollywood version, it would be much easier to fight. Certain standards, a genuine personal philosophy, whether from the home, church, school, or from reading is required before the shapes and forms of evil can be discerned. Intelligence and a conscience are necessary in order to perceive it. Any caricature of evil, any black-and-white account, must be suspect.

Another type of thinking to beware of is the *static-rebel* dichotomy. Those who are governed by a *static* conception of society have no real awareness of the constant change in society, or at least they do not realize the nature and character of social transformations and that no human endeavors can hold off alterations for any length of time. The *rebels,* paradoxically enough, suffer from the same disability, a failure to understand the real nature of change. Lacking an understanding of the strong bonds that make for continuity, the other half of the process, they know change only as cataclysms, as violent overturnings of society. Failing to appreciate the complexity of society, they believe that it can be fundamentally altered by their own will. They do not recognize that attempts by force do more harm than good.

A similar ailment afflicts those who evaluate and judge present-day society in its contrast to perfection. Most people are aware of how far our society, or any other, is from perfect justice and pure democracy. While the ultimate goals should always be kept in mind, it does not follow that a blanket condemnation of our society is in order: failure to achieve utopia should not induce cynicism. Those who do expect perfection—and youth is prone to it—also fail to understand the true nature of social advance. Occasional glances backward over the past journey of humanity offer reassurances that we are moving ahead and are a good corrective for this state of mind.

One other type of erroneous thinking is to some extent unavoidable. We automatically use *our* ideas and *our* motives when we visualize the actions of a historical figure. Although we would laugh at someone depicting Luther riding to Worms in a motorcar, we do not hesitate to impute twentieth-century thoughts to his sixteenth-century mind. It is well to remember how anachronistic this is and be equally wary of the reversed situation when someone tells us what Lincoln or Washington, or Karl Marx for that matter, would do in present circumstances.

Other forms of thinking are not as crude as those already mentioned, but they should still be employed with caution. They are devices which are used in learning to think historically and which continue useful even in mature meditation. The use of *analogy* is one of these. Analogies are helpful in the learning process, since they enable one to employ familiar ideas and objects in order to grasp the unfamiliar and to visualize it. The afore-mentioned reference to plant growth helps one to understand the organic theory, the process of sedimentation and erosion as studied in geology is roughly comparable to certain historical processes, and the analogy of the lever will be mentioned later in connection with employment of native governments by imperial powers. Each of these is of assistance in instant comprehension of the meaning. Yet this is only the beginning of the process, for an analogy can be pushed only so far and after that it becomes misleading. Once the fundamental idea has been grasped, the factual material must be used to modify and color the concept being studied.

Another type of thinking also necessary in the learning process is the use of *absolutes*. For example, we like to lump all persons of a given economic group in a certain category. We know that most of them will fit into it, psychologically and politically as well as economically, yet there are those who will not. We like to think in long-term trends—and we must —yet we should not let this practice obscure those things which do not fit the pattern. We would like to see inevitability in certain events, but perhaps it looks that way only *after* the event. We like to find some formula, some key, that will spare us the painful task of actually examining the evidence in each case. This book is partially devoted to the learning of the larger generalizations of historical reasoning, and it is a necessary step in one's development to learn how to think in these categories. If not, history remains a meaningless jumble of bare facts without relevance to each other or to ourselves. Once these patterns have been learned, however, the final step consists in developing moderation in their use lest they become absolutes. The facts must be used to modify the generalizations.

Every event in history is *unique*. Although a certain episode may bear startling resemblances to other similar events, it has, nevertheless, never happened in exactly a given way before. While we can, to a degree, learn lessons from history, we cannot predict because so many of the factors cannot be accurately gauged. Every event in history or any contemporary development must be investigated for itself. We cannot walk in with some pet formula and pronounce judgment. We can and must use our categories in searching for interrelationships. We try each and see how it fits. But the *facts*, the primary sources, the actual evidence, ultimately must guide our decisions. One should constantly ask, "What is the evidence?"

We must, in conclusion, revert to the point made above concerning the distortion of the past by the application of present-day attitudes to historical situations. When we first travel into the past, we cannot avoid seeing it through eyes accustomed to the twentieth century and, consequently, seeing it in reference to that which seems familiar. Perhaps the analogy of travel used in the beginning of the book is too optimistic an expression of the first experiences of the beginning student; the truth would be more closely approximated if it were suggested that he is examining the past through a telescope. As such, his observations are sorely limited because he is rooted to one point of observation, the present, and the spot being viewed must be related to its surroundings by the broad view as seen with the naked eye, that is, by generalizations.

This initial stage in the development of historical-mindedness is definitely over when we begin to sense that when we visit another century we are, in fact, foreigners in a strange land. We are then more ready to examine the surroundings as they really were. As we study the past, we obtain bases for perspectives on the present. While the beginning student must necessarily view the past from the present, a person has not attained truly mature historical-mindedness until he is able to see the present from various vantage points in the past.

14

Power

Every college student has undoubtedly been puzzled, at one time or another, by the results of school elections. In a contest for King and Queen of Homecoming Festivities, in a class election, or in a contest for a campus post the seemingly best-qualified or most popular candidate loses. Perhaps a certain fraternity or sorority seems able to win a disproportionate share of honors. It may be that this results in cynicism and bitter comments on how elections are controlled by certain groups. In situations of this kind, a student encounters one of the facts of life in the political sphere.

A college campus is a microcosm of the larger society in its rivalry among social groups, in the methods used by these groups to win and hold positions, and in the place occupied by individuals in these rivalries. The author once heard a prominent public official make the statement that he first learned the technique of gaining votes by his activities as a student on a college campus. He asserted that there is no essential difference between campus and public politics.

The reason why the best-qualified or most deserving candidate does not always draw the most votes is that he is not supported by the groups with the most power. Such power is based on a number of different factors, all of which, in total, amount to an ability to influence many people. One important asset is the presence in the organization of big-names that draw votes by the very fact of being well known. Money with which to finance an aggressive campaign is important. An efficient organization, which can devise and carry through such a campaign, is a necessity. Prestige, in itself, is a big help. Finally, and perhaps most crucial, it depends upon the capacity to make deals with other groups. Presence of these resources indicates possession of power.

Types of Power

Power is to society what energy is to the physical world. It holds the state and lesser organizations together and makes possible social action on a wide scale. The governmental apparatus is a formal structure established in order to regularize certain practices of the state and is, consequently, the product of the channelizing and crystallization of power processes.

That type of power which is likely to occur to one, first in reference to the state, is physical force itself, the use of strong-arm methods to achieve a purpose. History books contribute to that conclusion, for tales of violence make up many of their pages. Still—as we know—they tend to narrate the exceptional and sensational events and in so doing overemphasize the role of sword and cannon. A stable government always achieves most of its work through public opinion. It is axiomatic that a law should be a formal statement of what most people would do without that law, that is, the law becomes mostly self-enforcing, and compulsion is necessary only for a few. An excellent indication of the actual stability of any regime is the degree to which it is compelled to resort to physical violence to keep control. A consistent display of force, such as the existence of a strong secret police, is in itself an indication that the regime faces strong internal opposition.

It should be obvious from experience that force itself is seldom used in personal relationships among people. Verbal persuasion is by far the most customary means employed. Such persuasion may result from a logical discussion, it may consist in appealing to prejudices or idealism, or it may amount to an appeal for cooperation. Historically speaking, the state has increasingly restricted and then eliminated the use of physical force among individual persons or by any institution except itself. Physical force is, legally, a monopoly of the state.

Economic power is much less dramatic in its historical manifestations and is less visible in the events narrated in history, yet it is, as we know, all-pervasive in its insistent pressure. Economic strength is manifested in the ability of the upper middle class to lend money to others, to hire and fire laborers in their factories, and by similar means to gain considerable control over other segments of the population. It displays itself in the organized ability of the working classes to provide the necessary labor or to withhold such labor temporarily if their demands are not met. British capacity in the nineteenth century to lend money gave Britain a far more formidable weapon than its military might. The ability to provide manufactured goods was an equally strong weapon in dealing with its neighbors. The United States in the past thirty years has wielded enormous power. Its huge production, vast domestic market, and gold reserves have all influenced the countries of the world and inexorably drawn the United States into the foremost international position.

Spiritual power—control over the mind—has been described in the earlier chapters entitled "The Bases of Loyalty" and "The Role of Ideas." The effects of a religious or political belief, the magnetism of a creed for the human mind, were discussed. In addition to the above, the functioning of normal public opinion is also a major element of spiritual power in the community. Inasmuch as each person constantly manages his behavior according to what he sees of himself in the mirror of public opinion, it is a potent force. This automatic regulator of social conduct, lying below the usual level of political control is undoubtedly more effective in maintaining a functioning society than all other factors combined. Political influence, in this case, is indirect and exists largely to the degree that the state controls schools, churches, newspapers, and other agencies which mold opinion. The totalitarian states, differing from democracies in their constant use of violence, also differ here; while democracies normally leave the realm of public opinion substantially to associations and individuals, totalitarian states insist on rigid control of even the organs of public opinion.

Under the category of spiritual power may also be classified the consequence of habit itself. An institution or group which has held authority for a long time achieves prestige and benefits from the growing idea that it is a part of the natural order of things. Power tends to become a habitual fact, a sort of momentum which enables its holders to dominate the will of the individuals in their group.

Technological power is an emerging form which has not yet been brought fully into use. It may be that the spell of the magician over the superstitious could be considered an early version of it to the extent that he was believed to control the forces of nature. There are those who believe that the technologists and scientists will, at some time in the future, assume control of affairs because the rest of mankind is becoming increasingly dependent upon them. Part of America's strength derives from its superior capacity to originate and use new forms of technological power.

By using these various types of power (physical, economic, spiritual, and technological), social institutions enhance their own positions and acquire still more power. They employ them to bring individuals under their control, and they use them against other institutions in a series of conflicts. It does not follow, of course, that an economic group such as the middle class or the proletariat limits usage of power to only economic methods or that a church limits techniques to purely spiritual ones. A group whose original motive was ideological does not necessarily limit its methods to verbal persuasion once it can employ economic or other power.

We have said above that the governmental apparatus is a formalization of certain power processes. This apparatus is, in the higher levels at least, manned by individuals who have a strong desire to exercise power. A person who has no wish to wield authority is unlikely to seek public office, while if he does want the right to command, one of the best means available is in the higher echelons of the state. The men who rise to leadership in various nonstate associations are also likely to want power for its own sake, and these men indirectly help to influence governmental decisions by their pressures. Bertrand Russell writes, "Love of power is the chief motive producing changes which social science has to study."

Inasmuch as power-hungry persons tend to run the state and the constant temptation exists to extend one's own control further, perhaps even in the conscientious belief that it is necessary for efficient government, the curbing of government has furnished one of the central themes of modern history. A two-way process is perpetually at work, one in the direction of strengthening the government and the other in the constant struggle for liberty. Both arise directly out of the needs of social organizations. We can think of numerous historical instances where aggrandizement of additional control by the government was a necessity in view of conditions at the time. While personal liberty might suffer decline, broader considerations of welfare for the whole country overruled objections on this score. Where weakness of authority verged on anarchy, a seeming restriction of freedom might, in fact, produce opportunities for real liberty. Power, if not held by the state, must perforce be exercised by other institutions or associations or by individuals, and such authority can be just as arbitrary as that of the political organs themselves. Power is necessary for the state and for the various social institutions; too great reluctance in using it ultimately means the dissolution of society itself. Power or even naked force is not to be regarded as an evil in itself; it is the *uses* to which it is put and the *degree* of usage which are apt to be evil.

The other side of the process is the constant struggle by individuals and associations for escape from state controls. This balances the institutional trend toward concentration of power. Where the vigor of the fight for freedom is debilitated for one reason or another, the result will be tyranny. An alert and mature body of citizens, intent on maintaining their freedom, will be constantly on guard against misuse and overextension of governmental authority. In sum, state power and the drive for human liberty check one another and prevent deterioration into either tyranny or anarchy.

Power in Colonial Controls

Perhaps a better understanding of the nature and operation of state power will result from a glimpse at the manner in which colonies with large native populations were conquered and then kept under control. Some of these territories, such as India and Indonesia, represented dominion over populations many times larger than that of the conquering states themselves. How was it possible to achieve and hold such control? What power did the white man, numerically few in the colonies, wield against so many?

Colonies were founded for one or more of several reasons: strategic location, trading purposes, raw materials, missionary activity, prestige, and white settlement. The use of power would necessarily vary according to the purposes for which the colony was intended. The original penetration was in most instances by other means than physical force, the first encounter between the Europeans and the Africans or Asiatics usually taking place in the realm of commerce, and the merchants often being followed by missionaries. Their respective activities did not necessarily lead to any political rule whatsoever, but in the case of backward areas without strong local government it was likely to do so.

A strategic base might require no control of the natives except in such measures as would prevent their attacking the fort. In such an instance, a country would normally have some troops stationed there anyway as a protection against other countries, and these would suffice against the natives. Where the motives were those of commerce, the trade was frequently of benefit for the natives also, and it might well be in the economic interest of the native government to provide adequate safeguards for the traders. In regions with weak native states, however, commercial enterprise might gradually be transformed into a territorial holding. Such a project might have its inception simply as a string of outposts inland, where the traders needed them. The new bases then required adequate protection, and this meant treaties with neighboring tribes. Agreements of this type might well be voluntary and based upon mutual interests, but they often were the result of coercion. The treaties then became the basis upon which actual territorial domination was established. Almost always, except where Europeans settled in considerable numbers, the white men worked through already existent native political units. Where a country took control for reasons of prestige, usually to prevent another power from seizing the region, little interference with native institutions occurred.

If the white man settled himself as a plantation owner and employer of native labor, he was much more likely, after a time, to weaken and then abolish the native institutions above the village level, for a tribal group or a traditional monarchy could serve as a focus of resistance against himself and his labor practices. Once the structure of native society had been ruined, the whole burden of restraint fell upon the white authorities. A ruling minority group, determined to stay in power, must exhibit physical force from time to time. Force, for them, becomes a positive good. The ancient Spartans, in these circumstances, transformed their nation into an armed encampment. The present-day South Africans may feel themselves compelled to make the same choice.

Actual conquest of the colonies was accomplished by the use of all four types of power. In many instances, the physical power employed was remarkably slight, and few colonial enterprises involved any sizable fraction of the total military strength of the occupying country. The factor which made large-scale efforts unnecessary—and hence prohibitively expensive—was technological. The Europeans were not crushed beneath the larger number of natives because of their possession of superior weapons, in turn made possible by a superior technology. Along with this went the infinitely better military organization which had been built up as these weapons evolved. The individual European normally possessed as much fighting power as ten or twenty natives. This conferred prestige of such proportions as to render out of the question any resistance other than that born out of desperation. If the native had any realization of the (to him) mammoth strength possessed by the mother country, the thoughts of fighting would seem visionary. The very existence of overwhelming force in the background rendered the application of force unnecessary.

In spite of such military might, it may be questioned if the larger colonies would have been held for any length of time by force alone. A determined and united resistance over many years, such as the British met in Palestine in the 1930's or the French in Indo-China after the Second World War, destroys the commercial and strategic value of the colony. That such resistance did not develop in the nineteenth century was due to another reason than force.

This other element in the picture was the very effective lever of control provided by the afore-mentioned use of native institutions and customs which made it possible for the whites to limit their dealings to the native authorities, rather than their being compelled to create the machinery for imposing control over the whole population. A native military constabulary might be provided, thereby even releasing the whites from the necessity of using physical force themselves except in cases of a general insurrection. The essential structure of the native society, the habit of obedience to their own well-known authorities, the reverence for native symbols and for the native religion remained intact. This method brought the conquerors all the advantages of conquest without all the labors. It softened the harshness of the rule and blurred the true reality of the conquest. For the individual among the subjugated, the change was much less perceptible, and he may scarcely ever have come into direct contact with the conquerors. The spiritual powers of the conquered society, the habits of centuries, were added to the strength of the imperial authority.

Further, such indirect rule through local native authorities was already well known among the conquered from their dealings with one another. The necessity of accepting an overlord was far from a novel experience. The very prevalence of such conquests rendered a new conquest easier, and its acceptance natural for the conquered. Indirect rule, in fact, has been the classic pattern of conquest everywhere. The Romans, for instance, frequently permitted client kings to govern or city-republics to maintain their existence as semi-independent states. From the ancient Egyptians to the modern British, the conquerors have practiced a sort of conservation of energy in imperial affairs by permitting, within limits, the conquered to govern themselves. Even the Americans, in the conquest of Japan, permitted Hirohito to remain as emperor, as the most feasible method of keeping order and obedience.

Where the conquerors made use of native institutions, the prevailing power, in the last analysis, was not physical force. The complex of spiritual and economic balances which already existed in the community continued, with force remaining in the background to be used as a last resort only. In cases where the whites destroyed the native institutions, however, much more repressive measures became necessary.

Two or three other broad principles of colonial control need to be mentioned. Every effort was made to give the native traditional leaders a vested interest in maintaining European rule. They found cooperation with the whites advantageous, for their own position was more secure from rivals, and they were enabled to share in the economic benefits of the coming of the Europeans. In this fashion, the native society lost its natural leaders and was split for the advantage of the conqueror in the usual pattern of "divide and rule." It was also frequently deemed best not to give too much opportunity for education among the conquered, inasmuch as the recipients might become prospective leaders. The natives were kept strictly away from major offices, beyond their own traditional ones, in order to prevent their learning how to run the country or to be in a position to start trouble. Finally, only small native military forces were permitted, since native usage of the white man's weapons might lead to expert use of these arms against the Europeans.

During the past few decades, the colonial areas have been regaining their independence. The colonial edifice of power has been weakening and breaking down altogether in a process strikingly similar to that described in the chapter on revolutions. It will be recalled that domestic revolutions are much more likely to result from weakness of government than from tyranny: the ruling class loses confidence in itself. Similarly, the European spirit of imperialism has been sapped by theories which question their right to hold such control; the British, for instance, have lost their conviction that they are supporting the "white man's burden" and are now loath to use physical power against colonial peoples. In their case, a gradual transfer of power to the natives has been long under way before the actual grant of freedom occurs.

Ideas are necessary in order to give revolutionists a common cause. Western nationalism and ideas of democracy, as well as Marxist concepts, have provided Asiatics and Africans with a philosophy justifying their struggle for independence in the same way that these doctrines were used earlier by the Europeans themselves. Exerting pressure in the direction of changes are social groups which feel hampered by the restrictions of an old regime. A native middle class, working-class groups, and an intelligentsia have appeared in the colonies, and, in various proportions, these play the part exercised by the middle class in the French Revolution. Finally, in order to make a revolution successful, an organized party, like the Jacobins or Communists, is essential; in the colonies such political organizations as the Congress party of India have emerged, which have known how to propagandize and lead their own masses in a fight for independence.

Power and the Associations

A normal democratic community has a wide distribution of power. Not only are powers of government scattered among its various branches, but the remaining power in the community, the great bulk of it, is dispersed among the nongovernmental associations. Anglo-Saxon societies, in particular, have been characteristically prolific in the creation of associations. Americans are especially great "joiners," members of numerous clubs, lodges, and professional organizations. These associations perform functions which are elsewhere regarded as being primarily within the purview of the state.

We are accustomed to the thought that every American shares in his government through exercising the right of the ballot, but this occasional display of power is only a small part of the story. He is a sharer in the power of the community in other ways as well. As a member of several associations, he is constantly contributing to their strength and influence, and if he chooses to be an active participant, he may, in time, wield much more actual power than many public officeholders. (The same is true, of course, in the student community on a college campus.)

We have a saying that a man's home is his castle. The feudal lord possessed a power which was visible in the defiant bastions of his citadel and the clanking passage of his armored horsemen. Of such brute strength, the modern citizen's strength is not constituted. Yet, his home is a more secure castle than that of the baron. Ours is a more subtle prerogative, made up of the Bill of Rights, the ballot, personal economic resources, strength of personality, and leadership in associations.

Within a society the various associations and social groups are in a constant state of competition, latent or open. To repeat the words of an earlier chapter, "The conflicts are fought out primarily in the market place and in the various organs that influence public opinion. Such tension or conflict is usually an indication, in the modern society, of growth and vitality and emergence of new interests. Only if a conflict becomes so severe that it endangers the stability of the society and the well-being of its members does it become dangerous."

The associations display the usual characteristics of the institutional factor. They seek to expand their numbers and try to keep their membership loyal. Financial resources must be obtained. The creed of the group is phrased in a manner intended to evoke sympathy or active support from the general public. The more successful the association becomes, the greater will be its ambitions.

Of what, more specifically, is the power of the association composed? A brief examination of a couple of the more prominent ones, such as the Chamber of Commerce of the United States and the American Federation of Labor, should be instructive on this point. The Chamber of Commerce is a federation of state and local clubs, the local clubs numbering over 2,500, with a membership of about 20,000 firms and individual businessmen. Along with such other groups as the National Association of Manufacturers and the American Bankers' Association, it represents the point of view and policies of American business. The political program is well known: protection of private enterprise, prevention of socialist measures, elimination of state control of business, reduction of taxes, and decentralization of government.

Much of the power of the Chamber of Commerce lies in its ability to mold public opinion. Its own magazines, such as *Nation's Business,* the newsletters, reports and studies, help to unite the membership in a common program. The public is influenced in favor of this program by newspapers, magazines, radio, and television; these are also business enterprises and therefore sympathetic to the general policies of the group. Purchased advertising frequently combines the advocacy of a product with the larger program of the business community as a whole. With a network of local clubs made up of some of the more prominent and respected men of each town, the man-to-man influence of the Chamber of Commerce on Main Street is apt to be decisive. An added source of strength is the prevalence of many other associations (such as the fraternal societies) which were organized for other purposes, but whose viewpoints in general policy are very similar.

The strategic location of the businessman in the economy is an asset. Unless a labor union is very powerful, an employer possesses vastly more economic power than the employee. The banking element controls that commodity which is the very life stream of any economic enterprise; the

possibility of a banker's veto on credit for a new venture or expansion of
an existing one is a very strong weapon. Manufacturers and wholesalers
possess power over the retailer. The capacity to build laboratories and hire
scientists provides increasing technological power along with the basic
economic strength of the business community.

An efficient "selling job" of its viewpoint makes the Chamber of
Commerce (and similar groups) potent in state and national politics.
Through its research department and, more specifically, through its lobby,
the Chamber of Commerce influences legislation. Its representatives are
in constant contact with the men in public office. The Chamber's pam-
phlet *For the Long-range Good of America* says, "Because of its facilities
for discovering American business opinion, the Chamber speaks with
authority on public issues. It commands the respectful attention of the
Government when it speaks. Members of Congress often seek the Chamber's opinion on legislative matters."

Certain features of this association are typical of all. The Chamber
of Commerce is constantly attempting to mold public opinion. A network
of local clubs adds greatly to its power and provides, in fact, much of the
substance thereof. A lobby is maintained for the specific purpose of obtaining needed legislation and discouraging unwanted laws and directives.
The members are certain that the advancement of their program is for
the ultimate good of the country. No opprobrium should be attached to
such activity: its behavior is a typical—if conspicuous—example of what
all associations do on a greater or lesser scale. The powerful influence of
the Chamber of Commerce is a reflection of the fact that business does
possess enormous power—economic, technological, and spiritual—in
America.

The American Federation of Labor pursues similar activities, although for different purposes. It is a federation of about one hundred
unions, whose power and influence radiates to every part of the country
and includes widely separate sections of labor. Among its unions are the
United Brotherhood of Carpenters and Joiners, the International Ladies'
Garment Workers' Union, the National Association of Letter Carriers,
the Order of Railroad Telegraphers, the Retail Clerks International Association, and the International Brotherhood of Teamsters, Chauffeurs,
Warehousemen, and Helpers of America. While the unions are autono-
mous, each running its own affairs, the federation itself serves as a unify-
ing force, carries on research, provides information, tries to get its side of
the story before the public, and gives assistance in organizing and negoti-

ating. A magazine *The American Federationist* is published, and a news
service provides copy for labor newspapers.

Like the Chamber of Commerce, the labor unions maintain a lobby.
Their representatives talk to legislators and appear before Congressional
committees. Voting records of the members of Congress are maintained
and are duly placed before the voters at election time. Senators and representatives from areas with a large workers' vote will keep a good labor
record if they hope to win another term. That is an example of the efficacy
of power. The single strongest weapon of labor is the strike. The strongest
potential power, however, is the ballot box, laborers making up the single
largest segment of the population and, if united, would be able to outvote
any other group.

Descriptions of such other associations as the Farm Bureau, the
American Legion, the American Medical Association, and the American
Bar Association would show a basically similar pattern. Perhaps fifty associations, at a rough guess, are giants, in the sense that their power is constantly felt in public opinion and in legislative lobbies. An additional
thousand associations, perhaps, possess a certain amount of power in
specific circumstances. Some professional groups, for instance, will make
regulations for their own professions, and legislatures will pass such
regulations without change.

Why are some associations especially powerful? Larger numbers,
better organization, financial resources, a particularly powerful weapon
(such as the strike), and a strategic location within the economic order.
The powers of associations vary according to their nature. Some possess
economic power, while others are unable, for one reason or another, to use
it. Salaries and wages of individuals depend, to a large extent, upon the
strength and aggressiveness of the association rather than upon the intrin-
sic value of work done—as any schoolteacher knows. All associations
appeal to public opinion, and some, indeed, have no power except through
such appeals. The great debate within the democratic American society
never subsides.

Upon occasion a severe clash between two groups will occur and will
pass beyond discussions and negotiations. When such a struggle occurs,
some sort of adjustment must eventually be made between the contestants.
Peacemaking between them will usually take the form of an accommoda-
tion, each party granting certain concessions or one side gaining certain
advantages, but not enough to make the loser prefer to continue the
struggle. The policy of "unconditional surrender" is not normally followed

among social groups where the democratic tradition is strong. This type of procedure is reminiscent of the balance-of-power mechanism among nations studied in an earlier chapter. Over the past few centuries, most treaties between countries have been drafted in such a way that the two states are enabled to continue as equals, since only relatively minor concessions have been made.

Associations have sometimes grown too powerful, so much so that the welfare of the community as a whole has been jeopardized. Revolutions may be aimed more at the stranglehold of an association than at the government itself. The struggle for individual freedom in the French Revolution was aimed not only against the absolute monarchy but also against those associations which benefitted from the survival of the Old Regime. The radical actions of the revolutionists against the Church stemmed from this feeling, so did the abolition of the Three Estates, and the guilds fell victim to the same hostility.

What prevents an individual association from gaining complete control over American society? The answer is that other associations check it if it becomes too powerful. A situation in which any group becomes too selfish in its behavior and excessively dangerous to other interests inspires a coalition of other associations against it. The balance of power goes into operation in a manner not essentially different from that on the international scene.

In the United States competition among social groups, although often sharp, is usually carried on with adherence to the "rules of the game" and with a final underlying consciousness that all are members of the same community. Social clashes in American society have always been characterized by their complexity. The American system of political parties reflects this condition. Conservatives and liberals are found among both Republicans and Democrats, although the Republicans are considered the more conservative party. The landed interests of the South, in the past, have rallied to the Democratic side, while the Northern farmer was long traditionally Republican. The businessman in the North is frequently an enthusiastic Republican, but those who have achieved success since the depression of the 1930's have displayed a greater tendency to be Democratic. Labor leaders tend to be Democratic, but this does not prevent a sizable number of laborers from voting Republican. A large and independent number of professional people and others are likely to switch from one party to the other.

Each party consists of an alliance of groups which find it in their interest to combine at that particular period. Government policies, individual leadership, and national conditions will cause the line-ups to change from one decade to another. In these circumstances, the principal social groups have an opportunity to maneuver for group advantages, while a rough equilibrium prevents any one group from assuming undue advantages. Although, like the English cabinet system, it was not planned, the system has become an adequate device for expressing and curbing group desires, and it safeguards the existence of democracy. We might describe democracy in terms like these: Democracy is a well-proved method of adjusting differences among social groups without resort to violence or permitting the individual to be crushed by the jostling among these groups; a rough equilibrium exists, with the constant tensions and pressures being somewhat mitigated by the acknowledgment of certain rules of the game.

The Communist portrayal of twentieth-century American society in terms of class struggle is a staggering oversimplification of its actual shapes and of its social forces. The Marxists have taken one single type of social conflict, exaggerated it, minimized other conflicts, and emerged with a gross caricature of the true nature of society. Their point of view goes back to the days of a relatively simple community when the lord was master over his serfs. The portrayal of nineteenth-century capitalism by Karl Marx, when the reform movement was just starting, had considerable validity; with every passing decade, however, the growth of the modern economy has rendered the original picture, still used by Russian Communists, more and more absurd.

The Communists see our economy as a relic of the nineteenth-century bourgeois society which is doomed to perish. Americans see it as an evolving system so modified by the past half century as to be a new society, more revolutionary than communism and more adapted to the social forces and technology of our century. It is no longer possible to speak of *the* middle class or *the* laboring masses or *the* farmers. They have all proliferated into a variegated assortment of associations, each with its own values and goals. The Communist does not understand the role of the associations and how they express the diversified economic and social forces of our era. Instead, he dogmatically insists on an artificial division of society between capitalists and workers and places all other groups in one or the other camp. Aware of conflicts in democratic society, as there must be, the Communist deliberately exaggerates them into chronic civil war in which physical violence is permissible. Communism expresses an old-fashioned point of view which lags a century behind the veritable situation at present. An American must judge that it represents a rudimentary approach to an industrial society by those who do not understand the true nature of social forces or modern production.

Marxism (not necessarily of the Communist type) exercises some attraction for students because it does give some insights into economic forces. For a beginner in social science, it gives a new sense of reality, a more detailed perception of certain forces, perhaps, than his non-Marxist colleagues possess; it has opened a door to the whole fascinating vista of social and economic relationships; this view is *only* a beginning, however, a distorted and fragmentary glimpse of the whole scene.

Power and the State

For the average person in this country, the power of the state is not much in evidence, although it has increased immensely since the depression of the 1930's. We recognize its presence in the drafting of soldiers, the collection of taxes, and the policeman on the street corner, but the fear of such power is not in us unless it comes with the sound of the police siren when speeding or after running through a stop signal. We recognize in government officials men we ourselves have put into office and who are holding powers we have given them. By contrast, the fear of the police in many countries is an omnipresent terror that never leaves the person; government-by-terror has become a method of ruling in itself, a system that uses law for purposes of enslavement rather than for justice. Government officials increasingly become a caste possessing special privileges and elevated above the remainder of the populace.

While one of the principal themes of modern history is the progressive liberation of the individual from the abuses of power, the period since the end of the First World War has seen a dramatic reversal of this trend. The struggle for liberty has lost ground to a general movement to strengthen governmental controls. The more obvious examples of this have occurred in totalitarian states, but the state has also grown mighty in the free world.

One excellent indication of this change is offered by the altered meaning of the word *liberal*. Originally, a liberal was a person who advocated social reform through a lessening of state power. He wished to liberate the population from controls. In our century the liberal has increasingly looked to the state as the agency which can achieve necessary measures; consequently, liberal governments have frequently sought to strengthen the government as over against the associations. While such measures undoubtedly liberated some individuals from associational controls, the cumulative result was a great expansion of the central authority.

Lest the recent resurgence of absolutism lead to pessimism, one should note, once again, that no country where democratic government has become habitual has relapsed into totalitarianism. The Anglo-Saxon nations, France, the Low Countries, Scandinavia, Switzerland, and a few others have maintained genuine rule by the people. Latin America continues its slow and spasmodic progress toward democratic rule, and most of the former Asiatic colonies have at least adopted the democratic pattern. The regions where absolutism has its strongest grip today are the same areas where tsars and emperors formerly maintained an iron grip. The totalitarian regimes are a reversion to former patterns of absolutism. Where a monarch was once absolute, where a single person was enshrined with the seeming absolute power of the divine-right theory, a single political party is now given the same absolute power and the same absolute obedience is demanded.

One reason, then, for the seeming resurgence of absolutism is that it never actually vanished. Democratic ideals may have been proclaimed briefly, but they were never actually implemented, much less became habitual. Older habits of government, as in Russia, reasserted themselves. The people themselves continued to expect a "strong" government, one which exacted obedience. Democratic government requires a high rate of literacy, a population interested in politics, and a society which freely permits men to rise in various fields, who may, in turn, become leaders in politics. Where these conditions do not yet obtain, democratic government cannot flourish properly.

The very rapidity with which modern civilization has spread over the earth is partially responsible for the new totalitarianism. The swift growth of new social classes, of new drives and interests, has come too swiftly for peaceful adjustment. Every society is subject to a "cultural lag," the tendency for ideas to change more slowly than the physical environment, and this is particularly true of societies where ideas have been adhered to as dogma in the past. The increasing complexity of the modern social structure has outmoded the former ideas of government. Whereas the European societies of the nineteenth century consisted of certain well-defined social groups—the nobility, the bourgeois, the clergy, and the peasantry—a society like that of the United States is not divided into a few clearly delineated social groups

We know that a free society has many associations, each possessing the right to express its wishes and to form alliances with other groups in furtherance of a program. In the democratic community, there are many voices heard, many programs outlined, and pressure from every direction as to policies the government should follow. The varying demands and pressures check each other to the extent that no single group can seize complete power. In the totalitarian state, under communism and fascism, these associations are either crushed or brought into complete obedience to the state as agencies of it. The ruling party, in order to achieve national unity, or what it considers national unity, ends the free existence of the associations and in effect silences various vital segments of the population. Such a policy of frustration naturally sets up terrific tensions within the social body; only increasing usage of terrorism as a policy can keep the natural associations passive. In order to maintain control, one crisis after another must be simulated, in which the ostensible enemy may be the Jews, the capitalists, the United States, the British Empire, or some other convenient scapegoat. Finally conditions reach the point where the only way to keep society integrated is by fomenting the crisis of an actual war. Perhaps a modern, industrial society must possess many free associations and a democratic form of government. Perhaps this has become the only natural form of community.

The former apparatus of absolutism no longer suffices. In the older absolute monarchy, the greater part of the population, rural and illiterate, was not politically minded and the problem of repression was relatively easy. In the twentieth century, the ability to spread ideas has been tremendously amplified through the capacity of most of the population to read, plus the appearance of newspapers, the radio, the telegraph and the telephone, and television. The task of controlling public opinion has been rendered infinitely more difficult. Dictatorships have responded by rigid censorship and by elaborate propaganda. The enormous numbers of people who have been sent to concentration camps and labor camps is in itself a tribute to the twentieth century's distribution of ideas. The persistence of rigid controls in the Soviet Union is an indication that even there control of ideas is not wholly possible.

Present-day tyranny differs from the old in that the new absolutism must control the mass production of ideas, the spiritual element, or else lose control of the situation. It differs not merely in increased quantity of police for purposes of repression, but also in the thorough "thought control" which reaches to the most intimate core of the personality. The modern dictator issues far more than negative commands, for he also undertakes to prescribe which ideas shall be thought. Public opinion is played upon by the propaganda machine as an organist plays his pipe organ. Because of the higher development of education (which dictators must continue in order to keep the modern level of technology going) and the improved means of spreading ideas, the government must provide the masses with ideas or see the masses permeated by thoughts not to the liking of the authorities. "Ideas are weapons," and leaders of totalitarian countries use them just as they do physical means. These men deliberately create a *myth* and then use the propaganda machine to make the people believe in it. They employ all the means of propaganda available to convince the people that they are engaged in some great struggle for worthy ends, the net effect being to harness the people as a single disciplined army working with enthusiasm for a single purpose.

The American may look upon his politicians with considerable cynicism—perhaps too much so—but he still tends to take political programs seriously. He wants his leaders to be interested in the welfare of the people and to regard themselves as their servants. After making due allowance for politics, Americans still believe that the man who seeks public office is imbued with an idealistic hope of improving society. The people of democratic countries are repeatedly fooled by the difference in the usage of ideas by democratic and totalitarian leaders. The latter look upon ideas as tools, true in themselves only to the extent that they can be used to guide the people in the direction that the leaders wish them to go.

The men who govern in an absolute state are interested, first of all, in power for themselves. Whatever their claims may be, regardless of what they say, they are actually interested only in how to attain and then keep power. The totalitarian state is a power aggregation for its own sake, an accumulation of all available means of maintaining jurisdiction over others. It is the ultimate result of the institutional factor run wild when the struggle for human liberty is suppressed. The state then becomes a machine for exploitation, the army, police, courts, productive agencies, schools, churches, and newspapers (economic, spiritual, technological, and physical power) all being used for this purpose. The totalitarian state is simply a new form of exploitation by cynical men who know that they have a good thing and intend to hang on to it. They are the equivalent, on the national level, of the racketeers of the cities and with methods amazingly similar. The science of government becomes simply a science of how to keep the people working and how to keep them quiet.

Once a totalitarian state is imposed, no successful spontaneous uprising can be expected as long as that regime remains efficient and the army loyal. In these circumstances, conspirators are unable to organize properly, and even if they could, modern weapons of war place a great advantage in the hands of the dictator over against any rebels. The old-fashioned fight at the barricades, of the nineteenth century, is unlikely now. Germans who were anti-Nazi under Hitler testified that their only hope was for the army to do the job. A decisive split in the ruling party would possibly destroy a totalitarian state, but the only other method is by a defeat in war.

The Marxists claim, of course, that government, in the past, has been a means whereby a certain economic group, the middle class, has been able to use state machinery for purposes of its own. Up to a point, this argument of the Marxists has some validity. The fact is, however, that when they insist that the economic desires are the supreme guide for human conduct, they are wrong. The constant struggle for money is only one form of an even more pervasive struggle: to attain power. Once this is secured, luxuries are available, the desire to orders others around is satisfied, and prestige among one's fellows is assured. In a capitalist country, money will purchase these. In a socialist country, these same privileges may be obtained by being a member of the bureaucracy, for privileges, contrary to Marxist contentions, are not likely to be abolished—socialism merely transfers these rights, in a somewhat different form, to a new group.

In summary, power itself is necessary and cannot be abolished. The degree of it required for successful operation of government varies with the historical circumstances of the times. A concentration of power of such proportions as prevails in totalitarian states is abnormal and could perhaps be likened to a high fever in an individual: it is symptomatic of a grave ailment within the social body. A healthy community will have its powers distributed into an equilibrium which maintains stability while permitting change and which allows the government to exercise authority without encroaching on the right of freedom of the individual and of the associations.

15

International Organization

In the last chapter the nature and use of power within the national community was discussed. It was pointed out that physical force has, legally, become the monopoly of the state itself. The greatest aggregation of physical force is to be found in the modern state in wartime, and the single most crucial problem of our times is the use of power in international affairs. Some persons might be tempted to hazard a guess that if humanity manages to survive the present era without the destruction of civilization, the historians of the future will declare that the greatest political development of the twentieth century was the evolution of international organization for the prevention of war.

The various factors that are inexorably driving the peoples of the world toward a choice between a greater degree of cooperation or irredeemable disaster are so obvious that they scarcely need to be enumerated. The increasingly destructive nature of war poses the question whether modern civilization can survive these periodic cataclysms. Wars, at one time profitable for the victor, can now be only a defeat, economically, for all countries. In terms of rational behavior, war has ceased to be a useful activity.

Improvements in transportation and communications originally led to the closer integration of individual countries, economically, socially, and politically. The same pressures which erased provincial units in favor of national now are forcing statesmen of different countries to see national sovereignty, however reluctantly, in less total terms than formerly. Wars and depressions alike, in their impact upon the affairs of all lands, witness to the interdependence of the various countries. The existence of regional organizations like the Pan American Union, the Council of Europe, the Benelux customs' union, and the Schuman Plan constitutes recognition of the growing need for a greater unity.

The growing evolution of modern society over the past half century has undermined the basic assumptions of national sovereignty. Hitler's campaigns, particularly, revealed how obsolete national sovereignty had become when some European states fell in a week and even France collapsed in little over a month. Norway and Denmark, before the Second World War, had maintained little more than token armed forces, in full conviction that no army which they maintained would be effective. The ease with which the Soviets gained control of the eastern European countries is another example which prompts one to question if more than two or three countries are truly sovereign today. Many persons would assert that when armed forces can no longer offer a reasonably sure defense, other means, in the form of international organization, must be found to give proper protection.

One other factor must be mentioned. Repeated mobilization of a nation's resources for war tends to produce a continuing degree of control over a country's economy and population, which then becomes habitual. We saw in an earlier chapter how the peoples of continental Europe were often compelled to sacrifice personal liberty in order that their countries should remain strong. The same condition, unfortunately, now prevails all over the world, and one may legitimately wonder how long the tradition of liberty can be maintained under the circumstances.

The need for a strong defense of a country is a social force in its own right which has exerted a powerful influence in the domestic affairs of nations. The military establishment, subject to the same institutional psychology as all other institutions, tries to expand its own numbers, acquire a larger revenue, procure a greater voice in the affairs of the country, and perpetuate its own influence. The danger is that it may gain an undue dominance in public affairs and carry through a natural tendency to militarize a country. Continuing conditions of national rivalry have placed a premium on military growth to such a degree that it is extremely difficult for any rational individual to argue against very strong defenses: to disarm, under present conditions, is to invite catastrophe. Such power concentrations, however, can scarcely be maintained indefinitely without serious damage to democratic institutions and to the material welfare of the people.

In view of the above considerations, are we living in the midst of an evolutionary development leading to an ultimately successful international organization, whose principal purpose would be the maintenance of world peace? If this is the case, the successive steps are so close to us that they are difficult to discern, and the failures and half measures are so clearly apparent that any actual progress is overshadowed by them. In order to gain the proper perspective on what may be happening, it is necessary to recall the type of evolutionary process by which Parliament gained power in England or the way in which the cabinet system emerged.

It will be remembered that these developments occurred as a result of circumstances whose pressures and implications were not fully realized by the participants in the events of the time. Circumstances guided men more than men made circumstances. The forms which evolved were the results of trial and error. Practices appeared as makeshift attempts which worked and which were then repeated until they became customary. After they had been habitual for some time, they were formalized in actual constitutional structures. At all times, the innovations met opposition and were partially hammered into shape by the nature and exigencies of the opposition. A tendency to revert to the older type of government was always present, and there were men who sincerely believed that this was advisable. The forms and practices that eventually emerged were not the result of paper plans and visions as much as simply those which proved practical.

No man living in the midst of such a development can tell with any certainty what the ultimate results will be, nor can he select, with assurance, the most significant events. The pattern of change does reveal the trend, however, and a sequence of related events stretching over a span of several decades, as is the case with international organization, is sufficiently impressive to merit serious consideration. When governments themselves are influenced by past experiences in this sequence, the historians must take cognizance of it, even though they still lack proper perspective for foolproof judgments. Let us, then, scan the outline of the evolution of international organization as a believer in its ultimate success might visualize it, at all times remembering that the interpretation is tentative, represents no consensus of opinion, and will assuredly undergo drastic future revision.

The League of Nations

The necessity of curbing sovereignty had received some slight recognition early in the nineteenth century when the major powers of Europe, by formal statement, promised to abide by certain principles of international law in their dealings with one another. A series of international conferences issued a number of rules of conduct: no nation, for example, could cancel a treaty with another nation except by mutual consent; privateering was abolished by the Declaration of Paris (1856), and at this same time it was stated that other countries need not recognize a proclaimed blockade of a country unless the action was actually effective; in the Geneva convention of 1864, agreements were reached as to the treatment of wounded soldiers in battle; in the Treaty of London in 1871, the principle of unilateral renunciation of a treaty was again rejected.

The Hague conferences of 1899 and 1907 marked a decided step forward in the development of international law with the creation of a Court of Arbitration for international disputes. (After the First World War, the Permanent Court of International Justice was established at the Hague.) An attempt was also made to regulate the conduct of war by forbidding poison gas and the dropping of explosives from balloons [!] and by the regulation of naval warfare.

Another development of the nineteenth century, incidentally, was the clarification of the status of diplomatic representatives. In early modern times ambassadors from one power to another had been of a temporary nature and were appointed for only a specific purpose. During the seventeenth and eighteenth centuries the practice was adopted of stationing a representative permanently in the capitals of the more important countries. This intensified the wrangling of the powers over the precedence of their respective agents, the question of national prestige and honor being involved in these disputes. At the congresses of Vienna (1815) and at Aix-la-Chapelle (1818), a permanent arrangement was agreed upon whereby there were to be four categories of representatives: ambassadors, envoys extraordinary and ministers plenipotentiary, resident ministers, and chargés d'affaires. These are given in descending order of precedence. It was also agreed, in this period, to drop claims of superior precedence by certain countries in favor of operating according to the alphabetical order of the countries involved, and this procedure has been followed to the present time.

The real beginning of international organization dates from the time of the First World War. This struggle, beginning as one more in the long series of fratricidal conflicts among European countries, changed its character with the entrance of the United States into the war. Starting as another war between nations, the struggle was transformed into a crusade for world peace by Woodrow Wilson, the American President.

Wilson and the British, in the hope of achieving this aim, proposed the establishment of a League of Nations. The League was to be a voluntary organization which, presumably, all right-minded nations would join for the common purpose of keeping peace. Wilson hoped that public opinion and moral standards would be sufficient, although stipulations for sanctions (international coercive action to enforce the law), were included, which might be used against an aggressor. Wilson and the British were well aware that they were beginning an experiment the fate of which could only be conjectured. They anticipated that the League would gradually gain popular support and create precedents of behavior in international affairs.

The French—those Frenchmen who wanted an international organization at all—were in favor of a more powerful organization. They were in a much more exposed position than the British and Americans, having been invaded thrice in a century, and a League that did not function promptly and effectively would be worse than useless, for it might give a false sense of protection. The French argued for the establishment of an international army that could be mobilized at the first sign of danger. (After the Second World War, the French were again for a time strongly in favor of organizing a Western European army, only to balk later out of fear that the Germans would soon dominate it.) The British and the Americans, in far less danger, refused to go this far, since it involved a certain infringement on national sovereignty. The plain fact was that the nations of the world were not yet willing to countenance any genuine limitation on their freedom of action.

The League was established in the form which Wilson and the British wanted. A paper document had been produced, and presently the various councils and assemblies of the new organization were brought into being. Most persons were skeptical. The Americans refused to join at all, and that imperfect member of God's elect, Woodrow Wilson, the prophet of a new world order, was repudiated by his own country.

During the following decade, the League continued to go through the motions and in so doing, statesmen began to build up the habit of discussing their problems in the "Parliament of Man," to borrow Tennyson's famous phrase. The League did succeed in preventing some minor wars. It achieved a great amount of good in other directions, such as the collection of information and the suppression of slavery, whiteslavery, and the peddling of narcotics. In 1928, the Pact of Paris was signed, a pious statement of the renunciation of war as a means of national policy. But what would this paper organization, this assembly of talkers, do when confronted with a major crisis?

The first great test came when the Japanese invaded Manchuria in 1931. The Chinese immediately appealed to the League; if wholehearted support of the League had existed, it would have warned Japan, then applied progressively more severe measures as the warning went unheeded. It is not, as we know, in the nature of social institutions to acquire new patterns of conduct this rapidly. Just as the individual learns a new behavior pattern with difficulty, with hesitation, and many errors, so it was with the nations in the international organization.

No particular interest in halting the Japanese was displayed by the governments of the larger European powers, and the British, formerly allies of the Japanese, were especially reluctant to act. The League did what any organization is likely to do when action is called for but seems inadvisable or painful: it appointed a committee. This Lytton Commission visited Manchuria and eventually recommended that the area be restored to the Chinese, but with special provisions for safeguarding Japanese interests.

The Japanese still balked at giving up Manchuria. In the debates at Geneva, the Japanese delegate, Yosuke Matsuoka, used all possible arguments. He pointed out that his people, by engaging in colonial conquests, were only doing what the British, French, Germans, and Americans had done a few decades earlier, and he insisted that the Japanese were bringing civilization and Western techniques to backward peoples just as the Western countries had done. To American moral indignation against Japanese aggression, Matsuoka responded that if the Americans could proclaim a Monroe Doctrine in the Western hemisphere, the Japanese had the right to do the same in the Far East. He made out a strong argument—if the year had been 1900 instead of 1933.

Since the Age of Imperialism, a new set of values and a new moral code in international affairs had been emerging; the disparity between the Japanese arguments and the attitude of the League supporters was a measure of how far world opinion had advanced in a third of a century.

New values *were* beginning to influence the conduct of the nations, for early in 1933 the League voted the Japanese guilty of aggression, the first time in history that this had been done. The greater number of countries never did recognize the state of Manchukuo which the Japanese established.

The episode also revealed how far from effective the new code still was. One step had been taken, but the obvious next one, that of actual penalties against Japan, was never started. The governments of the major European powers were not ready for this step.

Two years later, Mussolini's Italian Fascists invaded Ethiopia, a flagrant act of aggression. The League of Nations met immediately, the procedure with the precedents of the earlier one worked much more easily this time, and in a matter of days Italy was declared guilty of aggression. After considerable discussion, sanctions were adopted by a vote of fifty-one to three. These sanctions included the severance of financial relations, a refusal to import Italian goods, the prohibition of shipment of certain types of possible war materials to Italy, and an embargo on arms.

This much, public opinion had achieved. The British Conservatives, involved in an election campaign at the time, recognized the political reality of the opinion by promising complete support for collective security. The election over, Sir Samuel Hoare of the Conservative cabinet joined with Premier Pierre Laval of France, later fascist chief of Petain's Vichy regime, in secret negotiations with Mussolini. This attempt to revert to old-fashioned secret diplomacy blew up in their faces when the press got wind of it. The public explosion forced Hoare out of office, and Laval soon had to resign as premier. Obviously the peace machinery was becoming something more than a paper document.

Nevertheless, the Italians won the Ethiopian war and sanctions were lifted soon thereafter. The major governments were never as enthusiastic about this novel procedure as the populace seemed to be. The British and French governments claimed that they were not prepared for actual hostilities with Italy, and they were even more afraid of what Hitlerite Germany might do. Various other complex factors entered into the failure to apply the dictum of the League covenant more effectively. The League had failed again, although from the point of view of its own development it had made considerable progress. The course of events was too rapid, the race against time was lost, and the forces of aggression had been permitted to get completely out of control. However, one more precedent the League established while it existed. When the Soviet Union invaded Finland in 1939, the aggressor was expelled from the League.

The League had been an experiment which failed in the impossible task of changing the conduct of nations in twenty years. Not only that, the rulers of Germany and Italy and Russia gave every indication of abandoning even the "rules of the game," the diplomatic law of the nations, established by the sovereign nations of the nineteenth century. During its brief existence, however, the League of Nations had accustomed the world to debate in an international forum with some degree of publicity. It had made an appeal to public opinion in various disputes. The League had established the principle that war was not morally acceptable, that aggression was a heinous international crime, to such an extent that the Japanese, Italians, and Germans all felt compelled to disguise their wars and annexations under other names. In a sense, even the most violent opponents were admitting the emergence of a new, a shadowy, but nonetheless potent element upon the international scene.

With the breakdown of faith in collective security, the world reverted to the style of diplomacy and *Realpolitik* characteristic of Europe before 1914. Some might claim to see an important difference however: the whole scene more nearly resembled an anarchy suddenly let loose by the collapse of a central authority. Hitler spoke and behaved like a rebel as he stormed against the Wilsonian dispensation. Although the Second World War had the superficial aspect of a war between sovereign nations, actually its character was as unlike the conflicts of the last century as the wars of the French Revolution were different from the previous dynastic hostilities; this was a rebellion against authority, even though the latter had not yet succeeded in establishing its position. It was something new, a pattern which could recur repeatedly until permanent international cooperation of some sort is effectuated.

The war that followed, in some ways, had the quality of a nightmare —as if people had been through it all before. With a sort of inexorable inevitability, events seemed to repeat themselves in a distorted fashion. German armies streamed into France, but there was no Battle of the Marne; once again the British came to Flanders—and the Tommies were driven into the sea; the sons of the Americans of 1918 were drafted and sent "over there" to far more places than northern France; and so it went with all the nations. A moralist would say that Providence seemed to be forcing each people to go back over its part again, each one paying in rough measure through natural punishment for its sins of omission and commission against the emerging code of the twentieth century. Each people again took up the weary burden of doing over again what had been done once before.

The life of an individual sees a constant process of adjustment to environment. When his surroundings change, he must also have the flexibility to make personal changes. The vast drama being played out on this planet concerned essentially the same rule, because technological change, already potent in preceding centuries, had by this time also produced a dramatic change in the physical surroundings of the nations. Certain political practices, developed in the earlier types of environment, continued to sway the minds of man with all the persistence that habits normally possess, despite the fact that modern technology had rendered some of these usages obsolete. Political habits had not been adjusted to conform to a rapidly evolving environment. An individual abandons a habit if he repeatedly is hurt when he practices it; in the Second World War all humanity suffered because it had not adjusted its political practices rapidly enough.

The United Nations

The lesson of the catastrophe seemingly at least partially learned, the United Nations was created. The League of Nations could scarcely have been resurrected by the victorious coalition because of the general impression of impotence it had created in the twenties and thirties. Furthermore, the Soviet Union, at that time an ally of the Americans and British against the Nazis, would never have consented to reenter an organization from which it had been expelled in 1939. Nevertheless, the United Nations, as it was ultimately established, was decidedly reminiscent of the original League, an association that seemed, for a time, to work somewhat better than the original organization. The most signal difference was that the United States was exercising a political directorship commensurate with its economic might. At the same time, the Soviets went into opposition and made abundantly clear that, while they did want a united world, it would have to be their kind of world. They replaced the fascists as the rebels against the emerging international society of nations.

The United Nations was able to prevent aggression in a number of instances. It brought such pressure to bear on the Russians, who had occupied Azerbaijan in Iran, that they evacuated that province. In Greece the Communist satellite states gave assistance to Communist rebels against the government; the United States supported the legal regime, and the United Nations again applied pressure to the Soviets. A long and bloody civil war followed, but did not expand into a greater conflict.

Several major crises were halted short of war. Syria and Lebanon asked for help in persuading the French to evacuate their countries; this was done. The United Nations played a very influential role in preventing the Indonesian-Dutch quarrel from degenerating into a real war, and the influence of the United Nations (strongly backed by the United States) procured actual independence for the Indonesians. In Palestine the United Nations once more exercised its conciliatory influence and undoubtedly prevented a general flare-up, although it could not prevent some fighting. The Kashmir controversy between India and Pakistan was also prevented from leading to war.

In several of these controversies strict justice may not have been done. The Arabs may have had cause for complaint in the Palestine affair, the Dutch in Indonesia, and the Pakistanis in Kashmir. These were quarrels settled by politics on the international level, and politics is imperfect. One could argue that the solutions were no more unjust than measures adopted in national parliaments where different pressure groups clash.

The League had failed when it was challenged by brute force, by aggression in Manchuria and Ethiopia. By refusing to give adequate support to collective security, the great powers had opened the way to further aggression and thus to the Second World War. This same challenge came to the United Nations in the invasion of South Korea in June, 1950. If the Communist forces were successful there, further outbreaks would be encouraged in other places, probably against Tito's Yugoslavia or in Germany, where a similar split between Communist and Western occupation existed as in Korea.

The United Nations, under strong inspiration of the United States, went to the assistance of the South Koreans. For the first time, an international organization replied to force with force, and an international army came into existence. Americans and South Koreans made up the bulk of the armed forces, but it did include contingents from Britain, France, Canada, Greece, and Turkey, and also from such countries as Colombia, Ethiopia, and Thailand. The machinery worked creakingly, it was far from perfect, all the countries in the United Nations were not adequately represented by any manner of means—but an international army did exist. After Communist China entered the war, it was

208 A PREFACE TO HISTORY

declared guilty of aggression in January, 1951, economic sanctions gradually being imposed on such strategic goods as petroleum, arms, ammunition, steel, and rubber. The upshot of the war was not a clean victory, not even the unification of Korea. The guilty were not brought to trial or punished, except as the heavy losses themselves were punishment. A segment of American public opinion vociferously voiced disapproval of the whole project. Nevertheless, aggression had failed, and the aggressors had been compelled to pay a heavy price without any reward for it.

Those who believe that we will succeed in creating a workable international organization are certain that the development of the modern means of warfare and the conquest of distances make some form of world organization inevitable. They might even argue that the question is no longer *whether* it will be established, but rather *what form* it will take—either a voluntary agency, like the United Nations, or, if voluntary cooperation should fail, a more coercive sort of union by virtue of conquest. Those Americans who hold this point of view regard the United Nations, essentially, as the American response to the need for greater world cooperation, one springing out of American tradition in that it is a conscious attempt to use our successful experience with the federation of our states as a model for the larger and more loose international organization. This type of relationship combines the greatest degree of freedom for the individual nation with the necessary cooperation among them all. The spirit of nationalism, hitherto so opposed to any lessening of complete sovereignty, would seem to be best served, they would say, by a common organization which assures the freedom of all countries.

Future Historians Will Rewrite the Pattern

A strong case could be made for the argument that the foregoing represents wishful thinking and that the pattern up to the present time is more indicative of failure than success. The League of Nations was abruptly created, without the necessary antecedent evolution in that direction; as an institution it lacked sufficient backing in the organized social forces of the times, and it consequently was unable to function properly. Furthermore, adequate support in the near future is difficult to foresee, since the main current of our century is so obviously running in nationalist channels. Despite the existence of the League or the United Nations, the balance of power, based upon national self-interest, has remained the basic device for ensuring protection, and the historian, in writing his account, should continue to center his narrative about it. Even though an international organization does exist, it is wholly dependent upon the vastly stronger institutions connected with the nation for its resources; any successes achieved are actually the work of an alliance of powers within the organization. Beyond all this, how can genuine and lasting cooperation possibly be attained, in the last analysis, until the exceedingly diverse nations of the world have attained more similar societies and a consequent basis for agreement? If there is any evolution, as claimed, toward international organization, it can be found, at most, in continental or semicontinental groupings of states. So might run the argument against the preceding outline.

Even if the tentative outline is accepted as a reasonably faithful portrayal of an important trend, one must constantly remember that events and developments of a few years can radically alter the perspective and in so doing change the emphases, spotlight hitherto obscure implications, in a sequence of related episodes. In the original conception of aggression, for instance, international society was visualized in terms of sovereign states whose quarrels were most usually caused by territorial disputes or other matters in which national prestige was involved. The nations were likened to individuals living in the same neighborhood, the problem being one of first creating public opinion against lawlessness and then of organizing an adequate police. What becomes of this analogy when Korea and Germany have two separate and hostile governments and Italy and France have strong Communist parties which might some-day revolt? Does the fact that a Communist party is actually a fifth column for a foreign power make such a rebellion an act of aggression? The point is this: the problem of maintaining international peace has been changed by the Communist strategy of expansion, and the historian must recast his historical account to include this new element in the situation. Over the years the intrusion of such new factors, hitherto unimportant, will force repeated revisions until little resemblance to the early interpretations may be visible. To some extent, of course, the appearance of new elements and new attitudes induces revision not only of recent history but also the story of preceding centuries.

Should an international organization eventually succeed in ending wars, humanity will certainly not be ushered into any never-never land of Utopia. Men will not abruptly become angels, although mankind will have taken another step—a long step—on its pilgrimage out of barbarism. The fact that armed force is taboo within the political framework of our own American union has not prevented the jostling and angry words and injustices of social groups competing with one another. On the international level, nations will still quarrel with nations and use the pressures that are available. Social forces will still furnish the muscles and individual ambitions will still be the fingers that write history.

Bibliographical Notes

Much of the material in this book, as is true of most elementary textbooks, belongs within the realm of common knowledge. The author, however, is conscious of an indebtedness to particular works in specific instances for more specialized information, for certain ideas, or for quotations.

Chapter 2

The traditional explanation for the Belgian ethnological border has been somewhat modified by the article by C. Verlinden, "Frankish Colonization: A New Approach," *Transactions of the Royal Historical Society*, Fifth Series, vol. 4, 1954, pp. 1–17. The statements on the time concepts of children at different age levels are based chiefly on N. C. Bradley, "The Growth of the Knowledge of Time in Children of School-age," *The British Journal of Psychology*, vol. 38, December, 1947, pp. 67–78.

Chapter 3

The section on Florence is derived from F. Schevill, *History of Florence from the Founding of the City through the Renaissance*, New York, 1936.

Chapter 4

The Plymouth episode is based upon the brief account in *Sir Francis Drake Revived*, edited by Philip Nichols, vol. XXXIII of *The Harvard Classics*, New York, 1910, p. 203. Two books used extensively for this chapter are F. A. MacNutt, *Bartholomew de las Casas: His Life, His Apostolate, and His Writings*, New York, 1909, and W. Foster, *England's Quest of Eastern Trade*, London, 1933. The Gilbert quotation is from the account of his voyage in *Early English and French Voyages, Chiefly from Hakluyt, 1534–1608,* edited by H. S. Burage, New York, 1906, p. 219. The excerpt from the Columbus patent is taken from *Documents of American History,* edited by H. S. Commager, 3d ed., New York, 1943, p. 1.

Chapter 5

The Cheyney quotation: E. P. Cheyney, *Law in History and Other Essays,* New York, 1927, p. 11. The Luther quotation: *Address to the Christian Nobility of the German Nation,* vol. XXXVI of *The Harvard Classics,* New York, 1910, pp. 291–292.

Chapter 6

The description of the evolution of football: L. H. Baker, *Football: Facts and Figures,* New York, 1945, and A. A. Stagg, *Touchdown!* (as told to W. W. Stout), New York, 1927.

The evolution of parliament and the cabinet system: G. B. Adams, *Constitutional History of England,* revised by R. L. Schuyler, New York, 1934; G. N. Clark, *The Later Stuarts, 1660–1714,* Oxford, 1934; K. Mackenzie, *The English Parliament,* revised edition, Mardmandworth, 1951; M. Powicke, *The Thirteenth Century, 1216–1307,* Oxford, 1953; F. Thompson, *A Short History of Parliament, 1295–1642,* Minneapolis, 1953; M. A. Thompson, *A Constitutional History of England, 1642–1801,* London, 1938; B. Wilkinson, *Constitutional History of Medieval England, 1216–1399;* two vols., London, 1948–1952; B. Williams, *The Whig Supremacy, 1714–1760,* Oxford, 1939.

Chapter 8

The ideas in this chapter are largely drawn from C. Brinton, *The Anatomy of Revolution,* revised edition, New York, 1952; L. P. Edwards, *The Natural History of Revolution,* Chicago, 1927; and the article by A. Meusel, "Revolution and Counter-revolution," vol. XIII of the *Encyclopaedia of the Social Sciences,* New York, 1934, pp. 375–376. Also consulted were the standard works by Madelin, Gaxotte, Gershoy, and Thompson. The quotation from Arthur Young is from his *Travels in France during the Years 1787, 1788, 1789,* London, 1924, pp. 153–154.

Chapter 9

The description of the coronation ceremony: The Coronation Record Number of *The Illustrated London News,* London, 1937, and the approved souvenir program, *The Coronation of Her Majesty, Queen Elizabeth II*, London, 1953. Some use was made of the flag issues of *The National Geographic Magazine*, October, 1917, and September, 1934.

Also, *Histoire de France contemporaine depuis la revolution jusqu'à la paix de 1919*, edited by E. Lavisse (vols. IV–V by S. Charléty), Paris, 1921; F. B. Artz, *Reaction and Revolution, 1814–1832*, New York, 1934; J. Lucas-Dubreton, *The Restoration and the July Monarchy*, translated by E. F. Buckley, London, 1929; C. Hayes, *Essays on Nationalism*, New York, 1926, and *The Historical Evolution of Modern Nationalism,* New York, 1931; F. Hertz, *Nationality in History and Politics: A Study of the Psychology and Sociology of National Sentiment and Character*, London, 1944.

Chapter 10

S. Hook, *The Hero in History: A Study in Limitation and Possibility*, New York, 1943; *Studies in Leadership: Leadership and Democratic Action*, edited by A. W. Gouldner, New York, 1950; P. Guedalla et al., *If: Or History Rewritten*, 1931.

Chapter 11

W. H. Boulton, *The Pageant of Transport through the Ages*, London, 1931; R. Burlingame, *Backgrounds of Power: The Human Story of Mass Production*, London, 1949; H. Butterfield, *The Origins of Modern Science, 1300–1800*, London, 1950; F. C. Dietz, *An Economic History of England*, New York, 1942; J. L. Hammond and B. Hammond, *The Rise of Modern Industry*, New York, 1926; P. J. Mantoux, *The Industrial Revolution in the Eighteenth Century: An Outline of the Beginnings of the Modern Factory System in England*, translated by M. Vernon, revised edition, London, 1948; S. T. McCloy, *French Inventions of the Eighteenth Century*, Lexington, 1952; L. W. Moffit, *England on the Eve of the Industrial Revolution*, New York, 1925; L. Mumford, *Technics and Civilization*, New York, 1934; A. Redford, *The Economic History of England (1760–1860)*, London, 1931; A. P. Usher, *Introduction to the Industrial History of England*, Boston, 1920.

Chapter 12

S. H. Thomson, *Czechoslovakia in European History*, Princeton, 1944; E. Wiskemann, *Czechs and Germans: A Study of the Struggles in the Historic Provinces of Bohemia and Moravia*, London, 1938; *Czecho-slovakia: Twenty Years of Independence*, edited by R. J. Kerner, Berke-ley, 1940.

Chapter 13

L. Gottschalk, *Understanding History: A Primer of Historical Method*, New York, 1950; A. Nevins, *The Gateway to History*, New York, 1938; G. J. Garraghan, *A Guide to Historical Method*, edited by J. Delanglez, New York, 1948. (These three inevitably influenced the author, indirectly, in some of the other chapters also.)

J. W. Thompson, *A History of Historical Writing* (with the collabo-ration of B. J. Holm), two vols., New York, 1942; A. H. Lybyer, "The Influence of the Rise of the Ottoman Turks upon the Routes of Oriental Trade," *Annual Report* of the American Historical Association, 1914, vol. I, Washington, 1916, pp. 127–133; G. L. Burr, "The Year 1000 and the Antecedents of the Crusades," in R. H. Bainton, *George Lincoln Burr: His Life*, selections from his writings edited by L. O. Gibbons, Ithaca, 1943, pp. 273–283; M. Ventris, "King Nestor's Four-handled Cups: Greek Inventories in the Minoan Script," *Archaeology*, vol. 7, No. 1, March, 1954, pp. 15–21. The description of the Kensington stone is drawn from two books by H. R. Holand, *The Kensington Stone*, Ephraim, Wis., 1932, and *America, 1355–1364: A New Chapter in Pre-Columbian History*, New York, 1946, and also from sporadic notices on the subject in *Time* magazine.

Chapter 14

B. Russell, *Power: A New Social Analysis*, New York, 1938.

Index